GENETIC
ENGINEERING
OPPOSING VIEWPOINTS

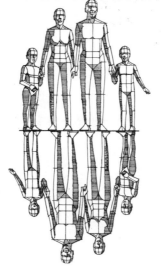

Other Books of Related Interest in the Opposing Viewpoints Series:
Animal Rights
Biomedical Ethics
The Environmental Crisis
Science & Religion

Additional Books in the Opposing Viewpoints Series:
Abortion
AIDS
American Foreign Policy
American Government
American Values
America's Elections
America's Future
America's Prisons
Censorship
Central America
Chemical Dependency
China
Civil Liberties
Constructing a Life Philosophy
Crime and Criminals
Criminal Justice
Death and Dying
The Death Penalty
Drug Abuse
Economics in America
The Elderly
Euthanasia
The Health Crisis
The Homeless
Israel
Japan
Latin America and U.S. Foreign Policy
Male/Female Roles
The Mass Media
The Middle East
Nuclear War
The Political Spectrum
Poverty
Problems of Africa
Religion in America
Sexual Values
Social Justice
The Soviet Union
The Superpowers: A New Detente
Teenage Sexuality
Terrorism
The Third World
The Vietnam War
Violence in America
War and Human Nature

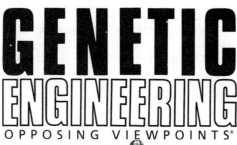

GENETIC ENGINEERING

OPPOSING VIEWPOINTS®

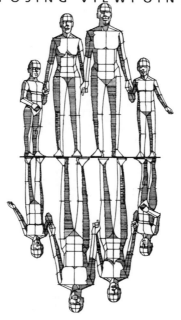

David L. Bender & Bruno Leone, *Series Editors*

William Dudley, *Book Editor*

OPPOSING VIEWPOINTS SERIES ®

Greenhaven Press, Inc.   PO Box 289009   San Diego, CA 92128-9009

Library of Congress Cataloging-in-Publication Data

Dudley, William, 1964-
    Genetic engineering : opposing viewpoints / William Dudley,
book editor.
        p.   cm. — (Opposing viewpoints series)
    Includes bibliographical references.
    ISBN 0-89908-477-X. — ISBN 0-89908-452-4 (pbk.)
    1. Genetic engineering. 2. Genetic engineering—Social aspects.
I. Title. II. Series.
TP248.6.D83   1990
179' .1—dc20   89-25765
                                                                          CIP

"Congress shall make no law...
abridging the freedom of speech,
or of the press."

First Amendment to the US Constitution

The basic foundation of our democracy is the first amendment
guarantee of freedom of expression. The *Opposing Viewpoints
Series* is dedicated to the concept of this basic freedom and the
idea that it is more important to practice it than to enshrine it.

Contents

Chapter 5: Will Genetic Engineering Lead to a Biological Arms Race?

Why Consider Opposing Viewpoints?

The Importance of Examining Opposing Viewpoints

The purpose of the Opposing Viewpoints Series, and this book in particular, is to present balanced, and often difficult to find, opposing points of view on complex and sensitive issues.

Probably the best way to become informed is to analyzc the positions of those who are regarded as experts and well studied on issues. It is important to consider every variety of opinion in an attempt to determine the truth. Opinions from the mainstream of society should be examined. But also important are opinions that are considered radical, reactionary, or minority as well as those stigmatized by some other uncomplimentary label. An important lesson of history is the eventual acceptance of many unpopular and even despised opinions. The ideas of Socrates, Jesus, and Galileo are good examples of this.

Readers will approach this book with their own opinions on the issues debated within it. However, to have a good grasp of one's own viewpoint, it is necessary to understand the arguments of those with whom one disagrees. It can be said that those who do not completely understand their adversary's point of view do not fully understand their own.

A persuasive case for considering opposing viewpoints has been presented by John Stuart Mill in his work *On Liberty*. When examining controversial issues it may be helpful to reflect on this suggestion:

> The only way in which a human being can make some approach to knowing the whole of a subject, is by hearing what can be said about it by persons of every variety of opinion, and studying all modes in which it can be looked at by every character of mind. No wise man ever acquired his wisdom in any mode but this.

Analyzing Sources of Information

The Opposing Viewpoints Series includes diverse materials taken from magazines, journals, books, and newspapers, as well as statements and position papers from a wide range of individuals, organizations and governments. This broad spectrum of sources helps to develop patterns of thinking which are open to the consideration of a variety of opinions.

Pitfalls to Avoid

A pitfall to avoid in considering opposing points of view is that of regarding one's own opinion as being common sense and the most rational stance and the point of view of others as being only opinion and naturally wrong. It may be that another's opinion is correct and one's own is in error.

Another pitfall to avoid is that of closing one's mind to the opinions of those with whom one disagrees. The best way to approach a dialogue is to make one's primary purpose that of understanding the mind and arguments of the other person and not that of enlightening him or her with one's own solutions. More can be learned by listening than speaking.

It is my hope that after reading this book the reader will have a deeper understanding of the issues debated and will appreciate the complexity of even seemingly simple issues on which good and honest people disagree. This awareness is particularly important in a democratic society such as ours where people enter into public debate to determine the common good. Those with whom one disagrees should not necessarily be regarded as enemies, but perhaps simply as people who suggest different paths to a common goal.

Developing Basic Reading and Thinking Skills

In this book, carefully edited opposing viewpoints are purposely placed back to back to create a running debate; each viewpoint is preceded by a short quotation that best expresses the author's main argument. This format instantly plunges the reader into the midst of a controversial issue and greatly aids that reader in mastering the basic skill of recognizing an author's point of view.

A number of basic skills for critical thinking are practiced in the activities that appear throughout the books in the series. Some of the skills are:

Evaluating Sources of Information   The ability to choose from among alternative sources the most reliable and accurate source in relation to a given subject.

Separating Fact from Opinion   The ability to make the basic distinction between factual statements (those that can be demonstrated or verified empirically) and statements of opinion (those that are beliefs or attitudes that cannot be proved).

Identifying Stereotypes   The ability to identify oversimplified, exaggerated descriptions (favorable or unfavorable) about people and insulting statements about racial, religious or national groups, based upon misinformation or lack of information.

Recognizing Ethnocentrism   The ability to recognize attitudes or opinions that express the view that one's own race, culture, or group is inherently superior, or those attitudes that judge another culture or group in terms of one's own.

It is important to consider opposing viewpoints and equally important to be able to critically analyze those viewpoints. The activities in this book are designed to help the reader master these thinking skills. Statements are taken from the book's viewpoints and the reader is asked to analyze them. This technique aids the reader in developing skills that not only can be applied to the viewpoints in this book, but also to situations where opinionated spokespersons comment on controversial issues. Although the activities are helpful to the solitary reader, they are most useful when the reader can benefit from the interaction of group discussion.

Using this book and others in the series should help readers develop basic reading and thinking skills. These skills should improve the reader's ability to understand what they read. Readers should be better able to separate fact from opinion, substance from rhetoric and become better consumers of information in our media-centered culture.

This volume of the Opposing Viewpoints Series does not advocate a particular point of view. Quite the contrary! The very nature of the book leaves it to the reader to formulate the opinions he or she finds most suitable. My purpose as publisher is to see that this is made possible by offering a wide range of viewpoints which are fairly presented.

David L. Bender
Publisher

Introduction

"The tools of molecular biology have enormous potential for both good and evil. Lurking behind every genetic dream come true is a possible Brave New World *nightmare."*

Philip Elmer-Dewitt, *Time*, March 20, 1989.

Genetic engineering encompasses several techniques developed within the last two decades which manipulate and alter the genes found in the cells of living organisms. Genetic engineering has turned heredity—the passing of inheritable characteristics from parent to offspring—from a natural, random event into a process that can be artificially controlled and exploited. It has the potential to give humanity unprecedented power over life itself, and its use has thus raised profound questions in such diverse areas as the environment, agriculture, biological warfare, and animal rights.

Ironically, one of the sharpest controversies involves a scenario that has yet to exist: the genetic engineering of humans. Present genetic engineering technology is limited to plants, bacteria, and some animals. Two events in 1989, however, point to a time when that could change. In January, the United States launched the Human Genome Project, a multi-billion-dollar research program under the direction of James D. Watson. The project's goal, expected to take years to complete, is to discover and map all of the estimated 100,000 genes found in every human cell. A second milestone occurred in May 1989 when a National Institutes of Health medical team led by Steven Rosenberg genetically altered human cells and injected them into a patient. The experiment marked the first time genetic engineering was applied directly to humans.

Both events foreshadow a future which many people believe will feature the genetic manipulation of humans. This prospect has drawn a variety of responses. Watson and other proponents argue that genetic engineering can help correct genetic defects and prevent suffering and death. Some forecast more drastic developments. Science lecturer Brian Stableford envisions a future in which humans are genetically altered for space travel and underwater living. "Until now, we have had to be content with the image in which evolution has shaped us," he writes. "Soon, we will have the capacity to remake that image in any way we choose." Science writers Sharon and Kathleen McAuliffe agree: "The human species as we know it may be replaced by a new bionic animal that controls its own evolution."

Many people, however, find these ideas profoundly unsettling and even immoral. Critics question both the utility and the value of genetic engineering. Some, such as V. Elving Anderson, question human genetic engineering for religious reasons: "Is it right to monkey with the genetic makeup that we assume was placed in us by an omniscient God?" Further objections have been raised by controversial activist Jeremy Rifkin, who asks, "Do we want our children to grow up in a world where the genetic codes of plants, animals, and humans are interchangeable and living things are programmed as engineered products with no greater intrinsic value than autos or microwave ovens?" Rifkin and others argue that the price of exploiting genetic engineering could be the cheapening of life and the loss of what it means to be human.

No one can predict when and if the genetic redesigning of humans will become a reality. But debating the questions raised by this and other aspects of genetic engineering becomes ever more crucial. The topics considered in *Genetic Engineering: Opposing Viewpoints* include the following: Is Genetic Engineering Beneficial? Can Genetic Engineering Improve Health? Does Genetic Engineering Improve Agriculture? Is Genetic Engineering Adequately Regulated? Will Genetic Engineering Lead to a Biological Arms Race? Underlying all the debates is the question: Can the cleverness which led to the discovery of genetic engineering be matched by wisdom in using it?

Is Genetic Engineering Beneficial?

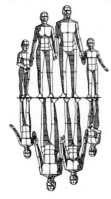

Chapter Preface

Most participants in the debate over genetic engineering would agree with the statement that genetic engineering carries the *potential* for both good and harm. Most proponents, for example, would concede that it is theoretically possible for genetically altered microbes to become environmental hazards, and most opponents would agree that genetic engineering could be used to develop vaccines to many diseases. Where they often disagree is in their confidence in the governments and corporations that govern genetic engineering. Proponents generally assume that genetic engineering can be developed to maximize its positive potential and minimize its harm. Critics have doubts as to whether such development is possible.

The viewpoints in this chapter debate whether genetic engineering is beneficial and whether humans are ready for it.

"Genetic engineering holds tremendous promise."

Genetic Engineering Is Beneficial

Monsanto Company

The Monsanto Company produces agricultural products and is a leader in industrial genetic engineering research. The following viewpoint describes the structure and function of DNA, and how genetic engineering works. The authors argue that genetic engineering will improve humanity's quality of life by improving agricultural plants and animals and by creating new medicines and chemicals.

As you read, consider the following questions:
1. How do the authors describe the process of genetic engineering?
2. How are bacteria used in genetic engineering, according to the authors?
3. According to Monsanto, what are some of the applications of genetic engineering relating to health and the environment?

From a Monsanto Company booklet, *Genetic Engineering: A Natural Science*, 1989. Reprinted with permission of the Monsanto Company.

Over billions of years, life has evolved into a fascinating array of structures, forms and functions. Of the 300,000 kinds of plants and more than a million kinds of animals that are known today, no two are exactly alike—yet within families there are marked similarities.

We take it for granted that children resemble their parents, and that other living things show a like continuity from generation to generation. The fact of family resemblance is so obvious, so natural, we rarely give it a second thought.

Farmers and plant breeders have used the obvious fact of family resemblance for centuries to improve the productivity of their plants and animals. By selecting and breeding the largest or the strongest or the most disease-resistant, they have mixed and combined genetic information in new ways to create better hybrids. Though they didn't know it, they were applying genetic engineering.

Gregor Mendel

But the rules governing the transmission of genetic information to progeny remained a mystery until about 150 years ago when Gregor Mendel began his studies of inheritance in garden plants.

Using carefully planned experiments and mathematical calculations, Mendel concluded that particles exist that carry hereditary traits, and that these traits are passed from generation to generation according to a constant ratio of dominant traits to recessive traits. This ratio is nature's law of inheritance for every living organism.

Though the scientific world failed to recognize the significance of Mendel's discoveries until long after his death, his work serves as a foundation for the science of genetics as we know it today.

Recent Discoveries

Over the last 30 years, molecular biologists have made great strides in understanding inheritance. Beginning with James Watson and Francis Crick's description of the structure of DNA, scientists now understand how genetic information is stored in a cell, how that information is duplicated and how it is passed from cell to cell, generation to generation.

Building on this knowledge, more recent discoveries have enabled scientists to move pieces of genetic information (genes) from one organism to another. This ability to transfer genetic information is known as "genetic engineering." Though still in its infancy, genetic engineering holds tremendous promise. It has enabled us to make crop plants naturally resistant to diseases and insects. It is providing new ways to treat human diseases, manufacture chemicals and eliminate wastes.

As scientists' discoveries about genetics and genetic engineering have made headlines in newspapers and magazines, a myriad of confusing terms have entered our language, and questions about this new science have been raised.

Many people believe that discoveries in molecular biology and genetic engineering can significantly improve the quality of our lives, but they also believe that intelligent use of this new knowledge depends on society's understanding of its potential—and its limitations.

This viewpoint is intended to help explain the facts about genetic engineering, and its realistic applications.

Two major discoveries led scientists to conclude that a universal chemical language unites all living things.

As early as the 1800s, it was known that all living organisms are composed of cells, and that the elements of all cells—whether they are from a human, a bacterium, a flower or a whale—are essentially the same.

Then in 1867, Friedrich Meischer noticed that all cells contain a slightly acidic substance in their nuclei. He called it nucleic acid. Meischer had unknowingly discovered the material that transmits hereditary information.

A Revolutionary Advance

Recombinant DNA technology is a revolutionary advance. According to classical biology, species are in part defined by their ability to mate sexually and exchange genetic material. The union of cows will result in cows and the union of horses will result in horses. But the union of a cow and a horse can produce nothing. The recombinant DNA technology discussed permits the transfer of genetic material not only across species lines but out of the animal kingdom (man's insulin gene) and into bacteria—a truly remarkable achievement. Although it now appears that certain natural viruses may shuttle bits of genetic material between animals and lower species, recombinant DNA technology for the first time gives man control over this kind of process and presages major possibilities for what has come to be called genetic engineering. The potential impact of this capacity on the health of man and on the social and commercial fabric of his world is hard to overestimate.

Richard Noel Re, *Bioburst*, 1986.

When its chemical composition was determined in the early 1900s, the substance was named DeoxyriboNucleic Acid—or DNA. By the 1940s it had been proven that the genes within cell chromosomes are made of DNA.

As a result of the work done by Watson and Crick in the 1950s, we now know that the DNA molecule is a double helix—two strands of DNA connected by chemicals, called bases. We also know that all DNA in all living cells has a similar structure, function and composition.

The order of the bases within two strands of DNA comprise a specific gene for a specific trait, like leaf shape or hair color. A typical gene has hundreds of bases.

The first letters of the chemical names of these bases—Adenine, Guanine, Cytosine and Thymine—are the scientist's "alphabet" of the language of life. These chemical bases are always arranged in pairs. When A occurs on one strand, T occurs opposite it on the other. G pairs with C. A, C, G, and T when strung together compose "sentences," or genes. It is these sentences that contain the DNA messages for maintaining cells and organisms, and building the next generation.

As with written language, the language of DNA can be "edited." If DNA is altered, then the message it delivers to the cell is changed, a natural event in evolution. Viruses, mistakes in duplication, and atmospheric radiation are among the influences that can change the DNA of an organism. Sometimes these changes in the DNA code are passed on to the next generation, and therefore are responsible for the variety of life forms we see today.

Two Functions

DNA plays an essential role in two processes that 1) allow the cell to reproduce and 2) maintain its life. The first is duplication. To create a new cell, or a whole new organism, DNA must be able to duplicate or "clone" itself.

Duplication begins when a special protein unwinds the DNA molecule and separates it at the base pairs. Each separate strand is now a blueprint for a new strand. With the bases of each half of the original molecule exposed, new bases which are floating in the cell nucleus can attach to them, according to the A-T/G-C rule. The result is two new double strands of DNA, each exactly alike. This process is essential for reproduction.

The second process produces the proteins—and through them the chemicals—necessary for a cell's maintenance and function. DNA is translated into messenger RNA which contains instructions for the production of the 20 amino acids from which all proteins are made. The order of the letters specifies the arrangement of the amino acids in the protein. These sequences can be hundreds of amino acids long.

Amino acids can be arranged in an almost infinite number of combinations to produce hundreds of thousands of different proteins. Proteins make up the structure of cells, produce chemicals essential to the cell and the organism's survival, and guide and facilitate chemical reactions in the cell. Hair, blood, muscle, antibodies, skin, enzymes—all the organs and functions of our bodies—are composed of or controlled by proteins. The same is

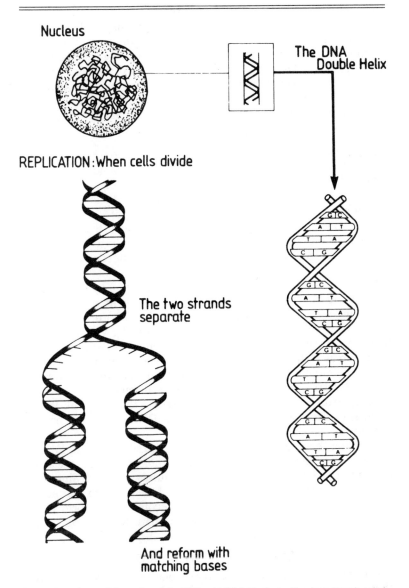

Nucleus

The DNA Double Helix

REPLICATION: When cells divide

The two strands separate

And reform with matching bases

The nucleus of every living cell contains DNA, which is in the form of two long strands spiraling around each other. The strands are joined by the bonding of four chemical bases: adenine (A) with thymine (T), and guanine (G) with cytosine (C). DNA replicates itself by first splitting the strands apart. Each strand then attracts and links with its complementary chemical bases. The result is two DNA double helixes identical to the original.

From *Reshaping Life*, copyright 1985 by Cambridge University Press. Used with permission.

true for plants, animals and microorganisms.

Once scientists had deciphered the language of life and understood the production and function of proteins, they began looking for ways to use nature's language to study gene function and regulation. They theorized that if the DNA in a cell could be specifically changed, then the cell could be given new instructions to produce desirable chemicals or proteins in large quantities, carry out useful processes or acquire valuable characteristics. . . .

Gene Splicing

Recently, scientists have developed the ability to transfer genetic material from one cell into another by using a common bacterium.

Most DNA in higher plants and animals is tangled in a large mass inside the cell's chromosomes, making it difficult to study. In the early 1970s, it was discovered that a bacterium called *E. coli* has closed circular pieces of DNA (plasmids) floating free in its cell liquid. Because of their shape and relative simplicity, plasmids appeared to be the vehicle scientists needed to transfer genes.

Before these plasmids could be used, though, a technique had to be found for "cutting" DNA molecules into gene segments and "pasting" the segments into the plasmid. Certain proteins—called enzymes—that "chew up" the DNA of invading viruses to protect the cell turned out to be nature's chemical "scissors."

Known as restriction enzymes, these special proteins attack and cut DNA molecules at specific sites. There are many different kinds of restriction enzymes and a large number of them have been carefully catalogued in terms of where they will cut. When a cut is desired at an exact spot along a DNA chain, the proper enzyme is selected to do the job.

By using these chemical scissors, specific sequences of DNA—genes—can be cut out of a complex DNA molecule. Then, the same enzyme is used to cut open the bacterium's plasmid. Since the cut ends of the plasmid and the cut ends of the gene are chemically "sticky," they will attach to each other—recombine—to form a new circular plasmid containing the new gene. This technique is called "gene splicing" or recombinant DNA technology. . . .

Using Bacteria as Factories

A number of years ago, scientists isolated the DNA sequence that directs human insulin production. By transferring that gene into *E. coli*, using the technology described earlier, they were able to turn the bacteria into insulin "factories."

Insulin is an essential therapeutic agent for diabetics. Until the advent of recombinant DNA technology, insulin could be obtained only in tiny amounts from animal pancreas tissue. Because animal insulin is not exactly the same as human insulin, some diabetics are allergic to it.

The technique used to grow the insulin-producing bacteria is called fermentation—a process that has been used for centuries in beer and wine making, cheese production and leavening.

The genetically engineered bacteria are placed in large containers, called fermentation tanks, which hold all the nutrients the bacteria require to grow and multiply. The environment in the tank must be carefully monitored and controlled to ensure that the bacteria flourish. In fact, genetically engineering bacteria so weakens them that they usually cannot survive outside the fermenter or the laboratory environment.

After a period of cell division and growth, the bacteria are "harvested" from the tank and broken open. The insulin proteins are separated—purified—from the other proteins and collected for use. Any remaining bacteria are destroyed.

As yet, relatively few organisms can be engineered to accept new genetic information, but research in this natural science promises us new ways to improve the productivity of plant and animal agriculture, find new therapeutic agents for human diseases, manufacture chemicals more efficiently and safely, and even help clean up waste. . . .

Genetics and Agriculture

Whenever a bee carries pollen from one flower to another or a plant breeder crosses one crop plant with another, genetic information is exchanged. Precision is the only difference between this kind of exchange and the kind effected by genetic engineering. In traditional cross breeding, all of the genetic information—both desired and undesired—from both plants is combined even though the breeder may be trying to transfer a trait controlled by only one gene. Because genetic engineering enables scientists to transfer specific genes controlling specific traits from one organism into another, they are able to improve crops in a less haphazard, less time-consuming way.

Molecular biologists are now able to transfer new genetic information into plant cells. They are doing on the molecular level what plant breeders have been doing for centuries: combining genes in new ways to improve crops. . . .

Recombinant DNA techniques also have been used for the production of proteins that enhance animal health and productivity. . . .

Genetic Engineering and Health

Vaccines for the prevention of diseases like smallpox and polio and antibiotics to cure life-threatening illnesses like pneumonia are significant milestones in man's ability to improve human health and the quality of life. More recent discoveries in human genetics, coupled with recombinant DNA techniques, may provide new ways to identify, cure or prevent disease.

The first application of genetic engineering for human health care has been in the production of pharmaceuticals, like insulin. In this approach, genes which have been selected for their ability to manufacture specific proteins are spliced into bacteria, viruses or animal cells. The microorganisms or cells then become protein factories, which manufacture the desired pharmaceutical in large quantities. All of the human health care products of genetic engineering now available or near commercialization are produced this way. Among the products under development are:

• Human growth hormone—Proteins that are under clinical study for the treatment of dwarfism;

• Factor VIII—A protein found in blood plasma that promotes clotting and is missing from the blood of hemophiliacs; . . .

Research in human health and genetics has led to recent discoveries that may enable scientists to develop new methods of diagnosing and treating inherited diseases, as well.

One possible way to treat inherited disease is to replace genes within a patient's body cells. One way involves the use of genetically engineered microorganisms to carry the required gene into the patient's cells. Acting as a messenger, the microorganism would inject the new gene into the patient's DNA, safely correcting the inherited disease. The benefit of this kind of treatment would not be passed on to the next generation.

Extensions of the techniques already developed should produce new human health care products efficiently and economically—probably by the 1990s. . . .

Industrial Applications

Recombinant DNA techniques may provide us with new ways to clean up our environment, and more efficient methods of producing chemicals.

Genetically altered bacteria have been developed that will feed on oil slicks—a potentially effective way to handle accidental oil spills. Other research is underway to speed the degradation of PCBs, dioxin, and a number of insecticides and herbicides that linger too long in soils and streams.

Equally attractive are the possibilities of converting waste materials into useful products. Studies are in progress on gene-spliced bacteria for converting organic wastes into sugar, alcohol and methane. Still other research aims at developing bacteria that will convert waste wood (cellulose) directly to grain alcohol. . . .

Although these applications of genetic engineering technology are only in the experimental stages, they illustrate the vast potential of this science for improving our lives.

*"Should biotechnology be allowed to play God?
The implications are frightening."*

Genetic Engineering Is Dangerous

Dick Russell

While many people are excited about genetic engineering, others
fear that this technology will cause more harm than good. In the
following viewpoint, Dick Russell outlines what he believes to be
the disturbing implications of genetic engineering. He argues that
genetic engineering causes environmental hazards and puts enormous power into the hands of a few genetic scientists and corporations. Russell is a free-lance writer specializing in environmental matters.

As you read, consider the following questions:

1. What does Russell consider unsettling about the patenting
   of life forms?
2. Who dominates genetic engineering research, according to
   Russell? What impact does he believe this will have?
3. How does Russell describe the policing of genetic
   engineering research?

Dick Russell, "A Molecular Auschwitz," *The New Internationalist*, April 1988. Reprinted
with permission.

Nature has been licked at last. Biotechnology, its fans say, will create a disease-resistant world of mega-crops and super-herds. Using genetic engineering we can now rearrange, synthesize and recombine genes in ways nature never dreamed of. Already this scientific revolution has become a multimillion-dollar business with transnational chemical, energy, agribusiness and pharmaceutical corporations virtually annexing US universities with massive research grants.

Playing God

But should biotechnology be allowed to play God? The implications are frightening. And alarm bells are being rung, not least by scientists themselves:

'We do not know what life is, and yet we manipulate it as if it were an inorganic salt solution,' says Dr Edwin Chagaff, Professor Emeritus of biochemistry at Columbia University Medical School. 'Science is now the craft of manipulation, modification, substitution and deflection of the forces of nature.'

And we are, he warns, heading toward 'human husbandry' in which embryos will be mass-produced for experimental purposes. 'What I see coming is a gigantic slaughterhouse, a molecular Auschwitz, in which valuable enzymes, hormones and so on will be extracted instead of gold teeth.'

But there is no guarantee that even 'human husbandry' would remain intrinsically human, as another major critic of biotechnology, Jeremy Rifkin, points out. It is already possible to transfer human growth genes into cattle, sheep and pigs to enable them to grow more quickly, thus bringing meat to market more cheaply. Scientists have even fused sheep and goat cells, creating an animal they call, not surprisingly, the 'gheep'.

Rifkin, who heads the Washington-based Economic Trends Foundation, is not overdramatizing when he asks: 'Do we want our children to grow up in a world where the genes of plants, animals and humans are interchangeable and living things are engineered products with no greater intrinsic value than microwave ovens?'

Animal Patents

In 1987 the US Patent and Trademark Office made the crucial—and disturbing—announcement that all forms of animal on earth, with the exception of *homo sapiens*, should be considered 'patentable' subject matter. 'All life,' proclaimed the patent officials, can now properly be regarded as a 'manufacture or composition of matter'.

The biotech companies were delighted: 'We're going to make animals that nature never made!' crowed Dr John Hasler, co-founder of an animal biotech outfit in Pennsylvania. And Bruce

Mackler of the Association of Biotechnology added in a more subdued but no less chilling tone: 'If we as a nation are to stay competitive in the world, we have to adopt new technologies. The ability to patent animals makes it more attractive economically to conduct research.' . . .

Power and Risk

Every new technological revolution brings with it both benefits and costs. The more powerful the technology is at expropriating and controlling the forces of nature, the more exacting the price we are forced to pay in terms of disruption and destruction wreaked on the ecosystems that sustain life. . . .

Genetic engineering represents the ultimate tool. It extends humanity's reach over the forces of nature as no other technology in history, perhaps with the one exception of the nuclear bomb. . . . With genetic technology we assume control over the hereditary blueprints of life itself. Can any reasonable person believe for a moment that such unprecedented power is without risk?

Jeremy Rifkin, *Declaration of a Heretic*, 1985.

But if the creation of 'transgenic animals' is permitted, can transgenic people be far behind? Already researchers are working on a project to decipher humanity's genetic endowment, the ultimate goal being to determine the location of each of the three billion chemical molecules that comprise human DNA. Everything from the way we look to how our brains are wired may, within a decade, become a computerized road-map.

The stated aim, of course, is to generate new medical strategies to combat diseases and ageing. But the competition to get there first is no less fierce than it was to develop the atomic bomb or get a person into space. Indeed, Harvard University researcher Walter Gilbert is starting his own company to sequence one entire human genome and has announced that he has a legal right to copyright what he discovers.

When life itself becomes subject to patents and copyrights, the world that Aldous Huxley foresaw in his *Brave New World* looms ever more like prophecy. And Rifkin's Economic Trends Foundation has emerged as the Cassandra of biotechnology, filing a series of lawsuits to delay release of genetically-altered organisms. What frightens Rifkin is that control of biotechnology is in potentially irresponsible hands. He can see the formation of an unprecedented combination of economic and political power: a multifaceted, multinational, 'life sciences' conglomerate; a huge company that will use genes just as earlier corporate powers used land, minerals or oil.

Even the futuristic linguistic terms now in operation are un-nerving. The Japanese, for example, are proposing an international research effort known as the Human Frontier Science Program. In 1987 they embarked on a 10-year investigation into making computers that would function like the human brain, possibly even using biological substances. The Mitsubishi Chemical Company, with a $233 million annual research budget, now devotes 40 per cent of it to biotechnology.

In the US the dominant powers are the chemical giants. Their contracts with universities have escalated from the six-million-dollar, five-year award that DuPont gave to the Harvard Medical School in 1981 to the seven-year, $50-million research deal Monsanto now has with Washington University. But such bargains may carry a Faustian price.

'Just as nuclear physicists are not trained to assess the effects of radiation on causing cancer,' says Cornell University ecologist Martin Alexander, 'molecular biologists are not usually qualified to evaluate the environmental consequences of releasing genetically-engineered organisms.'

Even if all such lab-created organisms were to prove harmless, the direction in which biotechnology's corporate pioneers appear to be moving is ample cause for alarm. Today the sale of weed-killing herbicides is worth four billion dollars worldwide. The Monsanto chemical company alone sold more than a billion dollars' worth in 1982, nearly half of which was from a herbicide called Round-Up. (Along with a prime competitor, Lasso, Round-Up has been shown to be a probable carcinogen in recent scientific studies.)

Corporate Priorities

Why, then, is Monsanto currently devoting about five million dollars to biotechnology? The reason is that many herbicides damage crops at the same time as wiping out weeds. Round-Up, for instance, causes no problems for corn. But soybeans, which are grown in rotation with corn, readily fall victim to the potent herbicide because it lingers in the soil. If soybeans could be implanted with a gene that tolerates Round-Up, one biotech consulting firm has predicted that farmers might triple their use of the herbicide and increase its sales by about $12 million a year.

That is precisely what Monsanto and other chemical outfits are hoping for. In the spring of 1987, scientists at the University of Wisconsin successfully inserted a gene for herbicide resistance into a woody plant. Thirty-three companies and at least a dozen private universities are embarked on similar research.

Dr Frederick Buttel, a prominent rural sociologist at Cornell University, believes the companies intend to use biotechnology 'to develop markets for broad-spectrum herbicides that might otherwise not be used. Attempts at even tighter packaging of seeds and agrichemicals are expected, where the use of a particular crop variety and an agrichemical are mutually obligatory.' In other words farmers will not be able to buy the seed without the herbicide that accompanies it. Since the chemical companies now own nearly all of the seed companies in the US, the scenario is scarcely far-fetched.

The multinationals which brought seed-pesticide packages to the Third World under the double-speak name of the 'Green Revolution' are now seeking a different brand of stranglehold: 'Seed Wars'. It centers around the fact that the US has no primary native crops, while the tropics and Southern hemisphere contain large numbers of useful seeds. For more than a century the West has garnered seeds freely from the underdeveloped countries.

Getting hold of the prime raw material is crucial to genetic engineers. Most varieties are stored in a US Department of Agriculture seed bank in Fort Collins, Colorado. The idea is for multinationals to withdraw a rare seed from, say, Bolivia from the seed bank, then genetically engineer and patent a new strain— then sell it right back to the farmers in Bolivia.

In anticipation of this, 100 Third World nations meeting in Rome late in 1986 accused the West of 'genetic imperialism' and threatened to seize control of other seed banks supported by the World Bank and the United Nations Food and Agricultural

Organization. The US retaliated by threatening to cut off its contribution to the FAO, which amounts to 25 per cent of its budget.

'Whoever controls germ plasm, and therefore genetic engineering, is now as important as who controls oil,' says Rifkin. 'With the big chemical companies moving in to collect seeds and patent animal embryos, they potentially will have power over many of the living things of the future. The US has now collected most of the rare seeds, making Fort Collins the Fort Knox of the genetic age. The biggest danger here is that they're preserving only those strains that have market value. With genetic engineering you can streamline monocultures of wheat and corn much more rapidly. But in breeding more and more for uniformity, we may not have the genetic diversity left to maintain resistance against changing conditions in the environment.'

If all this were not ominous enough, there is yet another chilling application of biotechnology. Responding to a lawsuit by Rifkin's organization, the Pentagon was forced to admit that it has been conducting 'defensive' research programs in biological warfare at 127 sites around the US. *Science* magazine subsequently reported that the Defense Department 'is applying recombinant DNA techniques in research and production of a range of pathogens and toxins, including botulism, anthrax and yellow fever.'

This effort increased dramatically under the Reagan Administration, undermining the Biological Weapons Convention of 1972. In an out-of-court settlement, the Pentagon agreed to file an Environmental Impact Statement on all of its biotech programs, indicating possible health risks to surrounding communities.

But what if there was an accident? 'A major concern is the potential of a virus to establish a reservoir that we have no experience with,' says the Boston-based Committee for Responsible Genetics. 'The virus could potentially live, without killing its host, providing a continual source of infection to the population, and be difficult—if not impossible—to wipe out.'

Clandestine Experiments

Similar questions continue to arise, of course, over the release of supposedly more benign genetically-manipulated strains into the environment. In 1987 the first three such outdoor tests overcame Rifkin's legal logjam. A company called Advanced Genetic Sciences conducted two controversial experiments on a strawberry patch in California with a lab-altered bacteria designed to prevent crops from freezing in hard frost.

So far no environmental problems have occurred. But once hundreds, even thousands, of new human-manipulated organisms are let loose, the results are unpredictable. Agronomists have noted that, while many non-native natural species brought to the US have adapted, others—such as the gypsy moth, kudzu vine, Dutch elm disease and chestnut blight—have unexpectedly run amok and wreaked havoc with other species. Genetic engineering vastly increases the chances of such eventualities.

Lax Regulation

And policing of biotechnology experiments is lax—to put it mildly. The potential for abuse surfaced in 1987 when Dr Gary Strobel, a plant pathologist at Montana State University, failed to wait for the required approval before experimenting. He used an engineered bacteria on 14 trees, seeking a new means to treat Dutch elm disease. Calling his action 'civil disobedience' in the face of 'almost ludicrous' standards, Strobel admitted having released another altered microbe three years earlier—also without Government permission or his university's approval.

While the Environmental Protection Agency slapped his wrists with what it termed a 'mild sanction', it was left to citizens like Tufts University Professor Sheldon Krimsky to express the outrage. 'You do not commit civil disobedience in the tradition of Gandhi and Martin Luther King by placing society at risk,' said Krimsky. A tearful, but not contrite, Strobel did agree to cut down the affected trees. . . .

It may be too late to put the genie of biotechnology back into the lamp. But one thing is clear. Biotechnology has no conscience. Only humanity can provide that—if we choose.

"There is a broad consensus among biologists that R-DNA techniques are safe."

Genetic Engineering Is Environmentally Safe

The National Academy of Sciences

To test the effectiveness of genetically altered organisms, researchers must release such organisms into the environment. Many people are concerned that releasing these organisms could damage the environment. In 1987 the National Academy of Sciences, a private society of scientists which officially advises the federal government on scientific matters, created a committee of biologists, geneticists, and ecologists to prepare a report on the safety of genetic engineering experiments. In the following viewpoint, which is excerpted from their report, the Committee argues that genetically engineered organisms are not inherently more dangerous than naturally occurring organisms, and that genetic experiments can be carried out with little risk to the environment.

As you read, consider the following questions:

1. What new powers does genetic engineering have that traditional plant and animal breeding lacked, according to the Committee?
2. What are the two broad categories of concerns surrounding genetic engineering, according to the authors?
3. What does the Committee conclude about the overall risk of genetic engineering?

Council of the National Academy of Sciences, *Introduction of DNA-Engineered Organisms into the Environment: Key Issues.* Washington, DC: National Academy Press, 1987.

Recombinant DNA (R-DNA) techniques offer exciting opportunities for the development of products in medicine, industry, agriculture, and environmental management. Vaccines are being made safer and produced more rapidly than ever before. Plants are being engineered to resist bacteria and viruses and to produce compounds that are toxic to pests. Bacteria are being modified to protect crops from frost damage and disease, to break down toxic pollutants, to increase the ability of plants to fix atmospheric nitrogen, and to aid in the recovery of metals from ores. To capture the benefits of these and similar developments, however, R-DNA-engineered organisms must be tested and used outside the laboratory, a procedure known as the "deliberate release" or "planned introduction" of genetically engineered organisms into the environment.

As with any intervention in the environment, there may be risks associated with the introduction of certain R-DNA-engineered oragnisms. There is a perception, however, that R-DNA techniques represent a means of alteration so distinct from other approaches that they will yield organisms that have completely unexpected and possibly deleterious properties outside the laboratory. This perception, along with experiences with certain previous introductions, has fueled public and scientific controversy. The result has been the formulation of regulations more stringent for organisms engineered with R-DNA techniques than for those produced with conventional genetic procedures.

This paper examines carefully the issues surrounding the introduction of R-DNA-engineered organisms into the environment. . . .

Historical Background

For thousands of years, humans have modified the organisms around them to meet practical needs. The development of agriculture included the selection and breeding of plants, animals, and microbes that provide greater yields of food and fiber or have other desirable traits. Such selective breeding was repeated many times to produce strains with strong expression of the desired traits; examples include corn with high oil content and dairy cattle with high milk yields. Artificial selection has been applied to thousands of traits in a vast array of organisms, ranging from the yeasts used in baking and wine making to the livestock and plants that constitute a major part of our diet. . . .

The accumulated experience in plant and animal breeding allows some generalizations. Although a breeder's genetically modified organism is useful in the managed ecosystem for which it was created, such as a farmer's fertilized and weed-controlled field, it is usually changed in such a way that it is not as fit as its natural progenitor to survive in "the wild" —its original, non-managed environment. For example, some plants, like corn, have lost their ability to disseminate their seeds; other plant varieties have a high requirement for fertilizers; and domesticated animals are often dependent on people for feed. Moreover, the genes of an organism do not function independently, but rather constitute a system of interacting components. Organisms that carry genes introduced from other species tend to be at a competitive disadvantage. With a few exceptions to the general pattern (such as the establishment of feral pigs and dogs), the conventional genetic manipulations done by human beings to increase an organism's utility are detrimental to the organism's survival outside the special environments provided.

Colors, Not Killers

If I have a petunia and I transfer a gene for a different color out of a bacterium, that's a big jump from a bacterium to a petunia. . . . [But] it's still a petunia. . . . It's not going to become a killer petunia.

Arthur Kelman, quoted in *The Christian Science Monitor*, June 3, 1988.

The R-DNA technology developed over the last 15 years has permitted a new and more precise kind of genetic manipulation. These techniques make it possible to isolate genes, to change the genes and how they are expressed, and, together with other techniques, to insert the genes into whole organisms. R-DNA techniques are unique because they permit genes isolated from almost any organism to be modified to function and be introduced into almost any other organism, regardless of the sexual compatibility of the organisms or the distance of their evolutionary relationship. Breeders who use traditional techniques change (or mutate) genes and move them, but they cannot change or move just one gene or a few at a time. Their methods are much less precise and controlled. A mutation made by traditional techniques may be accompanied by many unknown mutations, which often have deleterious effects on the organism. Furthermore, when genes are moved by traditional sexual crosses, unwanted genes may go along; thus, many cycles of selection are necessary to obtain the desired traits. The power of R-DNA techniques lies in their ability to make extremely precise alterations in an organism rapidly and to overcome the barriers of sexual incompatibility that have hitherto stymied breeders' efforts to move genes. It is precisely these features of genetic engineering with R-DNA techniques that have caused concern.

The ability of R-DNA techniques to expand the range of organisms among which genetic exchanges can be made and to increase the rapidity and precision of genetic manipulations has raised the number of practical applications for genetically modified organisms. But concerns have been expressed about the use of these techniques and about the possibility that their very availability will increase the frequency and scale of introductions of modified organisms into the environment. The two broad categories of concerns are whether distant genetic transfers and the use of R-DNA technology for genetic manipulations are inherently hazardous and whether the widespread introduction of organisms containing R-DNA can cause major ecological disruptions.

Some of the concerns are substantial; others are not warranted. To avoid the two extremes of paralyzing overregulation and inattention to significant potential hazards, the issues must be assessed in the light of scientific knowledge and accumulated experience. This section deals only with those questions that can be answered on that basis. It draws on our experience, largely in laboratory and agricultural applications, although future uses of R-DNA-engineered organisms will include the leaching of ores and degradation of pollutants, as well as agricultural applications outside our current experience. Nonetheless, for all applications the appropriate focus of concern should be the properties of the engineered organism, not the method by which it was produced. . . .

Is it inherently dangerous to use R-DNA techniques to move genes between unrelated organisms?

Are R-DNA technologies inherently hazardous? They have been used in hundreds of laboratories for more than a decade to produce R-DNA-engineered organisms on a small experimental scale and more recently on a large commercial scale in industrial fermenters. During that time, the transfer of innumerable genes between very different kinds of organisms has created untold numbers of individual transgenic organisms. No hazard peculiar to the use of R-DNA techniques has yet surfaced, and there is a broad consensus among biologists that R-DNA techniques are safe.

Gene Transfers in Nature

Considerable concern is voiced over the use of R-DNA techniques to move genes between organisms that do not generally exchange genes in nature. But are such transfers truly novel? Genetic exchanges brought about by unconventional, nonsexual means occur often in nature. Recent advances in molecular biology have revealed that the cells of most organisms can assimilate and incorporate genetic material from almost any source, and there is evidence that such exchanges have sometimes occurred naturally. They are usually unproductive because the genetic signals for gene expression function only when the recipient organism is closely related to the donor. To solve this problem, researchers have learned to alter the signals that enable a gene to be expressed in the recipient organism. Nature has done this too. For example, strains of the crown gall bacterium (*Agrobacterium tumefaciens*) carry genes that can be expressed only in plant cells. The bacteria have developed a mechanism for transferring certain genes to plant cells and for directing the plant cells to express the genes to make compounds that the bacterium can use as a source of food and energy. Thus, gene transfers among different types of organisms do occur in nature.

Are genetic transfers between unrelated organisms more likely to give rise to problem organisms than genetic transfers between closely related organisms? Also, is there scientific justification for designating as "novel" an organism containing a gene, or a small number of genes, from another species? Many thousands of distant genetic transfers have been carried out with R-DNA techniques, and the organisms with the new genes have the predicted properties: they behave like the parent organism, but exhibit the new trait or traits expected to be associated with the introduced gene or genes. Thus, an R-DNA modified organism is not a "novel" organism; rather, it is like a breeder's new variety of a flower. Occasionally, unexpected changes occur, but these have been detrimental to the organisms, making them less able to survive.

Ensuring Safety

As biotechnological research has progressed and techniques have been developed and refined, the initial concerns over the possible hazards implicit in this new field of industry have largely been put to rest. There has never been a biotechnology-related incident resulting in danger to humans, animals, or the environment. Nonetheless, the corporate community and government regulatory agencies alike recognize the need to set prudent standards for biotechnology research, and to periodically revise the standards as the industry matures. The overall aim of these efforts is to ensure that the benefits of biotechnology are reaped and that the health and safety of all living things is protected.

Industrial Biotechnology Association, *What Is Biotechnology?* 1984.

No evidence based on laboratory observations indicates that unique hazards attend the transfer of genes between unrelated organisms. Furthermore, there is no evidence that a gene will convert a benign organism to a hazardous one simply because the gene came from an unrelated species. The strong implication is that neither the source of the gene nor the method by which it is introduced warrants concern in assessing R-DNA-engineered organisms.

Are R-DNA-engineered organisms like nonnative organisms?

An analogy is frequently made between the potential consequences of introducing R-DNA-engineered organisms into the environment and the serious ecological disruptions that have been caused by the introduction of certain nonnative or alien organisms, such as the gypsy moth, the starling, and the kudzu vine. This comparison is based to some extent on the assumption that R-DNA modifications can change the properties of an organism in a wholly unpredictable way that will increase its ability to affect the environment adversely. Experience to date indicates that this is extremely unlikely. Engineered organisms, whether produced by traditional or R-DNA manipulations, resemble the parent organism in their reproductive and growth characteristics, and they are often at a disadvantage with respect to their parents in their ability to survive and to reproduce. Thus, it is not valid to regard all R-DNA-engineered organisms as nonnative.

Species invasions are among the most serious problems confronting environmental managers, and the nonnative or alien species model of introduction does provide a sound basis for extrapolation when the introduced species is not native to its target environment. But many of the currently proposed agricultural applications of R-DNA-engineered organisms will involve reintroducing modified organisms into the same or a similar environment from which they were taken, so they are not analogous to the introduction of a nonnative species.

New Pests?

Will the use of R-DNA techniques accidentally create new plant pests?

It has been suggested that the genetic engineering of crop plants might increase the potential for creating new pest plants, or "super-weeds." Weeds differ from crop plants in a number of traits. These include vigorous growth, production of large numbers of seeds, production of seeds that are long-lived and germinate readily, the capacity for either self- or crosspollination, and a mechanism for rapid dispersal. One published summary of the characteristics of an ideal weed includes 12 traits, most of which are determined by many genes. Although few weeds possess all these traits, most successful ones have a cluster of several. A single mutation can significantly enhance the potential of a given plant to become a weed, but the plant must already possess a number of the characteristics conducive to weedlike behavior. Moreover, although the mechanisms by which weeds have evolved will continue to operate, there is no evidence that plants engineered with R-DNA will behave differently from plants produced by traditional breeding procedures.

Care must be taken when genes conferring traits such as herbicide resistance are introduced into plants that can outcross with closely related wild and weedy species. Caution must also be exercised in the genetic manipulation of weeds, but the probability that R-DNA modification can inadvertently convert a crop plant to a noxious weed is negligible and warrants little concern.

Can R-DNA accidentally convert a nonpathogen to a pathogen?
Among the dangers envisioned in R-DNA genetic engineering of microorganisms is the inadvertent conversion of a nonpathogen into a new, virulent pathogen. How valid is this concept? It is important to recognize that virulent pathogens of humans, animals, and plants possess a large number of varied characteristics that in total constitute their pathogenic potential. The traits contributing to pathogenicity include the ability to attach to specific host cells, to resist a wide range of host defense systems, to form toxic chemicals that kill cells, to produce enzymes that degrade cell components, to disseminate readily and invade new hosts, and to survive under adverse environmental conditions outside the host. Together with the need to compete effectively with many other microorganisms for survival, these traits form an impressive array of requirements for pathogenicity. The possibility that minor genetic modifications with R-DNA techniques will inadvertently convert a nonpathogen to a pathogen is therefore quite remote. . . .

No Unique Risks

Several conclusions can be drawn from this review of the relationship between traditional genetic manipulation techniques and the R-DNA techniques developed during the last 15 years, and of the experience gained from the application of each.

• There is no evidence that unique hazards exist either in the use of R-DNA techniques or in the movement of genes between unrelated organisms.

• The risks associated with the introduction of R-DNA-engineered organisms are the same in kind as those associated with the introduction of unmodified organisms and organisms modified by other methods.

• Assessment of the risks of introducing R-DNA-engineered organisms into the environment should be based on the nature of the organism and the environment into which it is introduced, not on the method by which it was produced.

"Environmental scientists regard the safety of engineered organism products as a genuine concern."

Genetic Engineering Raises Environmental Concerns

Frances E. Sharples

Frances E. Sharples works in the Environmental Sciences Division of the Oak Ridge National Laboratory in Tennessee. She is also a former member of the Recombinant DNA Advisory Committee of the National Institutes of Health, a committee of scientists and other experts that formulates government guidelines for genetic engineering experiments. In the following viewpoint, she maintains that releasing genetically altered organisms could have negative effects on the environment. She argues that such organisms should be acknowledged as potential environmental hazards, and urges caution in the use of genetically engineered products.

As you read, consider the following questions:

1. Why does Sharples place little significance on the safety record of genetic engineering experiments in contained laboratories?
2. What example does Sharples provide of a minor genetic change causing major environmental damage?

Frances E. Sharples, "Regulation of Products from Biotechnology," *Science*, Vol. 235, Pages 1329-33, 13 March 1987. Copyright 1987 by AAAS. The Oak Ridge National Laboratory is operated by Martin Marietta Energy Systems, Inc., under contract DE-AC05-840R21400 with the Department of Energy. Reprinted with permission.

Proponents of biotechnology often assert that the safety of "genetically engineered" organisms has been established because adverse effects have yet to be documented after handling the organisms in contained facilities for a decade. But the past is not necessarily a reliable guide to the future. Although the absence of effects on the health of workers in biotechnology laboratories is admirable, it is not particularly relevant to the question of whether uncontained uses of modified organisms will be equally harmless. For various reasons, the concerns for environmental applications of biotechnology products are fundamentally different from those for laboratory uses.

Environmental vs. Laboratory Uses

First, in environmental applications, it is the myriad of nonhuman species in an ecological community that will be exposed to released organisms. Second, the spectrum of potential effects is not restricted to pathogenicity, although this, too, is certainly a significant concern. Additions of nonindigenous organisms can influence the structure (population size and species diversity) and function (energy and material dynamics) of ecological communities through a variety of mechanisms that sometimes displace or destroy indigenous species. Such events are copiously documented in the literature of ecology, and experience with the ecological dislocations and economic losses that sometimes result when organisms are introduced into environments where they are not normally found is too abundant to be trivialized or ignored.

Third, the degree of control afforded by experiments conducted in containment differs from that involved in releases in the field. Once released, modified organisms that find suitable habitats may not only reproduce and spread, but can be expected to evolve in ways that are beneficial to their own survival. The evolutionary process can allow modified organisms to escape constraints imposed by debilitating them before their release, so that both physical and biological containment may be nullified outside the laboratory. Fourth, differences of scale become important as the transition from research to commercial products is made. It is one thing for trained experimenters to apply novel organisms to a 0.2-acre field under close supervision. It will be quite another matter to market commercial products for widespread use by applicators whose major qualification for using them is possessing the cash to acquire them. To assert therefore, that we are merely thrashing over issues that were laid to rest years ago is to ignore all these important differences.

Biologists in the molecular and ecological fields disagree in the application of "evolutionary principles" to arguments about safety issues. All biologists are, to some degree, "evolutionary biologists" in the sense that all scientists who study living systems receive schooling in the basics of evolutionary theory. Because evolution deals with changes in the genetic structures of populations of organisms, both those whose primary interest in genes and those whose focus is on whole organisms and the higher systems of which they are a part (populations, communities, and ecosystems) can lay claim, if they choose, to the title of "evolutionary biologist." In fact, many scientists whose research interests are in such sub-disciplines as "ecological genetics" prefer to call themselves "evolutionary biologists" rather than ecologists. In short, no one discipline in the biological sciences corners the market on the use and interpretation of "evolutionary principles." Both major factions in the biotechnology controversy can support their cases with evolutionary arguments.

Courting Disaster

The environmental risks posed by genetically engineered organisms are not unlike the risks posed by the past introductions of exotic and hybrid species to the environment. The difference is that genetic engineering makes possible the introduction of a greater number of new species, with more specific and precise genetic changes, and at a more rapid rate, than with the "old biotechnology" of plant breeding and species importation.

Whether a particular new species in a particular environment will cause damage is extremely difficult to forecast. For each of those past introductions of exotic and hybrid species that have been problematic, many other introductions have occurred without any problems. So many factors interact in the environment to determine where there will be trouble, that prediction of just which species introductions will cause ecological disruptions is nearly beyond the ability of ecologists and population biologists. Yet we must try to enlist a strong level of involvement among scientists to critically evaluate new organisms designed for release, and give them the opportunity to anticipate problems, or as a society we are courting disaster.

The National Center for Policy Alternatives, "Regulating Environmental Release of Genetically Engineered Organisms: The State Perspective," June 1, 1988.

Take, for example, the question of whether a novel organism is likely to survive and spread after release. It is frequently argued that "genetically engineered" organisms will not have superior ability to survive in the environment because the addition of the engineered genetic material is likely to disrupt the coadaptation of the natural genomes of the organisms or because the added genetic material is likely to pose a physiological burden and thus be a handicap, or both. Given the evolutionary principle that a "new" organism must have an advantage in order to survive and

41

spread in the environment, and interpreting engineered modifications as disadvantages, it is not difficult to deduce that engineered organisms should not survive. But there is more to it than this relatively superficial view suggests.

The fundamental premise of evolutionary theory is that natural selection, the dominant force responsible for adaptations of organisms to their environments, operates on genetic alterations or novelties—mutations, rearrangements, and acquired accessory elements, such as plasmids—to produce evolutionary change. It follows that at least some genetic alterations improve the abilities of organisms to survive, reproduce, compete for resources, or invade new habitats. A general assertion that genetic alterations, be they natural or man-made, always lower the fitness of organisms is therefore not warranted and runs counter to basic evolutionary principles.

The Effect of Mutations

Some kinds of genetic alterations may be more apt to lower the fitness of organisms than others. In each of the major categories mentioned, some kinds of alterations probably do consistently lower fitness. Simple mutations that disrupt the production of necessary enzymes should, for example, certainly produce serious disadvantages. But what of mutations that do not affect essential proteins or that do not disrupt protein function? The existence of high levels of allelic diversity for many different proteins in many kinds of organisms is interpreted by some evolutionary biologists to mean that many simple mutations are not "perceived" by natural selection. And some simple mutations are clearly advantageous. Slight modifications in only one or a few genes are implicated or clearly documented in many phenomena involving changes in environmentally important phenotypes in all manner of organisms. Examples include expansions of the host ranges of insect and microorganism pests or parasites and acquisition of resistance to chemical control agents in insects and bacteria.

Mutations may also be associated with abilities of organisms to overcome natural limiting factors. Such changes may allow organisms to invade new habitats, which, in turn, may produce concomitant changes in their surrounding ecological communities. An example involves cheatgrass, a plant once restricted to moderately moist habitats. The Agricultural Research Service reported that because of a mutation that must have occurred about 10 years ago, cheatgrass is now able to colonize rangelands with dry sandy soils in which it was previously unable to survive. The overall result has been that millions of acres of western rangeland that were once considered unburnable are now subject to wildfires that destroy valuable grazing resources. Many of the engineered organisms being considered for environmental use also will have been purposely designed to overcome natural limiting factors such as low nitrogen, low temperatures, or predation by insects. Such changes, although accomplished with minor genetic modifications, can nevertheless be expressed as major shifts in properties of ecological significance. . . .

Ecological Roulette

Because they are alive, genetically engineered products are inherently more unpredictable than chemical products. Genetically engineered products can reproduce, mutate, grow, migrate. And once released, it's virtually impossible to recall living products back to the laboratory, especially microscopic viruses and bacteria.

Whenever a genetically engineered organism is released, there is always a small chance it will run amok. Each synthetic introduction is tantamount to playing ecological roulette. While there is only a small chance of it triggering an environmental explosion, if it does, the consequences can be thunderous and irreversible.

Jeremy Rifkin, *USA Today*, September 8, 1987.

Another favorite argument for dismissing concerns about the environmental products of biotechnology deals with "domesticated" species. Domesticated plants and animals are supposed to be familiar and their behavior predictable; unable to survive in the wild as a result of artificial selection for traits of use only to their "masters"; and, above all, harmless. Most of the agricultural and horticultural plant species common in the modern western world provide reasonable examples of just these characteristics. If the benign successes of modern agriculture furnished the only experiences on record, the conclusion one would draw is that domesticated species are not capable of inflicting ecological harm. Such is not the case, however. Feral populations of domesticated animals, particularly goats and rabbits, have repeatedly been responsible for massive damage to natural vegetation in both island and continental settings all over the world. Domestic cats are associated with dozens of cases of harmful predation on other animals, including more than 30 cases of complete extinction, in places where cats have been released by humans. To claim that all domesticated species are debilitated and harmless is simply incorrect. In addition, the assertion that the products of biotechnology can be construed as the equivalent of domesticated species is dubious, at best. Among bacteria, probably only two or three taxa, such as the human gut commensal, *Escherichia coli*, and the various species of nitrogen-fixing symbionts in the genus *Rhizobium*, have been studied well enough to qualify for the "domesticated" label. If these familiar organisms

43

represented the limits of biotechnology's horizons, there might indeed be little cause for concern, but they do not. The spectrum of organisms suitable for genetic engineering is already broad and, as technical capabilities continue to develop, may eventually include almost any organism deemed to have useful properties worth manipulating. It is not uncommon these days for genetic engineering efforts to begin on bacterial species that have only just been described and even before their basic physiological properties have been determined. In addition, most of what is known of the basic biological properties of bacteria is information that has been determined from laboratory work with single-species cultures. Knowledge of the biotic and abiotic interactions of most species in mixed populations in natural ecological systems is extremely limited. Currently the unknowns far outweigh the knowns where the ecological properties of microbes are concerned.

Harmful Natural and Engineered Modifications

Finally, there is the argument that no ecological harm will result from any man-made modifications that merely duplicate genotypes that already occur in nature. The basic premises are usually (i) that something must be truly "unique" (that is, not found in nature) to have potential for harm; and (ii) that in the 3 to 4 billion years over which life has evolved, nature herself has no doubt already produced organisms with all possible gene combinations. Since most of these have already failed the test of survival, there is no reason to be concerned that their man-made duplicates will be any more apt to survive and be harmful. Premise (ii) serves, in effect, as a neat "catch-22" for (i).

The premise that all possible gene combinations have already been tested in nature cannot be true. It has been estimated that there are 10^{70} atoms in the universe, whereas a single organism that is heterozygous at only 232 structural gene loci can produce 10^{70} different kinds of gametes. The sudden appearance of the virus that causes acquired immune deficiency syndrome should serve to convince us that nature occasionally does produce something with "new" and unanticipated properties. Equating "natural" with "harmless" makes no more sense than equating "artificial" or "manmade" with "harmful." Nature is full of harmful phenomena that would not be to mankind's benefit to duplicate or promote. And genetic modifications may be only one element contributing to an ecologically "unique" situation. Frequency-dependent effects and the influences of shifting environmental contexts are also important. To assert, for example, that the number of organisms released is not relevant to the magnitude of potential effects is to ignore a great deal of evidence to the contrary from both epidemiology and ecology. A basic principle of epidemiology is that the spread of an epidemic is dependent on, among other things, the size of the source pool of pathogens—the larger the source pool, the more effective the transmission of the disease agent. Ecologists have repeatedly observed threshold effects in the abilities of populations to survive. Large and concentrated numbers of organisms above critical population sizes may gain footholds where small populations cannot. To state that the scale of an introduction or application is only important for chemicals, but not for organisms, is absurd. Chemicals are invariably diluted, and are often degraded as they disperse among various environmental compartments. A population of released organisms that finds itself in a suitable environmental setting, however, may reproduce, evolve, and transfer genetic material to other organisms in the environment. Mistakes, therefore, can have permanent consequences.

The Risks of Genetic Engineering

Environmental scientists regard the safety of engineered organism products as a genuine concern that requires evaluation of associated risks. Regulation of biotechnology products is a means of ensuring that adequate consideration is given to risk assessment. This situation does not differ from that which pertains to new chemicals and drugs. Regulation of biotechnology products is justified and should be supported. . . .

Ecologists who have voiced their reservations about biotechnology's environmental products have done so for reasons of professional integrity and because of their concern for the environment. We are not Luddites or alarmists, but merely skeptics who wish to consider what the hidden costs of this promising new technology might be.

"Genetic engineering has revealed the universality, beauty and order of the rules of biology."

Research in Genetic Engineering Must Proceed

G.J.V. Nossal

G.J.V. Nossal is director of the Walter and Eliza Hall Institute of Medical Research in Melbourne, Australia. He has written several books on medicine. In the following viewpoint, he argues that many critics of genetic engineering are skeptical of all scientific progress. Nossal considers genetic engineering to be typical of new scientific technologies in that while it has risks, it promises ultimately to have great rewards in improving people's lives. He concludes that the risks of genetic engineering are manageable and research in genetic engineering should continue.

As you read, consider the following questions:

1: Why are some people afraid of science and genetic engineering, according to Nossal?
2. How does the author respond to those who argue that genetic engineering research should be stopped because it might one day cause harm?
3. Why does Nossal believe scientists' increasing knowledge of human genetics is inherently good?

G.J.V. Nossal, *Reshaping Life*. New York: Cambridge University Press, 1985. Reprinted with the permission of Cambridge University Press.

How far should scientists go in exploring the secrets of life? Who should decide what is an ethical and safe experiment? What concerns should influence a decision to move from laboratory bench to commercial application or clinical practice? Above all, how will the awesome power to manipulate the very fabric of life affect mankind's perception of the universe and man's place in it? These are just a few of the ethical, moral and philosophical issues arising from genetic engineering. None of them are entirely new, but the intensity with which they are being raised and the widespread nature of the debate exceed anything witnessed previously for the biological sciences. The picture is reminiscent of the agony of the atomic scientists over forty years ago. . . .

Distrust of Science

It is a fact that this technology, and extensions of it which can be logically foreseen, give mankind the possibility to find out more about the basic processes of life than ever before, and to create life forms in ways that nature never intended. These vast new powers frighten many people.

In fact, there is nothing new about a distrust of science. In his brilliant essay, 'Reflections on the Neo-Romantic Critique of Science', Leo Marx reminds us that many of the eighteenth-century writers questioned 'the legitimacy of science both as a mode of cognition and as a social institution'. Alfred North Whitehead saw this romantic reaction as 'a protest on behalf of the organic view of nature, and also a protest against the exclusion of value' from the sober array of facts which are the fruits of scientific work. Somehow, the Arcadian vision of nature as good, supreme, bountiful, was challenged by the impersonal machines of technology that were eroding nature's grip on human destiny. While the reliability of scientific knowledge within its own frame of reference has really not been seriously questioned since the days of Galileo, Whitehead sees a discrepancy between what science provides in the way of knowledge, and what mankind actually wants by way of a meaningful existence. Strangely, the romantic writers make scant mention of the effects of science and technology on the crushing burdens of work which the poor were forced to assume in order to eke out a meagre existence. More recently, C.P. Snow lamented the gap between the 'two cultures', but even he did not foresee the intensity of the dissident movement, the intelligent anti-science counter-culture, which reached its crescendo in the Vietnam war era. This saw science as the villain responsible not only for the tools of destruction but for fostering a mentality that could allow them to be used.

Basically, the opposition to major technological change, and thus indirectly to science, comes in two forms. On the one hand, there is a tendency for people to fear the unknown, to resist change, to preserve comfortable preconceptions, to resent new circumstances not of their own making. This kind of objection is best countered by modulating the rate of technological change, and while this is a major challenge for politicians and other decision-makers, the body politic has the capacity at least to address the issue and make appropriate choices.

Not Inherently Evil

Many people assume that the ability to change living beings is something that is new, complex, and therefore inherently dangerous. But mankind has been altering living species since before recorded history began, both accidentally and purposefully. Corn, wheat and nectarines are all examples of this kind of alteration.

The new techniques result from our better understanding of the process of life. They permit us to alter certain life processes in a defined way, instead of simply taking pot luck with the mutations and genetic accidents that Nature supplies as a starting point for many generations of laborious inbreeding, hybridizing and selection. Biotechnology techniques by themselves are neither good nor evil—but they can be used toward either end.

American Council on Science and Health, *Biotechnology: An Introduction*, 1988.

The second class of objection is more difficult to counter. It is more abstract, and relates to whether a scientific view of nature, after all a rather recent event in human affairs, somehow robs mankind of other ways of finding truth or knowledge. Theodore Roszak wonders whether an ingrained commitment to science as the reality principle 'frustrates our best efforts to achieve wholeness'. He links mankind's recent flirtation with science and technology to the sometimes terrifying trend to urbanization, and deplores the 'technocratic elitism' which characterizes not only the industrialized countries but also dominates the leadership of most developing countries.

It would be altogether too facile to dismiss this category of opposition to science as being Luddite responses of disaffected minorities. Many able and intelligent people perceive a genuine threat. For example, Pope John Paul II, in an address to UNESCO, expressed the following view:

> The future of man and mankind is threatened, radically threatened, in spite of very noble intentions, by men of science. . . . Their discoveries have been and continue to be exploited—to the prejudice of ethical imperatives—to ends . . . of destruction and death to a degree never before attained, causing unimaginable ravages. . . . This can be verified in the

realm of genetic manipulations and biological experiments as well as in those of chemical, bacteriological or nuclear armaments. . . .

This vision of science as somehow anti-human, coldly perverting people from a truly satisfying destiny, must be refuted, because it offends common sense—it is simply not true. If fault there be, it lies in mankind's nature and the uses to which power may be put.

In Defense of Scientific Truth

Science and technology have been embraced by people all over the world for one simple reason: they work. Sir Peter Medawar has argued that 'science, broadly considered, is incomparably the most successful enterprise human beings have ever engaged upon'. We do not have to go all the way with Marcelin Berthelot who declared that science 'will provide the truly human basis of morals and politics in the future'. Nevertheless, it is unfair to blame science and technology for ills in the human condition that are as old as mankind: for undue aggression, selfishness, greed and a chronic incapacity to live up to one's highest aspirations. It is as illogical to blame science and technology for not slaking our thirst for spirituality and transcendence as it would be to blame literature, art and music for not feeding, clothing and sheltering us. Science can only address part of the phenomenon of man. In my experience, few people realize this more fully than the scientists themselves, who, as a group, are better read and more concerned with humanistic values than many other technical and professional groups.

There are undoubtedly some who will say that genetic engineering research offends nature, that the creation of new life forms should be left in the hands of evolution, not in mankind's. We must listen to this view, but also be careful to explain to its proponents that conventional genetic techniques employed by civilizations for ten thousand years have already had a formidable impact on the ecosystem, and it might indeed be difficult to distinguish, say, a disease-resistant strain of wheat created by scientific breeding and selection pre-1975 from one fashioned tomorrow through the new technology. Should we really stop ourselves from accelerating the search for moulds making better or cheaper antibiotics because DNA splicing is somehow intrinsically bad? Well, if it appears that this makes little sense, should we at least declare 'hands off' genetic engineering of higher life forms such as mammals? But if genetic manipulation of growth hormones were to allow a steer to grow to full size in six months rather than three years, is it evil to create such animals given that we already have feed lots, and that the world is hungry for first class protein?

49

What, then, about human beings as genetic guinea pigs? This is clearly the area that has caused the most concern and also confusion. At the moment, the only realistic possibilities that can be foreseen are manipulations of cells and tissues of a given sick human individual, one of whose genes is unhealthy. This seems worth while and noble if it can be achieved. There is currently no approach which can cure single gene defects inside a person so as to repair the genes in all the sperms or all the ova. Accordingly, the only way of eradicating bad genes (or repairing them) for the benefit of future generations is to contemplate treatment of sperm, ova or early embryos in the test tube, prior to artificial insemination or embryo transplantation. Given that practical ways of doing this may be decades away, and that sperm or ovum selection may be more practical in many situations involving recessive gene traits, there still appears to be nothing that mankind should fear in this approach.

The Danger of Being Too Cautious

Many members of Congress and the biotech industry worry that overly oppressive safety regulations could threaten the nation's international leadership in the field. . . .

A more profound worry among some scientists and policymakers is not that the United States will come in second but that some of the potential benefits of biotechnology will not be realized at all if the field is bottle-necked at the level of small-scale research, especially in the nation's universities. If there is value in approaching a new technology with caution, there is also a price to be paid for clinging too long to the status quo.

Yvonne Baskin, *Business and Society Review*, Fall 1988.

Now we come to the famous 'thin edge of the wedge' style of argument. 'If you are curing thalassaemia today, will you not be tackling social rebelliousness tomorrow? If we allow this kind of thing to start, where will it all stop?' The first defence, but not the most important one, I believe, is that we still have only the sketchiest of notions about the processes of inheritance that govern complex features of character, or even most physical attributes such as strength, beauty, tendency to obesity and so forth. These are clearly the results of the interplay of a multiplicity of genes; and of societal and environmental forces impinging on each individual. They are therefore simply not amenable to gene therapy, and may never be. Even were this not the case, I find myself out of tune with a line of reasoning which says: 'I will not do this good thing, because it might lead me on to do that bad thing'. The whole history of mankind has been to probe, to examine, to explore, to seek the limits of understanding and then to exceed them, each generation building on the legacy of its predecessors. To deny that thirst for knowledge is to destroy mankind's wholeness, more surely than anything else.

Knowledge Is Good

And what if the chemical nature of man is the object under study? Is it healthy for us to know that we are 'just' a few DNA molecules being copied and read? The answer again is blindingly clear. Of course it is good for us to know more about what we are; at worst, this knowledge might allow us to prevent and cure our most obvious ailments; at best, it might even help us to deal more effectively with one another. No knowledge of a natural truth gained by objective search can be harmful, though its misuse obviously can. Furthermore, no depth of insight into the physical nature of man that we can derive from scientific experimentation will detract from or compete with the insights that we gain through the humanities, though indeed a complementation is an eventual possibility. . . .

Groundless Fears

Speculations about the future of genetic engineering tend to fall into groups, each possessing able and vocal proponents. There are those most excited about the industrial and commercial potential, who see new Silicon Valleys emerging, capable of jetting whole nations into a new golden age of prosperity. Then there are those whose dominant concern is with twin dangers. They fear a wilful or accidental release of highly pathogenic species into the biosphere. They also worry that an excessively mechanistic appreciation of the nature of life may further drive mankind towards materialism and a sterile, stereotyped view of the universe, devoid of subtlety or value. . . .

A fuller understanding of man's biological nature, not by a few experts, but by large masses of people, could prove to be a very liberating influence. Ignorance, superstition, fear of unknowable dark forces, oppression by the few gifted with knowledge and power—these have been the impediments which over the centuries have fettered the human spirit. A conviction that even the most profound and obscure realities—the nature of consciousness, the uniqueness of each individual—are the results of orderly processes, which obey rules and possess structure, must allow a person to confront his or her destiny with a heightened awareness and strength. If, further to that, a belief grows that these rules and structures are knowable, this surely permits man to walk into the future tall and free-striding, more determined to shape that future himself. As the biological basis of the phenomenon of man is gradually revealed, I have no doubt that, far from leading to a sterile or uniform vision, a richly-patterned, fine-grained mosaic will emerge, dazzling in its complexity, diversity and subtlety. We are a long way from that point, groping about as we are at this taxonomic and descriptive stage of gene research. We cannot yet pick Einstein from a dullard or Mozart from a tone-deaf philistine on the basis of DNA sequence data. But we have made a beginning. We can describe the differences between the genetic make-up of two people more fully than ever before. We can say profound things about the diseases each is more likely to get, and the biochemical weaknesses each is capable of passing down to offspring. Of necessity, our first concern has been with abnormalities, potentially capable of detection, but analysis of variances between normal people, as a problem in its own right, has also begun. The correlation of these with those physical or mental characteristics that matter to us will be an awesome task, the work of centuries rather than decades, but we need certainly not fear what the search will uncover.

Our Cultural Heritage

Genetic engineering has revealed the universality, beauty and order of the rules of biology. These rules create the diversity of life that we revere and cherish. It now appears a matter of prime importance that the central truths which are emerging find their way into the school curricula, not only for that small proportion of children and youths who choose to study biology as a specialty, but indeed for all future citizens. In the deepest sense, DNA's structure and function have become as much part of our cultural heritage as Shakespeare, the sweep of history, or any of the things we expect an educated person to know. The era in which the fundamentals of molecular biology and genetic engineering are taught in high school could well prove to be the era when man finally becomes comfortable with science, one of his prize creations, and more mature in ensuring that its power is harnessed towards noble ends.

"I don't think [genetic engineering is] an acceptable or necessary risk."

Research in Genetic Engineering Should Be Halted

Linda Bullard

Linda Bullard is a feminist and social activist who has worked with the Foundation on Emerging Technologies, a Washington, D.C. organization that seeks to restrict genetic engineering research. In the following viewpoint, she argues that genetic engineering represents humanity's latest attempt to control and dominate nature, and that it could lead to social and ecological catastrophe. While acknowledging that genetic engineering has potential benefits, she concludes that its risks are so great that the technology should be banned.

As you read, consider the following questions:

1. What irony does Bullard see in the promised benefits of genetic engineering?
2. Why does Bullard believe genetic engineering is a feminist issue?
3. What makes genetic engineering uniquely important and dangerous, according to the author?

From Linda Bullard, "Killing Us Softly: Toward a Feminist Analysis of Genetic Engineering," chapter nine of *Made to Order*, Patricia Spallone and Deborah Lynn Steinberg, editors. New York: Pergamon Press, 1987. Reprinted with permission of Pergamon Press.

If the present trend continues, genetic engineering will very soon permeate every facet of human activity, having profound social, political, legal, and economic ramifications. Reproduction technologies represent one of the more visible manifestations of the new industry. Perhaps more subtle, but not less dramatic, will be applications in agriculture, pharmaceuticals, animal husbandry, energy production, pollution control, and the military, to cite only a few. The US Patent Office has received to date more than 5500 applications for patenting biotechnology products, and issued 850 such patents in 1986. It is estimated that by the year 2010, 70 percent of the US Gross National Product will be linked to biotechnology. That means Big Business, and the Big Businessmen are well aware of it. When the first biotechnology company, Genentech, made its initial public offering on the stockmarket in 1980, it set the Wall Street record for fastest increase in price per share (from $35 to $89 in 20 minutes). The next year Cetus set another Wall Street record for the largest amount of money raised in an initial public offering. Here are some of the kinds of things they're investing in.

Health Products

About 83 percent of all capital investment in biotechnology is in the field of human health-related products. Many drugs and vaccines will be produced by living factories, drugs such as insulin, growth hormone, and interferon, which are already on the market. In one of these living factory experiments, biologists at Monsanto have transplanted a human gene into a pink petunia with the aim of getting it to secrete a female reproductive hormone. . . .

In the area of animal husbandry, the US Department of Agriculture is conducting experiments to engineer new super-breeds of livestock by transplanting the gene for human growth hormone into the animals. By so doing they hope to be able to produce cows the size of elephants and pigs the size of cows, which grow to maturity in half the time it now takes. This has already been successful with mice, and so there is now a variety of mice in our world which expresses the human trait for growth hormone. In West Germany a pig has been developed which has no eyes, so that it is not distracted from eating. . . .

In the area of information technology, computers of the new Age may have their chips replaced by proteins called "biochips." Part of the Pentagon's Star Wars budget is devoted to research on this kind of "molecular computer".

In the field of environmental engineering, microorganisms have already been created which can eat up oil spills and consume wood pulp, as well as mine copper. . . .

And last but not least, we must not forget that gene technology opens up marvelous new possibilities in the field of weaponry. In fact, genetic engineering itself is in a very real sense the direct descendent of the Bomb. When we entered the Atomic Age with the bombing of Hiroshima and Nagasaki in 1945 scientists and some government officials realized that radiation could have harmful effects on human gene mutation. This sparked a renewed interest in genetics research, and the Atomic Energy Commission began to pour funds into this field. One of their grants went to James Watson and Francis Crick, who, in 1953, unraveled the molecular structure of DNA, the key to genetic engineering. . . .

The Biological Weapons Convention (BWC) was concluded in 1972, *before* the discovery of recombinant DNA, cloning, and the other major techniques of genetic engineering; had it been delayed only slightly, it probably would not have been concluded at all. Despite the existence of this treaty, there are clear indications that a dangerous new spiral of the arms race has already begun using the technology of genetic engineering.

The first and most striking indication is how much money is being spent by the military on biological weapons and genetic engineering research. . . .

The second indication of a new kind of arms race is the marked shift in what Defense Department and administration officials have been doing and saying in public. . . .

Two Futures

Two futures beckon us. We can choose to engineer the life of the planet, creating a second nature in our image, or we can choose to participate with the rest of the living kingdom. Two futures, two choices. An engineering approach to the age of biology or an ecological approach. The battle between bioengineering and ecology is a battle of values. Our choice, in the final analysis, depends on what we value most in life. If it is physical security, perpetuation at all costs, that we value most, then technological mastery over the becoming process is an appropriate choice. But the ultimate and final power to simulate life, to imitate nature, to fabricate the becoming process brings with it a price far greater than any humanity has ever had to contend with. By choosing the power of authorship, humanity gives up, once and for all, the most precious gift of all, companionship.

Jeremy Rifkin, *Algeny*, 1983.

Two reports from the Pentagon to the US Congress make the reevaluation of the military significance of biological weapons abundantly clear. In August of 1986 the Deputy Assistant Secretary of Defense for Negotiations Policy, Douglas Feith, told the US House of Representatives, "The technology that makes possible

choose for our journey into the Age of Biology—the path of genetic engineering or the path of deep ecology. Our opponents are already gearing up for a massive and precisely calculated propaganda campaign to win hearts and minds over this issue. . . .

Challenging the dominant worldview and power structures on a fundamental level is nothing new for feminists. We have been doing it in a relatively organized way for more than 100 years. We need only look to our own history for the lessons to inform our development of a strategy against this latest onslaught of the patriarchy, genetic engineering.

In addition, I think we might do well to consider a method of decision making employed by people native to the northeastern part of what is now the United States. Whenever they were faced with a major and difficult problem, these Iroquois Indians would come together in a Tribal Council and ask themselves a single question: What will be the effect of the action which we take today on the seventh generation of our children? And they wouldn't take a decision until they could answer that question.

I don't think we can answer that question today for gene technology—we simply don't have a predictive ecology methodology which enables us, and until we can answer it, I don't think it's an acceptable or necessary risk.

Distinguishing Between Fact and Opinion

This activity is designed to help develop the basic reading and thinking skill of distinguishing between fact and opinion. Consider the following statement: "American universities spend $5 billion every year on genetic engineering research." This is a factual statement because it could be proved by checking the amount of money allocated for this type of research in university budgets. But the statement, "American universities spend too much money on genetic engineering research," is an opinion. Someone who is a genetic engineer and thinks more money should be spent to refine the technologies would not agree.

When investigating controversial issues it is important that one be able to distinguish between statements of fact and statements of opinion. It is also important to recognize that not all statements of fact are true. They may appear to be true, but some are based on inaccurate or false information. For this activity, however, we are concerned with understanding the difference between those statements which appear to be factual and those which appear to be based primarily on opinion.

Most of the following statements are taken from the viewpoints in this chapter. Consider each statement carefully. *Mark O for any statement you believe is an opinion or interpretation of facts. Mark F for any statement you believe is a fact. Mark I for any statement you believe is impossible to judge.*

If you are doing this activity as a member of a class or group, compare your answers with those of other class or group members. Be able to defend your answers. You may discover that others come to different conclusions than you do. Listening to the reasons others present for their answers may give you valuable insights in distinguishing between fact and opinion.

> O = opinion
> F = fact
> I = impossible to judge

1. Biotechnology will create a disease-resistant world of mega-crops and super-herds.

2. Scientists have fused sheep and goat cells, creating an animal they call the "gheep."

3. When life itself becomes subject to patents and copyrights, the world that Aldous Huxley foresaw in *Brave New World* looms ever more like prophecy.

4. One hundred Third World nations meeting in Rome in late 1986 accused the West of "genetic imperialism."

5. Strength, beauty, the tendency to obesity, and so forth are the results of the interplay of many genes.

6. The vision of science as somehow anti-human must be refuted, because it offends common sense—it is simply not true.

7. DNA's structure and function have become as much part of our cultural heritage as Shakespeare.

8. If the present trend continues, genetic engineering will very soon permeate every facet of human activity.

9. It is estimated that by the year 2010, 70 percent of the U.S. gross national product will be linked to biotechnology.

10. Biologists at Monsanto have transplanted a human gene into a pink petunia with the aim of getting it to secrete a female reproductive hormone.

11. Genetic engineering is the most important and disturbing technological change in recorded history.

12. By the 1940s, it had been proven that the genes within cell chromosomes are made of DNA.

13. Genetic manipulations done by human beings to increase an organism's usefulness are detrimental to the organism's survival outside the special environments provided.

14. Genetically altered bacteria have been developed that will feed on oil slicks—a potentially effective way to handle accidental oil spills.

15. As early as the 1800s, it was known that all living organisms are composed of cells.

16. The probability that R-DNA modification can inadvertently convert a crop plant to a noxious weed is negligible and warrants little concern.

Periodical Bibliography

The following articles have been selected to supplement the diverse views presented in this chapter.

V. Elving Anderson   "Good and Harmful? Genetic Engineering," *Eternity*, April 1987.

C. Keith Boone   "Bad Axioms in Genetic Engineering," *Hastings Center Report*, August/September 1988.

Erwin Chargaff   "Engineering a Molecular Nightmare," *Nature*, May 21, 1987.

Robert K. Colwell   "Another Reading of the NAS Gene Report," *BioScience*, June 1988.

Stanley T. Crooke   "Knowledge and Power," *Vital Speeches of the Day*, September 15, 1988.

Bernard D. Davis   "Bacterial Domestication: Underlying Assumptions," *Science*, March 13, 1987.

James A. Drake, David A. Kenny, and Timothy Voskuil   "Environmental Biotechnology," *BioScience*, June 1988.

William A. Durbin Jr.   "Should Christians Oppose Genetic Engineering?" *Christianity Today*, September 4, 1987.

Richard Godown   "The Edge of Discovery," *American Legion Magazine*, March 1988.

Charles Hagedorn   "Potential and Risk in Commercial Use of Microorganisms," *Forum for Applied Research and Public Policy*, Fall 1989.

John Leo   "Genetic Advances, Ethical Risks," *U.S. News & World Report*, September 25, 1989.

Thomas H. Maugh II and Kevin Davis   "Genetically Engineered Organisms Not Dangerous, Science Panel Finds," *Los Angeles Times*, September 21, 1989.

Leslie Roberts   "Ethical Questions Haunt New Genetic Technologies," *Science*, March 3, 1989.

Edward Tivnan   "Jeremy Rifkin Just Says No," *The New York Times Magazine*, October 16, 1988.

Gerry Waneck   "Safety and Health Issues Revisited," *Science for the People*, May/June 1985.

Can Genetic Engineering Improve Health?

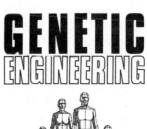

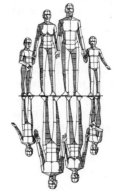

Chapter Preface

Scientists have envisioned several ways in which genetic engineering can be used to improve human health.

Currently, biotechnology companies have succeeded in engineering bacteria for the manufacture of drugs and chemicals that are otherwise hard to produce. Products now available include insulin and human growth hormone. These developments have raised relatively little controversy.

Scientists have also envisioned the direct use of genetic engineering on human patients. This process, also called gene therapy, is still in the experimental stage, but because it has the potential for permanently changing a patient's genes and those of his or her descendants, it has raised much controversy.

Proponents of gene therapy argue that it could provide a cure for many genetically caused diseases. Some envision a future in which humans can be redesigned and improved. But opponents of gene therapy assert that any genetic tinkering with humans is ethically wrong and should be avoided. They argue that instead of changing a person's genes, doctors should focus on improving a person's environment and diet. Opponents also assert that attempts to redesign and "improve" humans raise profound ethical dilemmas.

The viewpoints in this chapter discuss whether genetic engineering, and especially gene therapy, can improve human health.

"Soon, we will have the capacity to remake . . . [our] image in any way we choose."

Humans Should Be Genetically Redesigned

Brian Stableford

Brian Stableford is a lecturer at the University of Reading, England, and the author of several books on science. In the following viewpoint, he argues that future advances in genetic engineering will enable scientists to redesign the human body. Stableford views this as a positive development, and explains how human health, metabolism, and sensory perception can be improved.

As you read, consider the following questions:

1. How does Stableford respond to the argument that genetic engineering is unnatural?
2. What possible improvements of the human body does Stableford describe?
3. Why does the author believe that genetic engineering of humans must be accepted?

Until now, we have had to be content with the image in which evolution has shaped us. Soon, we will have the capacity to remake that image in any way we choose. Many people find this a horrifying idea. Most of us would be prepared to sanction the use of genetic engineering techniques on human beings in order to repair damaged or diseased bodies, and even to extend our lifespan. But to many people, it would be a very different matter to alter men crucially in form and structure—to modify what 'nature' has determined and produce new kinds of human being.

The new kinds of people discussed in this [viewpoint] *are* unnatural, but so are we. Popular ideas of what is 'natural' and what is 'unnatural' are to some extent arbitrary. Everything that makes us human as well as animal is 'unnatural', the product of human knowledge and not of genetic destiny. Agriculture, cooking, wearing clothes, reading books, science, technology, medicine and even language can be seen as unnatural if observed with a dispassionate eye. Modern man is not the product of nature, but the product of his own attempts to remake himself and to reshape his life. What we are today is the result of millions of choices made by millions of men over the last few tens of thousands of years. If we have achieved relatively little in the way of altering the form of our bodies, it is because of the limitations of our power rather than the dictates of our collective conscience.

Even if we do not like the idea at all, we should still be willing to accept that when the technology does exist for transforming human egg cells in such a way as to produce new kinds of human being, it is likely to be used. As long as there are purposes to be served by such a technology, it will be put into practice; and it is not too difficult to imagine motives which the people of the future might have that would lead them to play at being God. No doubt the first individuals who decide they want to do it will meet powerful and outspoken opposition, but it is difficult to believe that in the long run such opposition can prevail. If there are any mankinds at all a thousand years from now, there will be many mankinds. There are no grounds for doubting it.

Improving on Nature

In one of the most widespread modern hero-myths, an Everyman figure called Clark Kent harbours within an innocent disguise his true identity: Superman, the man of steel. The notion that a meek victim of circumstance can be transformed into an omnicompetent demigod is an appealing one; but designing new human species cannot give us the power of instant self-transformation, nor will it enable us to produce people invulnerable to injury, capable of levitation or possessing X-ray vision. Nevertheless, many improvements to our capabilities will be within the compass of the genetic engineers of the future, affecting not only the structure of our bodies, but also their metabolism and powers of perception. The desire to improve on nature will probably be one of the first motives to encourage them to design the seed of a new kind of man.

Genetic Intervention Is Ethical

While some people object to all genetic intervention, others only object to genetically designing human beings—not to repairing genetic faults *after* they are conceived or born. In short, they justify it for treatment but not for prevention.

This is somewhat more humane than the blanket condemnations but hardly any more rational. It is absurd to be willing to cure human ills or lacks but unwilling to avoid or supply them before they afflict us. Such a strange posture is ethical nonsense. For example, in the relatively benign area of cosmetic surgery for disfiguring physical traits, who would prefer to have it done over and over again from generation to generation when it could be obviated once and for all by genetic intervention?

Joseph Fletcher, *The Ethics of Genetic Control*, 1988.

What appals us most when we contemplate the human condition is probably our frailty: the ease with which we can be damaged, and our vulnerability to disease. Nature, like contemporary commercial technology, seems overfond of planned obsolescence, and human bodies suffer the double disadvantage of being soft and brittle at the same time. If one were laying down specifications for a new kind of man, one would probably ask first that he should have flesh which would not tear so easily and bones which would not snap so readily. Next, one might ask that he be given the capacity to recover much more completely from inflicted damage, by regenerating tissues and regrowing limbs and organs.

Why, if regrowing damaged parts is such a wonderful idea, has natural selection not already endowed us with such a capacity? Partly, this is because natural selection usually works in the most economical way available. It makes good sense for an organism to maintain repair facilities for skin—skin is very likely to be torn or scratched, but such tears and scratches are unlikely to be fatal. On the other hand, organs deep within the body are much less likely to be injured, and if they are injured the likelihood is that the injury will prove fatal anyhow. The cost-effectiveness of endowing individuals with great powers of self-repair also has to be compared with the cost-effectiveness of simple replacement of a whole individual by another grown from a new egg. This does not mean, though, that such repair would be impossible.

It would undoubtedly be hard to give redesigned people the

67

chance to regenerate completely if they suffer great damage. Regenerating bodies might not be too difficult, but regenerating minds is another matter: if the brain is starved of oxygen for only a few minutes, the person is destroyed, even though the cells can be revived. We will not be able to produce a race of people who could afford to be casual about massive blood loss or temporary heart failure, but it would be a significant step forward if a new kind of people could be given the power to seal off leaking blood vessels and the power to keep their hearts pumping even in the most difficult circumstances. This would allow time for sophisticated regrowing mechanisms to come into place, restoring lost limbs and smashed organs, or simply time to reach medical aid. The more effective our methods of medical care become, the more it will be to our advantage to adapt ourselves to make the maximum use of them.

Even when not subject to accident or disease, the human body is an imperfect structure made out of imperfect materials. For instance, people are especially prone to back trouble, because one of the weakest aspects of human bioengineering is the spine. Natural selection cannot be held entirely to blame for the design faults of the human spine, largely because it had such unpromising material to start with: there were limitations on what could reasonably be done in modifying our quadrupedal ancestors for upright life. The careful human engineer would surely try to do better in providing his creations with a backbone sturdy enough, yet flexible enough, to answer the various demands made of it.

The main function of a skeleton is to provide rigid support and protection for the soft parts of the body, while at the same time providing adequate jointing and manual dexterity. One wishes occasionally, though, that there were more freedom of action permitted by some of the joints, and that the rigidity of the long bones could be temporarily modified. If redesigned man could have the capacity to modify the properties of his skeleton (however slightly) at will, that might be greatly to his advantage.

A New Metabolism

As well as modifying the body's structural properties, it would also be convenient to pay serious attention to its metabolism. An engaging notion would be to increase the range of substances which the body can utilize as food. There are all kinds of organic molecules which we cannot digest, because we lack the enzymes which would be necessary to break them down into smaller molecules that can be used directly for energy production.

One unusable substance of which we eat quite a lot is cellulose, the principal structural substance in plant tissue. It becomes the 'roughage' in our diet, passing all the way through our digestive system. There is no reason in principle why cellulose should not be a useful food; it is a long-chain molecule whose individual units are glucose. If our bodies could make an enzyme to break up the chain, the glucose units could then be handled very conveniently by metabolic apparatus which we already produce. Actually, there are no higher organisms which possess such an enzyme. Herbivorous animals which live primarily on grass or leaves rely on microorganisms which live in their gut to break down cellulose for them.

Adapting men to digest cellulose would be a very minor modification in biochemical terms—as long as the required enzyme could in fact be designed—but it would be of very considerable significance. It would be very difficult for such redesigned people to find themselves facing starvation. As long as there was live plant material around, they could get by. . . .

There are other aspects of metabolism which might be modified productively. Control of metabolic rate might be a useful talent to have. Routine hibernation is not something that would be useful to most human beings, but the ability to slow the metabolic rate voluntarily to suit particular situations could be valuable. The most frequently suggested use for such an ability is to allow people to sustain themselves economically through long journeys in interplanetary—perhaps even interstellar—space.

Passing on Biological Heritage

For thousands of years now, people have had to accept responsibility for passing on to their children some material wealth and some wealth of knowledge. We have grown used to the problems attached to these responsibilities, though we may still feel them to be uncomfortable. In the future, the responsibilities will not only become heavier still, but will widen in scope. Future generations will have to decide not only what cultural heritage to pass on to their children, but what biological heritage. Even a refusal to intervene with the systems of human genetic inheritance would be an exercise of that responsibility: the choice will soon be there, and to refrain from using our opportunities is simply one way of exercising that choice.

Brian Stableford, *Future Man*, 1984.

It is likely that none of these modifications would be very sweeping in biochemical terms. None of them would require the wholesale alteration of the system we have inherited; it is a matter of tinkering. The consequences of such changes, in terms of human abilities and lifestyles, would nevertheless be profound.

The third general area in which modifications might profitably be made to human capability is the area of sensory perception. The information provided by the five senses about what is going on around us is the raw material on which our intelligence works, and any improvement in its quality would be an advantage.

It is easy enough to imagine our senses working better—clearly, we do not smell as well as dogs or hear as well as bats—but there is a catch in the naive argument that each and every one of our senses might simply be able to take in more information. There is such a thing as too much information; the brain's capacity to cope with it can be overloaded. The intelligent use of the eyes, for instance, involves the capacity to ignore most of what falls within the field of vision, and the intelligent use of the ears involves blotting out of consciousness most of the sounds that are actually there. The human sensorium has been 'finely tuned' by natural selection to pick out most of the information relevant to our decisions, while neglecting much that is relatively unimportant.

A simple increase in the sensitivity of one or more of the senses could easily be counterproductive, because it would throw out this delicate filtering mechanism. Optimizing the capabilities of the five senses is therefore a much more complicated matter than it might initially seem. Even taking these arguments into account, though, there are some additional facilities for recovering information which it would certainly be useful to have.

Night-Vision

One point which immediately calls itself to mind is that humans are not good at seeing in the dark. There are many animals which are better at making use of low levels of light than we are—cats, for example. It would be very useful to enhance the ability of humans to see by night, provided that any modifications made to the eyes for that purpose are not prejudicial to the ability to see by day.

There are two ways by which night-vision might be enhanced. One strategy would be to rearrange the proportion and distribution of the receptors in the retina. The retina contains different kinds of light-sensitive cells—rods, which perceive dim light, and cones, which discern fine detail in bright light and are used in colour vision. In man, cones are concentrated in the centre of the retina and rods predominate round the edges. By this means the human eye can adjust moderately well to very different light intensities. Improving night-vision by rearranging the receptors might, however, have a detrimental effect on daytime vision.

The second strategy would be to increase the spectrum of radiation to which the eye is sensitive. If the eye were sensitive to radiation in the infra-red range, it would have far less difficulty in discriminating between objects in the dark—especially living objects which are radiating heat in those wavelengths. Again, the problem would be one of improving night-vision while not harming day-vision. In daylight, infra-red sensors might simply be overloaded. Some kind of internal 'switch' would be required which could activate some receptors and deactivate others, so that the eye could operate in one mode by day and another by night. How such a mechanism could be biochemically designed is not clear, but something along these lines might be managed. Another solution to the problem would be to have the night-vision eye, or eyes, separate from the day-vision eyes. This is the strategy followed by a certain kind of snake which has heat sensors as well as eyes.

Other Sense Organs

The eyes are not the only sense organs which can be recruited to solve the problem of getting around in the dark. Bats find their way around not by using their eyes, but by using their ears, and some marine mammals which have to cope with the murky ocean depths use a similar system of echo-location. Sonar and radar are technological versions of this method of sensing which we have found extremely useful in extending our powers of perception artificially.

It might conceivably be possible to equip redesigned human beings with some kind of system akin to that used by bats. This would involve whole new anatomical structures being added to the head, and it would mean also that people so equipped would have to learn to make use of a new kind of incoming information. . . .

Using the New Power

Biotechnology will develop, over the next few decades and the next few centuries, into an awesomely powerful force of social change. In refining it and applying it, we must think very carefully about the consequences of what we are doing. We must also think very carefully about the consequences of *not* doing things. It is not sensible to refuse opportunities to do good simply because the tools and techniques we would need might also be used to do harm. It is not sensible to regret the increase of man's dominion over nature, because it is to the increase of that dominion that we owe everything we possess and everything we value. The possession of great power requires us to exercise great responsibility, and to shrink from that responsibility is a kind of failure. It might, indeed, prove to be the case that our power over nature will eventually be used to destroy the world, but we already have enough power to annihilate ourselves, and if we did not have it in the past, we also did not have the power to defend ourselves against other annihilating forces. Our best hope for the future is that we can learn to turn our new powers to our advantage, building better defences against the forces of destruction, whether they be within or without.

"With human genetic engineering... we are forced to accept the idea of reducing the human species to a technologically designed product."

Humans Should Not Be Genetically Redesigned

Jeremy Rifkin

Jeremy Rifkin is one of the most prominent opponents of genetic engineering. As president of the Foundation on Emerging Technologies, an organization in Washington, D.C., he has sponsored numerous lawsuits against genetic engineering experiments, organized public protests against biotechnology, and written several books, including *Algeny*. In the following viewpoint, he argues that the potential to redesign the human race is one of the most disturbing aspects of genetic engineering. Rifkin worries that future humans might be redesigned to change racial or socially undesirable traits.

As you read, consider the following questions:

1. How does Rifkin define eugenics?
2. Why does the author argue that eugenics is inherent in all applications of genetic engineering?
3. According to Rifkin, what is the price humanity will pay for genetically engineering humans?

Jeremy Rifkin, *Declaration of a Heretic*, London: Routledge & Kegan Paul, 1985. Reprinted with permission of the William Morris Agency, New York.

Any thoughtful probe of genetic engineering technology must eventually wind its way toward a discussion of eugenics. Genetic engineering technology and eugenics are inseparably linked. To grapple with one requires a willingness to wrestle with the other.

The term eugenics was conceived by Sir Francis Galton in the nineteenth century and is generally dichotomized in the following way. Negative eugenics involves the systematic elimination of so-called biologically undesirable traits. Positive eugenics is concerned with the use of genetic manipulation to "improve" the characteristics of an organism or species.

Eugenics History

As a social philosophy, eugenics found its first real home here in America at the turn of the century. The rediscovery of Mendel's laws spurred renewed interest in heredity within the scientific community which, in turn, ignited a eugenics flame in the popular culture. . . .

Before running its course, the early eugenics movement imprinted its image directly on state and federal laws. Many states adopted sterilization statutes, and the US Congress passed a new immigration law in the 1920s based on eugenics doctrine. In the years that followed, thousands of American citizens were sterilized so they could not pass on their "inferior" traits, and the Federal Government locked its doors to certain immigrant groups deemed biologically unfit by then-existing eugenics standards.

The American experience with eugenics was soon dwarfed by the eugenics campaign initiated by the Third Reich. Determined to rid the world of all but the "pure" Aryan race, Adolf Hitler orchestrated a campaign of terror and mass genocide of such overwhelming magnitude that it is likely to remain the darkest shadow ever cast over the human experience. Over six million Jews and members of other religious and ethnic groups were rounded up from all over the European continent and interned in giant concentration camps. Convinced that these human beings were biologically unfit, the Third Reich committed itself to expunging their genetic inheritance from the human gene pool. The high command called it the final solution—the systematic elimination of an entire people by gassing in crematoria all over the continent.

At the same time, the Nazis launched an ambitious positive eugenics campaign, in which carefully screened Aryan women were selected to mate with elite SS officers. The pregnant women were housed and cared for in specially designated state facilities, and their offspring were offered up to the Third Reich as the representatives of the new super race that would rule the world for the next millennium.

After World War II, many voiced the hope that eugenics had finally come to rest alongside the mass unmarked graves that scarred the European landscape. Their hopes were to be short-lived. Beginning early in the 1970s the world began to hear scattered reports of great scientific breakthroughs occurring in the new field of molecular biology. By the mid 1980s those reports have cascaded into a torrent of new discoveries, so astonishing in scope that a somewhat bewildered public is finding itself unprepared to assess the full social implications. Of one thing, however, the public is fast becoming aware. Our scientists are developing the most powerful set of tools for manipulating the biological world ever conceived. This newfound power over the life force of the planet is raising once again the spectre of a new eugenics movement. After all, eugenics is defined as the systematic effort to manipulate the genetic inheritance of an organism or group of organisms to create a more "perfect" species. Now our scientists are providing us with tools that are, by their very nature, eugenic. This is the terrible reality that so few policy makers are willing to grasp.

The new genetic engineering tools are designed to be eugenics instruments. Whenever recombinant DNA, cell fusion and other related genetic techniques are used to improve the genetic blueprints of a microbe, plant, animal or human being, a eugenics consideration is built into the process itself.

The Perils of Germ-Line Gene Therapy

Underlying the altruistic aims of germ-line therapy lies the potentially dangerous perception that a troublesome gene can somehow deliberately be erased from the human gene pool. The history of eugenics suggests that once a human characteristic—such as a particular skin color or mutant hemoglobin molecules or poor performance on IQ tests—has been labeled a genetic "defect," we can expect voices in society to eventually call for the systematic elimination of those traits in the name of genetic hygiene. But the notion that the human genome is like some sort of genetic garden from which hereditary defects can simply be plucked like so many weeds is both mistaken and dangerously naive.

David Suzuki and Peter Knudtson, *Genethics*, 1989.

Much of genetic engineering is concerned with changing the genetic characteristics of a species. In laboratories all across the globe, molecular biologists are making daily decisions about what genes to alter, insert and delete from the hereditary code of an organism. These are eugenic decisions. Every time a genetic change of this kind is made, the scientist, the corporation or the state is tacitly, if not explicitly, making decisions about what are the good genes that should be inserted and preserved and what are the bad genes that should be altered or deleted. This is exactly what eugenics is all about. Genetic engineering is a technology designed to enhance the genetic inheritance of living things by manipulating their genetic code.

The Desire to Improve

Some might take offense at the idea that eugenics is built into the new genetic engineering technology. They prefer to equate eugenics with the Nazi experience of four decades ago. The new eugenics movement, however, bears no resemblance to the reign of terror that culminated with the holocaust. The US and the world is unlikely to witness the emergence of a new social eugenics movement in the foreseeable future. It is more likely that we will see the emergence of a wholly new kind of eugenics movement, one in which there are no evil conspirators, no faustian figures, no machiavellian institutions which we could conveniently point to as instigators and purveyors. The new eugenics is commercial eugenics, not social eugenics. The evil, if there is any, is the human compulsion for a better way of life, for a brighter, more promising future for succeeding generations.

Is it wrong to want healthier babies? Is it wrong to want more efficient food crops and livestock and improved sources of energy? Is it wrong to seek new ways to improve our standard of living? Genetic engineering is coming to us not as a sinister plot, but rather as a social and economic boon. Still, we ought not to confuse the good intentions of the creators of this science with the logic of the technology. Try as we will, there is simply no way to get around the fact that every decision that is made to alter the hereditary make-up of an organism or a species is a eugenics decision.

In the decades and centuries to come scientists will learn more about how the genes function. They will learn how to map more of the individual genetic traits and they will become increasingly adept at turning the genes on and off. They will become more sophisticated in the techniques of recombining genes and altering genetic codes. At every step of the way conscious decisions will have to be made as to which kind of permanent changes in the biological codes of life are worth pursuing and which are not. A society and civilization steeped in ''engineering'' the gene pool of the planet cannot possibly hope to escape the kind of ongoing eugenics decisions that go hand in hand with each new technological foray.

Social Pressure

There will be enormous social pressure to conform with the underlying logic of genetic engineering, especially when it comes to its human applications. Every prospective parent will be forced to decide whether to take their chances with the traditional genetic lottery or program specific traits in or out of their baby at conception. If they choose to go with the traditional approach, letting genetic fate determine their child's biological destiny, they could find themselves in deep trouble if something goes dreadfully wrong from a genetic perspective: something they could have avoided had they availed themselves of corrective genetic intervention at the embryo stage.

The Limits of Our Understanding

Our knowledge of how the human body works is still elementary. Our understanding of how the mind, both conscious and subconscious, functions is even more rudimentary. The genetic basis for instinctual behaviour is largely unknown. Our disagreements about what constitutes "human-hood" are notorious. And our insight into what, and to what extent, genetic components might play a role in what we comprehend as our "spiritual" side is almost nonexistent. We simply should not meddle in areas where we are so ignorant.

W.F. Anderson, quoted in *Modern Biotechnology*, 1987.

Consider the following scenario. Two parents decide not to program their fetus. The child is born with a deadly genetic disease. The child dies prematurely and needlessly. The genetic trait responsible for the disease could have been deleted from the fertilized egg by simple gene surgery. In the Genetic Age, a parent's failure to intervene with corrective genetic engineering of the embryo might well be regarded as a heinous crime. Society will undoubtedly conclude that every parent has a responsibility to provide as safe and secure an environment as humanly possible for their unborn child. Not to do so would be considered a breach of parental duty for which the parents would be morally if not legally culpable.

With the introduction of an array of new human reproduction technologies, the choices become even more problematic. In the coming decades molecular biologists will map the specific genes for hundreds of monogenic disorders, providing prospective parents with a complete and accurate listing of the specific genetic defects they will likely pass on to their offspring. In the past, a parent's genetic history provided markers for speculation, but there was still no way to know for sure whether specific genetic traits would be passed on. In the future, the guesswork will be increasingly eliminated posing a moral dilemma for prospective parents. Parents will have at their disposal a more and more accurate readout of their individual genetic make-ups, and will be able to predict the statistical probability of specific genetic disorders being passed on to their children as a result of their biological union.

At that point, parents will have to make critical choices. Whether to go ahead using their own egg and sperm, knowing their children will inherit certain "undesirable" traits, or whether to substitute either egg or sperm with a donor through in vitro fertilization, embryo transfers and other emerging human reproduction techniques.

While ethicists contend that these artificial reproduction procedures have, at best, only a limited market, they ignore the commercial compulsion to expand and create a universal marketplace for new technologies. Prospective parents will be cautioned that if they have any significant risk factor in their genetic make-up that might adversely affect their offspring, they would be better off purchasing either untainted sperm or healthier eggs rather than relying on their own biological assets. . . .

Advocates of human genetic engineering argue that it would be irresponsible not to use this new tool to help prevent deadly, disabling and disfiguring diseases. What they apparently overlook is the fact that there are at least 2,000 monogenic diseases alone. Should they all be eliminated from the hereditary code of our species over the coming centuries? Does it make sense to monoculture the human germ line as we have with domestic plants and animals, eliminating recessive traits that our species might need in the future to adapt to changing environmental conditions?

No Place to Stop

Once we decide to begin the process of human genetic engineering, there is really no logical place to stop. If diabetes, sickle cell anemia, and cancer are to be cured by altering the genetic make-up of an individual, why not proceed to other "disorders": myopia, color blindness, left-handedness? Indeed, what is to preclude a society from deciding that a certain skin color is a disorder? In fact, why would we ever say no to any alteration of the genetic code that might enhance the well-being of the individual or the species? It would be difficult to even imagine society rejecting any genetic modification that promised to improve, in some way, the performance of the human race.

The idea of engineering the human species is very similar to the idea of engineering a piece of machinery. An engineer is constantly in search of new ways to improve the performance of a machine. As soon as one set of imperfections is eliminated, the engineer immediately turns his attention to the next set of imperfections, always with the idea in mind of creating a perfect piece of machinery. Engineering is a process of continual improvement in the performance of a machine, and the idea of setting arbitrary limits to how much "improvement" is acceptable is alien to the entire engineering conception.

Whenever we begin to discuss the idea of genetic defects, there is no way to limit the discussion to one or two or even a dozen so-called disorders, because of a hidden assumption that lies behind the very notion of "defective." Ethicist Daniel Callahan penetrates to the core of the problem when he observes that "behind the human horror at genetic defectiveness lurks . . . an image of the perfect human being. The very language of 'defect,' 'abnormality,' 'disease,' and 'risk,' presupposes such an image, a kind of proto-type of perfection."

What Is the Price?

The question, then, is whether or not humanity should begin the process of engineering future generations of human beings by technological design in the laboratory. What is the price we pay for embarking on a course whose final goal is the "perfection" of the human species? How important is it that we eliminate all the imperfections, all the defects? What price are we willing to pay to extend our lives, to ensure our own health, to do away with all the inconveniences, the irritations, the nuisances, the infirmities, the suffering, that are so much a part of the human experience? Are we so enamored with the idea of physical perpetuation at all costs that we are even willing to subject the human species to rigid architectural design?

With human genetic engineering, we get something and we give up something. In return for securing our own physical well-being we are forced to accept the idea of reducing the human species to a technologically designed product. Genetic engineering poses the most fundamental of questions. Is guaranteeing our health worth trading away our humanity?

"The tools of genetic engineering are increasingly being applied toward... dramatic new ways of treating (perhaps even curing) afflictions such as cancer and birth defects."

Genetic Engineering Can Cure Inherited Diseases

Jim Merritt

Cystic fibrosis and sickle-cell anemia are two of more than four thousand inherited diseases believed to be caused by missing or defective genes. In addition, many researchers believe diseases such as cancer and Alzheimer's might have genetic roots. In the following viewpoint, Jim Merritt argues that genetic engineering holds great promise in curing many of these diseases. Merritt is a science writer and co-editor of *Princeton Today*, an alumni publication of Princeton University in New Jersey.

As you read, consider the following questions:

1. What do genes control, according to Merritt?
2. What are some of the advances in medicine and genetic engineering that Merritt believes may lead to curing genetic disorders?
3. How many people carry defective genes, according to the author?

Jim Merritt, "Design of Life," *Modern Maturity*, June/July 1989. Reprinted with the author's permission.

Invisible to the naked eye, the image of a fertilized mouse egg looked enormous when projected by a powerful microscope onto the television monitor. From the right of the screen, a hair-thin glass syringe appeared and nudged against the egg's outer envelope. The jellylike egg resisted briefly, then yielded as the syringe broke through and penetrated to one of its two pronuclei, darker round objects that would later fuse into the nucleus and begin the cell division leading to a fully formed fetus. The syringe punctured the pronucleus, which swelled noticeably as the syringe injected its contents and withdrew.

"Perfect," said Rachel Sheppard, the Princeton University biologist at the controls of the microscope. "Is this not extraordinary?"

Routine Operations

Extraordinary, but also astonishingly routine. Sheppard had just performed a standard operation carried out countless times a day in the laboratories of molecular biologists around the world. Over the next two hours she would repeat the procedure, known as "microinjection," on several hundred mouse ova. The material squirted into each contained copies of a foreign gene. In a little more than half the ova this gene would successfully insert itself among the thousands of other genes in the mouse's DNA (deoxyribonucleic acid), the long molecular chain in which an organism's genetic code is written. In this case the implanted gene came from another breed of mouse, but it could just as easily have come from another species; organisms as evolutionarily distant as yeast and humans have been fused with mouse DNA.

Later, reimplanted in female mice, the eggs would develop. Most of the mice born three weeks later would carry the foreign gene in every cell and would be "transgenic," meaning that if mated they would pass the gene on to their offspring.

Genetic Engineering

Microinjection is just one of many mind-boggling techniques available to biologists exploring the fantastically complex rules by which genes orchestrate life. While developed in university laboratories to further basic research, the tools of genetic engineering are increasingly being applied toward practical ends that promise longer and healthier lives through increased food production and dramatic new ways of treating (perhaps even curing) afflictions such as cancer and birth defects. . . .

The father of genetics, Austrian monk Gregor Mendel, would hardly recognize the science he founded in the 1860s, when his experiments in the crossbreeding of pea plants uncovered the fundamental rules governing how an organism inherits physical traits from its parents. Later, biologists named the elements controlling these traits *genes* (after the Greek word for stock or descent) and linked them to chromosomes, the squiggly objects microscopes have revealed to be present in all cell nuclei.

Scientists knew chromosomes were largely made up of DNA, but not until the 1950s did they discover the structure of DNA and how it carries the instructions for life. The DNA molecule is built like a long, twisted ladder, whose "rungs" are assembled from bases known as A, T, G and C. These are the four "letters" of the genetic alphabet from which words and sentences—the genes themselves—are formed. If the genetic code for making a human being were typed on paper, it would fill a thousand thick volumes, the equivalent of a small library.

Genes not only determine a person's physical characteristics (the color of his skin or eyes, for instance), they control the whole chemistry of life through the production of proteins. Each of the estimated 100,000 human genes carries the instructions for making a protein essential to some bodily function. Structural proteins in skin, bone and cartilage hold us together. Muscle proteins store and release energy. The protein hemoglobin carries oxygen from lungs to tissues. Hormones that regulate growth and sex drive are proteins, as are the antibodies that fend off disease, and enzymes necessary for digestion.

New Weapons

The fruits of gene therapy may be here before anyone had expected—and they will be enjoyed by more of us than had ever been dreamed. And just as the advent of antibiotics transformed medicine by giving doctors weapons to fight infectious diseases, so gene therapy promises weapons to fight inherited, chronic, and degenerative diseases. The rare Lesch-Nyhan syndrome and severe combined immune deficiency are still high on the priority list because of their straightforward genetics. But medical researchers are already beginning to think about therapies for more common conditions, including heart disease, emphysema, diabetes, cancer, and Alzheimer's disease.

Science Impact, April 1989.

Scientists also recognize the central role of genes in an embryo's development from a single-celled fertilized egg to the miraculous complexity of a newborn baby, and in the regulation of cell growth throughout life. The DNA in all our nonreproductive cells contains our entire genetic repertoire, yet somehow a cell manages to "switch on" only those genes needed to fulfill its purpose, and at precisely the right time and in the correct sequence. When this clockwork mechanism goes awry, the result can be birth defects or the rampaging cell growth known as cancer. In ways biologists are only beginning to grasp, genes also play a key part in aging.

Radiation and foreign chemicals can cut or scramble DNA, and one theory of aging suggests that over time, the body loses its ability to repair this damage. Another theory proposes that genes in aging cells become inefficient at disposing of no-longer-needed proteins.

Gene Therapy

In the early 1970s scientists developed the process of gene-splicing: chemically snipping genes out of the DNA of one organism, joining them to the DNA of another, and inserting the composite into a cell (usually that of a bacterium). "Cloning" the altered bacterium—reproducing endless identical copies, each containing the foreign gene—created a source for producing large quantities of the gene's protein. Insulin, the hormone essential for metabolizing sugar, became the first protein made by such methods. Marketed since 1982, it has proved a blessing to those diabetics allergic to insulin derived from its traditional source, the pancreases of cows and pigs.

With the advent of gene-splicing, the biotechnical revolution was off and running. Scientists were quick to realize the new technology's potential for treating certain genetic diseases. Although it's still some years in the future, doctors envision a time when they will practice "gene therapy," actually entering cells to repair their genetic machinery. One way of doing this is by enlisting viruses to transport normal versions of a gene to cells in which the gene is missing or defective.

The first human experiments with gene-splicing are likely to be carried out soon, and medical scientists look forward to its becoming a clinical weapon against inherited disorders in which the lack of a functioning gene prevents production of some vital protein. Type A hemophiliacs, for example, are missing portions of the gene responsible for the blood-clotting enzyme known as Factor VIII. If normal versions of the gene were inserted into their marrow cells, they might produce the missing enzyme in sufficient quantity for a cure. (Currently, these hemophiliacs must rely on transfusions of blood serum with concentrations of Factor VIII. Because the serum is derived from human blood it can carry harmful viruses, including those for hepatitis and AIDS.)

Hemophilia is only one of more than 4,000 inherited diseases, a few of which are hopeful subjects for genetic research. Among the most common are cystic fibrosis, Huntington's and Tay-Sachs diseases, sickle-cell anemia and retinal cancer, as well as some forms of Alzheimer's disease, muscular dystrophy, heart disease and mental illness.

Medical scientists have taken the first steps toward understanding some of the worst hereditary illnesses' genetics by finding the responsible gene's general location on a "map" of a human's 23 chromosome pairs. Huntington's chorea, a severe nervous system disorder that comes on in middle age and killed folk-singer Woody Guthrie, results from a defective gene on the short arm of chromosome 4. The gene for retinoblastoma, a devastating eye cancer, lies on chromosome 13. The suspected gene for the familial form of Alzheimer's disease is on chromosome 21. And some types

How Gene Therapy Might Work

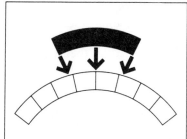

1. New gene inserted into virus.

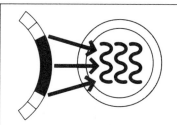

2. Virus infects endothelial cell, and is incorporated in DNA along with new gene.

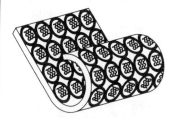

3. Cell is grown in culture into sheets of cells, which curl up to form a tiny capillary.

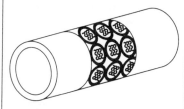

4. Capillary is spliced into existing blood vessel in the body.

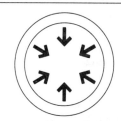

5. Insulin or other protein produced by new gene is released into blood vessel.

Wayne Vincent, copyright 1989 by Impact Publications. Used with permission.

of schizophrenia and manic depression have been traced to chromosomes 5 and 11.

For each of these diseases, scientists thus far have found only the defective gene's approximate location among the hundreds of other genes in its chromosomal neighborhood. This is sufficient, however, to allow screening of individuals with family histories of the disease. Pinpointing the exact location of the gene—its "street address" among all the other genes in its neighborhood—is a more daunting task; but once accomplished, it could lead to a screening test for a broad population. Among other benefits, genetic screening could help identify couples at risk of having children with genetic disorders. A couple could then conceive several embryos *in vitro* (outside the womb) and test for one that is defect-free. Reimplanted in the womb, the embryo would grow to become a normal baby.

In many cases, of course, environment and personal habits play key roles in inherited diseases. At least one form of colon cancer, for example, has been traced to a faulty gene, although eating fatty foods over many years may trigger it to begin making tumors. Cigarette smoke and other carcinogens can also act in concert with genes to cause cancer. According to Eric Lander, a fellow at the Whitehead Institute for Biomedical Research in Cambridge, Massachusetts, genetic screening could allow people "to practice a kind of personalized preventive medicine by tailoring their lifestyles in accordance with their genetic predispositions."

Decoding a Gene

Once isolated, a gene can be "sequenced" or decoded, revealing the specific order in which its bases (A, T, G, C) are assembled. This in turn allows scientists to decipher the gene's product—an enzyme, perhaps, critical to some cellular function. The cause of Duchenne muscular dystrophy, a crippling disease that strikes one of every 4,000 American male children, was completely unknown until 1986, when scientists succeeded in finding and decoding the gene, which turned out to be the blueprint for a structural protein in muscles. From such basic understanding of a disease can emerge new ways of treating it.

Scientists have known for years that Alzheimer's disease, an affliction in which the victim suffers a gradual loss of memory, is linked in some way to the buildup of amyloid peptide in the brain. Possible villains include the genes that code either for the peptide itself or for an enzyme that breaks down the peptide. Researchers have succeeded in creating a screening test for a few families with a history of the disease. However, any broader test is still probably years away, and researchers emphasize the need for more basic information on the biochemistry of Alzheimer's and how environment may influence it.

Finding and sequencing the Alzheimer's gene (or genes) will yield vital clues about the disorder, but this can only be done through a tedious process called "chromosome walking," in which successively smaller bits of DNA are examined. "We have a rough idea where it is," says research scientist Peter St. George-Hyslop of Massachusetts General Hospital, "but there are probably 30 or more genes in the general area. Isolating the one for Alzheimer's will take several more years of hard slogging." . . .

A Giant Step

Science will take a giant step toward understanding the entire rogues' gallery of inherited diseases with the expected launching of a massive federal effort, projected to take 15 years and cost $3 billion, directed at mapping and decoding all of the estimated 100,000 human genes. The project's end result will be a detailed construction manual for the genome, the entirety of genetic material that defines us as a species.

In the view of the Hastings Center's Kathleen Nolan, one result of the genome project may be to show that faulty genes are ubiquitous throughout the population. "We already know that most people carry at least a few potentially harmful genes, although usually in a recessive form that only causes trouble if it occurs in double dosage." (A person carries two copies of a gene, one passed on from each parent. With recessive traits, the abnormal version does not become evident so long as the other gene is present and healthy.)

Correcting Disorders

Biotechnology presents the possibility of correcting genetic disorders. Caused by an insufficient amount of a single protein, severe combined immune deficiency is the hereditary disorder brought to public attention by David, the "Boy in the Plastic Bubble." Children with this disease cannot fight off simple infections, and they rarely survive the first two years of life. The condition may be cured by replacing the gene that codes for the deficient protein.

Industrial Biotechnology Association, *Medicine and the New Biology*, 1988.

Early in the 1980s, a joint statement from top officials of three national organizations of Catholics, Jews and Protestants warned, "History has shown us that there will always be those who believe it appropriate to 'correct' our mental and social structures by genetic means, so as to fit their vision of humanity."

Most would agree that genetic engineering is already being used for good. Time will tell whether it will also be used for ill.

"Even in those rare cases in which the replacement of a single gene might ameliorate a particular disease, introducing new working genes into the tissues of mature individuals has proved to be exceptionally difficult."

Genetic Engineering Cannot Cure Inherited Diseases

Stuart A. Newman

Stuart A. Newman teaches cell biology and anatomy at New York Medical College in Valhalla. In the following viewpoint, first published in the journal *Science and Nature*, he argues that genetic engineering has limited potential for curing inherited diseases. Newman asserts that the role of DNA in determining human traits, including disease, is not as great as many scientists believe. He argues that many genetic diseases can best be treated by changing a person's environment and diet rather than changing one's genes.

As you read, consider the following questions:

1. What metaphors describing the function of genes does Newman reject?
2. What central mystery about embryos have scientists been unable to decipher, according to the author?
3. Why does Newman believe some genetic diseases can also be labeled environmental diseases?

Stuart A. Newman, "Genetic Engineering as Metaphysics and Menace," *Science and Nature*, nos. 9/10, 1989. Reprinted with the author's permission.

Molecular genetics, the reigning paradigm in biology, promises to transform the living world through manipulation of the DNA molecule. Genetic engineering of plants and nonhuman animals is already well underway, and proposals for genetic engineering of humans and human embryos for medical purposes are increasingly frequent. Genetic manipulations confined to the body cells of individual persons ("somatic" gene modification), if found to be effective in treating rare, life-threatening diseases, would almost certainly come to be advocated as a therapeutic procedure for more common health-threatening conditions such as obesity and hypertension. And genetic modification of the reproductive cells, or the early embryo, for the purpose of prospectively correcting inherited defects or predispositions to disease ("germ-line" genetic engineering), while not on the short-term medical agenda, is considered by many to be a reasonable prospect because of recent dramatic results along these lines in animal experiments. According to one prominent medical geneticist "the animal studies raise the possibility of future genetic manipulations in humans." . . .

In what follows I will attempt to show that the standard view of the accomplishments and capabilities of molecular biology, held by the general public, as well as by many scientists, is informed by a conceptual framework that is a poor representation of biological reality. As a consequence, justification of the technological application of molecular genetics is increasingly fraught with dogmatism and hype. Such mystification of biological science and technology increases the leverage of the commercializers over the general public, and provides a smokescreen for activities with unexamined hazards and social consequences. In particular, I will discuss the implications of a genetic engineering approach to human biology, given the current level of scientific understanding in this area. . . .

What Are Genes?

Gregor Mendel, whose work laid the foundations for the science of genetics, was interested in certain features of plants and animals that appeared to be transmitted across generational lines with predictable, but not absolute, regularity. In the case of the pea plant, which Mendel studied most carefully, these features included traits such as smooth or wrinkled seeds, white or gray seed coats, yellow or green pods, and long or short stems. Mendel suggested that certain "factors" existed in the peas which were associated with one version or another of these traits, and which were transmitted according to definite laws from parent to offspring. The most important of these laws were that each individual receives an equal number of such factors from each parent, and that each factor can exist in more than one version. These factors later came to be known as "genes," and have since become identified with specific sequences of DNA.

Note that Mendel conceived of his factors as influencing the *choice* between complex alternatives, not as determining the *nature* of these alternatives. However, a very different view had come into prominence when physicist Erwin Schroedinger published his influential book *What Is Life?* "The chromosome structures" he wrote, "are instrumental in bringing about the development they foreshadow. They are law-code and executive power—or, to use another simile, they are architect's plan and builder's craft in one." These "chromosome structures," the repositories of an organism's DNA, had taken on a significance in both scientific and popular thought about living organisms that far exceeded the role for which Mendel had proposed the gene concept. Since Schroedinger's statement, the claimed role for DNA has become even more inflated. According to molecular biologist David Baltimore, DNA is the "brain of the cell."

Many Difficulties

Even if there were no ethical questions about human genetic engineering, it is highly unlikely that this procedure could be attempted in our lifetimes. Genetic engineering is extremely difficult technically and has had a low success rate in experimental animals. It can also create genetic damage in the fertilized egg rather than correcting it. It would involve repeated surgical procedures which would pose health risks for the mother. There is not a hospital or clinic anywhere in the United States, and most likely anywhere in the world, that would allow such a risky procedure to be done in its facilities.

Gerald R. Campbell, *Biotechnology: An Introduction*, 1988.

But when we look at how DNA actually functions, it becomes apparent that this substance is no more responsible for a cell's activities or traits than a menu is responsible for a meal. That portion of a cell's DNA whose role is understood (which actually comprises only a few percent of this substance in a complex organism), represents the cell's means of keeping a record of the complement of protein and RNA molecules it is capable of producing. These molecules play a role in the cell analogous to the bricks and beams of a building, and to the tools that can help cut and join them. DNA performs its role not by issuing commands or coordinating functions, but simply by virtue of the fact that certain complex cellular activities make use of a correspondence between the linear sequence of the subunits ("nucleotides") of a portion of the cell's DNA, and the nucleotide and "amino acid" subunits of RNAs and proteins, respectively. . . .

Insofar as the presence of specific proteins and RNA molecules can be considered "traits" of an organism, DNA serves the role of the Mendelian factors for these traits. This is because changes in some DNA sequences are ultimately reflected in structural changes in the corresponding proteins and RNAs. This satisfies Mendel's stipulation that the factors should influence the choice among different versions of a trait. However, most identifiable traits of an organism, such as size, shape, and behavioral characteristics, are the outcomes of complex interactive development processes involving numerous proteins and RNA molecules, along with molecules from the environment, such as sugars and ions. Occasionally, there will be a reliable correspondence between a DNA change and a change in the expressed version of one of these traits. Under these rare circumstances a DNA sequence serves as this trait's Mendelian factor. But in most cases there will be no such simple factor for a given trait. . . .

Considering the wealth of data available on the cellular role of DNA, it is difficult to understand why the facile metaphor that likens this molecule to a computer program has persisted for so long. Although the cells of multicellular organisms like ourselves contain much more DNA than is required to specify the totality of their proteins, no one has convincingly suggested a function for this molecule beyond its bookkeeping role in RNA and protein synthesis. In effect, it constitutes a list of ingredients, not a recipe for their interactions. . . .

Nevertheless the view that DNA acts as the organism's program or blueprint remains fashionable.

Is Genetic Engineering Possible?

The attractive idea that organisms are programmed by DNA, and thus can be reprogrammed by manipulating DNA, and that diseases and other infirmities can be treated in a piecemeal genetic fashion, has been seized upon by those who seek to commercialize and profit from biotechnology. Yet it is far from clear whether this idea will yield concrete results in the form of therapies that actually work.

Even in those rare cases in which the replacement of a single gene might ameliorate a particular disease, introducing new working genes into the tissues of mature individuals has proved to be exceptionally difficult. Consideration of the normal mechanisms of gene expression, insofar as they are understood, shows why this is the case, and casts profound doubt on the idea, touted by some investigators and many commercializers, that organisms are susceptible to reprogramming with predictable results.

The chromosomes of each cell type are generated in sequential steps that occur during embryonic development, including chemical modification of the DNA itself. The result of these steps is that some DNA sequences wind up in functional chromosomal regions and some are packed away into nonfunctional regions. Current techniques cannot select where in a chromosome a particular piece of foreign DNA will be inserted, and thus cannot ensure that it will be active in the cell. Insertions that fortuitously result in an active foreign gene risk disrupting normally active genes or reactivating normally quiescent ones.

Mice Are Not Humans

Researchers have succeeded in changing the genetic constitution of mice so that new genes are passed down from generation to generation. But it is not now possible to do this with humans, and technical and ethical problems inherent in such work are likely to keep it from being attempted for years.

Steve Olson, *Biotechnology: An Industry Comes of Age*, 1986.

In the case of gene modification of the cells that constitute the body (i.e., somatic cells) these difficulties could lead to disruption of the patient's physiology by a variety of effects, including overproduction of proteins, desired or undesired, or suppression of normal ones. In the worst case the genetically modified cells could acquire cancerous properties, and eventually kill the patient. This is not to deny that appropriate expression of a desired protein can occasionally be achieved in target cells, or that implantation of such cells into a patient's body might ameliorate the symptoms of a gene-related disability. Such therapy may offer hope in some rare, desperate cases. But scientific principles that would allow one to predict the long-term behavior of bodily tissues that express foreign genes do not at present exist.

Additional Problems

The introduction of foreign DNA into the egg or sperm prior to fertilization, or into early embryos, presents an additional set of problems. These procedures are collectively referred to as "germ-line genetic engineering" for the reason that, whatever the intent of their application, they have the probable result that the altered genes will become incorporated into the embryo's own germ-line, or reproductive cell precursors, and thence conveyed to subsequent generations. The success that investigators have achieved in introducing functional genes into the eggs and embryos of experimental animals might appear to be a result of a deeper understanding of the process of gene expression during early development than currently exists for the analogous process in somatic cells. Quite the opposite is true.

Early embryos have long been known to have the capability of enduring major traumas and insults and still develop into normal looking organisms. Embryos of sea urchins, frogs, and even mammals can be experimentally dissociated into their constituent cells; if this is done at an early enough stage, each cell gives rise to a fully formed individual. If two unrelated early mouse embryos are jumbled together into a single aggregate, the constituent cells will readjust their fates to yield a single individual with four parents. Phenomena of this sort, which are more a tribute to biological prodigiousness than to human ingenuity, led the embryologist Hans Driesch to his mystical concepts of goal directedness or "entelechy" when he could not explain them physically. A hundred years later we still do not understand the mechanisms.

New Genes

Therefore it was not completely unexpected when it was reported that foreign genes injected into fertilized mouse eggs were expressed in the resulting embryos, which then developed into recognizable animals, occasionally with new characteristics, such as increased size. In some cases the new gene was expressed in the appropriate tissue types, in some cases, not; in still other cases there were unforeseen interactions that influenced the expression of genes different from the one inserted. Moreover, it was evident that certain embryos could incorporate the new genes with absolutely no outward signs.

Because of the extraordinary homeostatic capacities of the embryo, phenotypically normal or even "improved" development may occur in embryos that have been rendered genetically abnormal by these procedures. But in such cases the cryptic genetic defect has been known to show up in the phenotypes of subsequent generations. A recent study, for example, found that the normal-looking offspring of one genetically modified mouse developed cancer by the middle of their lives at more than 40 times the rate of the unmodified strain.

Who Needs Genetic Engineering?

Despite these potential problems, the specter of human genetic engineering clearly hovers over the medical industry, and basic research devoted to overcoming the technical obstacles is one of the most glamorous areas of science. The potential constituency for gene correction or replacement therapies, as currently perceived by those developing the procedures, is everyone with a "genetic disease." In the view of David Baltimore, speaking at a National Academy of Sciences forum:

> When such therapy becomes possible, there is little doubt that afflicted individuals will seek it. And not to make it available, if it is a feasible scheme, seems inhumane to me. In general,

genetic diseases are one of our most serious medical problems, and if gene therapy could be used, many lives could be enriched by better health.

What then, is a *genetic disease*? According to current understanding of genetic mechanisms, polymorphisms, i.e., DNA sequence variants, can occur in thousands of locations in the human genome. Such sequence variants can lead to qualitative functional alterations or variations in the quantitative levels of specific proteins or RNA molecules. The degree of phenotypic divergence between individuals carrying these variants is of course a different question from molecular changes that may be caused in this way. Often, identical changes in a specific cellular component can have radically different effects in different individuals.

Genes Not a Full Explanation

It would be a great tragedy if the general public would come to accept the simplification that variation in a single gene causes diseases. The complex interaction of the individual with his environment—which over time can result in the pain, suffering and isolation of disease—will never be successfully explained or dealt with if our understanding is reduced to explanations dealing only with sub-microscopic chemicals called genes.

The new tests that promote genetic explanations of disease have limited applicability and benefits. Multiple factors modify the experience of ill health for the individual in our society. Non-genetic factors such as quality of housing, income, availability of health insurance, employment status and education are usually more important to the ability to cope with infirmity and flourish than are one's genes. To study the complexity of human emotion and behavior, along with psychiatric illness, will always reveal the limited role of genetic effects on life experience.

Paul R. Billings, *Los Angeles Times*, March 18, 1987.

Sickle cell anemia, the earliest described disease associated with a single amino acid substitution in a known cellular constituent, hemoglobin, is a case in point. This condition is highly variable in its severity in affected patients. The reason for this is unclear, but an important aspect may be individual differences in the quantity of hemoglobin per red blood cell, which in turn influences the propensity of red blood cells with abnormal hemoglobin to take on a sickled shape (not all of them do so). The sickled cells clog the body's capillaries, so anything that affects their numbers affects the course of the disease. Contributing conditions, such as the amount of hemoglobin per cell, can be influenced by numerous genetic and nongenetic differences between individuals. Moreover, the possibility exists for drugs to mitigate the condition by acting on parameters, such as cellular hemoglobin concentration, that leave the underlying genetic condition leading to sickle cell anemia unchanged.

Environmental Causes

Phenylketonuria (PKU), an "inborn error of metabolism" that leads to mental deficiency, is certainly a genetic disease: the enzyme that normally converts one amino acid, phenylalanine, into another, tyrosine, is lacking due to a mutation. However, PKU is also an "environmental disease": the toxic effects of accumulated phenylalanine can be obviated entirely by dietary means.

Just as sufferers from some so-called genetic diseases can be successfully treated with drugs or diet, victims of other diseases long thought to result from gene defects, such as Parkinsonism and amyotrophic lateral sclerosis (Lou Gehrig's disease), may in fact have acquired their conditions by ingesting certain unusual toxic substances. Of course, there may be individual genetic variations in susceptibility to such exotic toxins. There is really no inconsistency in considering the same disease as simultaneously genetic and environmental. Many individuals, for instance, are resistant to the cancer-causing properties of tobacco smoke; those who are vulnerable to this environmental carcinogen could correspondingly be considered genetically impaired. Indeed, even such patently infectious agents as the AIDS virus and the *Haemophilus influenzae* bacterium preferentially attack genetically susceptible individuals, and under conditions of widespread exposure can come to be considered genetic diseases.

Limits of Genetics

None of this should be surprising in light of the previous discussion of the highly complex, nonprogrammatic relationship between changes in DNA sequence and changes in an organism's traits. But the virtually tautological presence of a genetic aspect to every healthy or unhealthy condition opens the door to an overemphasis of this aspect by interested parties with genes to sell, in both the commercial and intellectual senses. If a problem is defined as genetic, the implied solution tends to be genetic as well. . . .

No one would deny that altering an organism's DNA will often change its characteristics. For this reason, research conducted within the genetic programming paradigm will continue to generate facts and fill research journals. But isolated facts do not add up to a scientific understanding of the laws that govern the construction of organisms, and their susceptibility to dysfunction and disease.

"Better knowledge of the genome could speed development of gene therapy—the actual alteration of instructions in the human genome to eliminate genetic defects."

Mapping the Genetic Makeup of Humans Would Improve Health

Leon Jaroff

In January 1989 the human genome project was formally launched. Sponsored by the U.S. government, other countries, and private organizations, the project will attempt to locate and catalog all the genetic chemicals in human DNA. In the following viewpoint, Leon Jaroff argues that the project will greatly increase understanding of human health and perhaps lead to breakthroughs in treating many genetically based diseases, including mental illness, cancer, and heart disease. Jaroff is a contributing writer for *Time*, a weekly newsmagazine.

As you read, consider the following questions:

1. How does the author define what the human genome is?
2. According to Jaroff, how many human genes exist in one person? How many have been identified so far?
3. What are some of the diseases that could be treated with more knowledge of the human genome, according to the author?

Know then thyself . . . the glory, jest, and riddle of the world.
—Alexander Pope

In an obscure corner of the National Institutes of Health (NIH), molecular biologist Norton Zinder strode to a 30-ft.-long oval conference table, sat down and rapped his gavel for order. A hush settled over the Human Genome Advisory Committee, an unlikely assemblage of computer experts, biologists, ethicists, industry scientists and engineers. "Today we begin," chairman Zinder declared. "We are initiating an unending study of human biology. Whatever it's going to be, it will be an adventure, a priceless endeavor. And when it's done, someone else will sit down and say, 'It's time to begin.'"

With these words, spoken in January 1989, Zinder formally launched a monumental effort that could rival in scope both the Manhattan Project, which created the A-bomb, and the Apollo moon-landing program—and may exceed them in importance. The goal: to map the human genome and spell out for the world the entire message hidden in its chemical code.

Genome? The word evokes a blank stare from most Americans, whose taxes will largely support the project's estimated $3 billion cost. Explains biochemist Robert Sinsheimer of the University of California at Santa Barbara: "The human genome is the complete set of instructions for making a human being." Those instructions are tucked into the nucleus of each of the human body's 100 trillion cells [except red blood cells, which have no nucleus] and written in the language of deoxyribonucleic acid, the fabled DNA molecule.

In the 35 years since James Watson and Francis Crick first discerned the complex structure of DNA, scientists have managed to decipher only a tiny fraction of the human genome. But they have high hopes that with new, automated techniques and a huge coordinated effort, the genome project can reach its goal in 15 years.

The achievement of that goal would launch a new era in medicine. James Wyngaarden, director of the NIH, which will oversee the project, predicts that it will make "major contributions to understanding growth, development and human health, and open new avenues for therapy." Full translation of the genetic message would enable medical researchers to identify the causes of thousands of still mysterious inherited disorders, both physical and behavioral.

With this insight, scientists could more accurately predict an individual's vulnerability to such obviously genetic diseases as cystic fibrosis and could eventually develop new drugs to treat or even prevent them. The same would be true for more common disorders like heart disease and cancer, which at the very least

95

have large genetic components. Better knowledge of the genome could speed development of gene therapy—the actual alteration of instructions in the human genome to eliminate genetic defects. . . .

An Enormous Opportunity

The proposal to map in extensive detail and then sequence the human genetic material (DNA) excites me enormously. It represents an opportunity to establish definitively the genetic program which makes possible our development into human beings as well as our successful functioning as adults. Knowledge of the human genetic program will have profound consequences both for our ability to understand our existence as healthy men and women, as well as for how imperfections in our genetic messages lead to genetic diseases. Until recently, the thought that we might soon know all of the precise details of our genetic instructions had to seem an impossible dream that only much later generations would ever be able to realize. The extraordinary possibilities allowed by the procedures of recombinant DNA, however, have turned these fantasies into potential reality.

James D. Watson, Testimony before the U.S. Congress, April 27, 1988.

The very thought of being able to read the entire genetic message, and perhaps alter it, is alarming to those who fear the knowledge could create many moral and ethical problems. Does genetic testing constitute an invasion of privacy, for example, and could it lead to more abortions and to discrimination against the "genetically unfit"? Should someone destined to be stricken with a deadly genetic disease be told about his fate, especially if no cure is yet available? Does it demean humans to have the very essence of their lives reduced to strings of letters in a computer data bank? Should gene therapy be used only for treating disease, or also for "improving" a person's genetic legacy?

Although scientists share many of these concerns, the concept of deciphering the human genome sends most of them into paroxysms of rapture. "It's the Holy Grail of biology," says Harvard biologist and Nobel laureate Walter Gilbert. "This information will usher in the Golden Age of molecular medicine," says Mark Pearson, Du Pont's director of molecular biology. Predicts George Cahill, a vice president at the Howard Hughes Medical Institute: "It's going to tell us everything. Evolution, disease, everything will be based on what's in that magnificent tape called DNA." . . .

DNA is found in the human-cell nucleus in the form of 46 separate threads, each coiled into a packet called a chromosome. Unraveled and tied together, these threads would form a fragile string more than 5 ft. long but only 50 trillionths of an inch across.

96

And what a wondrous string it is. As Watson and Crick discovered in 1953, DNA consists of a double helix, resembling a twisted ladder with sidepieces made of sugar and phosphates and closely spaced connecting rungs. Each rung is called a base pair because it consists of a pair of complementary chemicals called nitrogenous bases, attached end to end, either adenine (A) joined to thymine (T) or cytosine (C) attached to guanine (G).

Fundamental to the genius of DNA is the fact that A and T are mutually attractive, as are C and G. Consequently, when DNA separates during cell division, coming apart at the middle of each rung like a zipper opening, an exposed T half-rung on one side of the ladder will always attract an A floating freely in the cell. The corresponding A half-rung on the other section of the ladder will attract a floating T, and so on, until two double helixes, each identical to the original DNA molecule, are formed.

Even more remarkable, each of the four bases represents a letter in the genetic code. The three-letter "words" they spell, reading in sequence along either side of the ladder, are instructions to the cell on how to assemble amino acids into the proteins essential to the structure and life of its host. Each complete DNA "sentence" is a gene, a discrete segment of the DNA string responsible for ordering the production of a specific protein.

Reading these genetic words and deciphering their meaning is apparently a snap for the clever machinery of a cell. But for mere scientists it is a formidable and time-consuming task. For instance, a snippet of DNA might read ACGGTAGAT, a message that researchers can decipher rather easily. It codes for a sequence of three of the 20 varieties of amino acids that constitute the building blocks of proteins. But the entire genome of even the simplest organism dwarfs that snippet. The genetic blueprint of the lowly *E. coli* bacterium, for one, is more than 4.5 million base pairs long. For a microscopic yeast plant, the length is 15 million units. And in a human being, the genetic message is some 3 billion letters long.

Like cartographers mapping the ancient world, scientists over the past three decades have been laboriously charting human DNA. Of the estimated 100,000-odd genes that populate the genome, just 4,550 have been identified. And only 1,500 of those have been roughly located on the various chromosomes. The message of the genes has been equally difficult to come by. Most genes consist of between 10,000 and 150,000 code letters, and only a few genes have been completely deciphered. Long segments of the genome, like the vast uncharted regions of early maps, remain terra incognita.

To complicate matters, between the segments of DNA that represent genes are endless stretches of code letters that seem to spell out only genetic gibberish. Geneticists once thought most of the

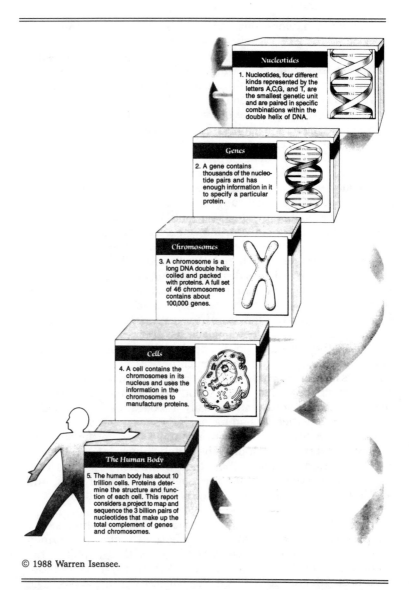

Nucleotides

1. Nucleotides, four different kinds represented by the letters A,C,G, and T, are the smallest genetic unit and are paired in specific combinations within the double helix of DNA.

Genes

2. A gene contains thousands of the nucleotide pairs and has enough information in it to specify a particular protein.

Chromosomes

3. A chromosome is a long DNA double helix coiled and packed with proteins. A full set of 46 chromosomes contains about 100,000 genes.

Cells

4. A cell contains the chromosomes in its nucleus and uses the information in the chromosomes to manufacture proteins.

The Human Body

5. The human body has about 10 trillion cells. Proteins determine the structure and function of each cell. This report considers a project to map and sequence the 3 billion pairs of nucleotides that make up the total complement of genes and chromosomes.

© 1988 Warren Isensee.

unintelligible stuff was "junk DNA"—useless sequences of code letters that accidentally developed during evolution and were not discarded. That concept has changed. "My feeling is there's a lot of very useful information buried in the sequence," says Nobel laureate Paul Berg of Stanford University. "Some of it we will know how to interpret; some we know is going to be gibberish."

In fact, some of the nongene regions on the genome have already been identified as instructions necessary for DNA to replicate itself during cell division. Their message is obviously detailed and complex. Explains George Bell, head of genome studies at Los Alamos National Laboratory: "It's as if you had a rope that was maybe 2 in. in diameter and 32,000 miles long, all neatly arranged inside a structure the size of a superdome. When the appropriate signal comes, you have to unwind the rope, which consists of two strands, and copy each strand so you end up with two new ropes that again have to fold up. The machinery to do that cannot be trivial."

One of the most formidable tasks faced by geneticists is to learn the nature of that machinery and other genetic instructions buried in the lengthy, still undeciphered base sequences. To do so fully requires achievement of the project's most challenging goal: the "sequencing" of the entire human genome. In other words, the identification and listing in order of all the genome's 3 billion base pairs.

That effort, says Caltech research fellow Richard Wilson, "is analogous to going around and shaking hands with everyone on earth." The resulting string of code letters, according to the 1988 National Research Council report urging adoption of the genome project, would fill a million-page book. Even then, much of the message would be obscure. To decipher it, researchers would need more powerful computer systems to roam the length of the genome, seeking out meaningful patterns and relationships. . . .

Tracking down the location of a gene requires tedious analysis. But it is sheer adventure when compared with the task of determining the sequence of base pairs in a DNA chain. Small groups of scientists, working literally by hand, have spent years simply trying to sequence a single gene. This hands-on method of sequencing costs as much as a dollar per base pair, and deciphering the entire genome by this method might take centuries.

The solution is automation. "It will improve accuracy," says Stanford's Paul Berg. "It will remove boredom; it will accomplish what we want in the end." The drive for automation has already begun; a machine designed by Caltech biologist Leroy Hood can now sequence 16,000 base pairs a day. But Hood, a member of the Genome Advisory Committee, is hardly satisfied. "Before we can seriously take on the genome initiative," he says, "we will want to do 100,000 to a million a day." The cost, he hopes, will eventually drop to a penny per base pair.

Hood is not alone in his quest for automation. That is also the goal of Columbia University biochemist Charles Cantor, appointed by the Energy Department to head one of its two genome centers. "It's largely an engineering project," Cantor explains, intended to produce tools for faster, less expensive sequencing and to develop data bases and computer programs to scan the data. Not to be outdone, Japan has set up a consortium of four high-tech companies to establish an automated assembly line, complete with robots, that researchers hope will be capable of sequencing 100,000 base pairs a day within three years. . . .

One of the early benefits of the genome project will be the identification of more and more of the defective genes responsible for the thousands of known inherited diseases and development of tests to detect them. Like those already used to find Huntington's and sickle-cell markers, for example, these tests will allow doctors to predict with near certainty that some patients will fall victim to specific genetic diseases and that others are vulnerable and could be stricken.

University of Utah geneticist Mark Skolnick is convinced that mapping the genome will radically change the way medicine is practiced. "Right now," he says, "we wait for someone to get sick so we can cut them and drug them. It's pretty old stuff. Once you can make a profile of a person's genetic predisposition to disease, medicine will finally become predictive and preventive."

Eventually, says Mark Guyer of the NIH's Human Genome Office, people might have access to a computer readout of their own genome, with an interpretation of their genetic strengths and weaknesses. At the very least, this would enable them to adopt an appropriate life-style, choosing the proper diet, environment and—if necessary—drugs to minimize the effects of genetic disorders.

The ever improving ability to read base-pair sequences of genes will enable researchers to speed the discovery of new proteins, assess their role in the life processes, and use them—as the interferons and interleukins are already used—for fighting disease. It will also help them pinpoint missing proteins, such as insulin, that can correct genetic diseases.

Mapping and sequencing the genes should accelerate progress in another highly touted and controversial discipline: gene therapy. Using this technique, scientists hope someday to cure genetic diseases by actually inserting good genes into their patients' cells. One proposed form of gene therapy would be used to fight beta-thalassemia major, a blood disease characterized by severe anemia and caused by the inability of hemoglobin to function properly. That inability results from the lack of a protein in the hemoglobin, a deficiency that in turn is caused by a defective gene in bone-marrow cells.

To effect a cure, doctors would remove bone-marrow cells from a patient and expose them to a retrovirus [a virus consisting largely of RNA, a single-stranded chain of bases similar to the DNA double helix] engineered to carry correctly functioning versions of the patient's faulty gene. When the retrovirus invaded a marrow cell, it would insert itself into the cellular DNA, as retroviruses are wont to do, carrying the good gene with it. Reimplanted in the marrow,

100

the altered marrow cells would take hold and multiply, churning out the previously lacking protein and curing the thalassemia patient.

Easier said than done. Scientists have had trouble getting such implanted genes to "turn on" in their new environment, and they worry about unforeseen consequences if the gene is inserted in the wrong place in a chromosome. Should the gene be slipped into the middle of another vital gene, for example, it might disrupt the functioning of that gene, with disastrous consequences. Also, says M.I.T. biologist Richard Mulligan, there are limitations to the viral insertion of genes. "Most genes," he explains, "are too big to fit into a retrovirus."

Undaunted, researchers are refining their techniques in experiments with mice, and Mulligan believes that the first human-gene-therapy experiments could occur in the early 1990s. Looking further ahead, other scientists are experimenting with a kind of genetic microsurgery that bypasses the retrovirus, mechanically inserting genes directly into the cell nucleus.

Not only those with rare genetic disorders could benefit from the new technology. Says John Brunzell, a University of Washington medicine professor: "Ten years ago, it was thought that only 10% of premature coronary heart disease came from inherited abnormalities. Now that proportion is approaching 80% to 90%."

Harvard geneticist Philip Leder cites many common diseases—hyper-tension, allergies, diabetes, heart disease, mental illness and some (perhaps all) cancers—that have a genetic component. Unlike Huntington's and Tay-Sachs diseases, which are caused by a single defective gene, many of these disorders have their roots in several errant genes and would require genetic therapy far more sophisticated than any now even being contemplated. Still, says Leder, "in the end, genetic mapping is going to have its greatest impact on these major diseases."

Of all the enthusiasm that the genome project has generated among scientists and their supporters in Washington, however, none matches that of James Watson as he gears up for the monumental task ahead. "It excites me enormously," he says, and he remains confident that it can be accomplished despite the naysayers both within and outside the scientific community. "How can we not do it?" he demands. "We used to think our fate was in our stars. Now we know, in large measure, our fate is in our genes."

"The genome project has been overhyped and oversold."

Mapping the Genetic Makeup of Humans Would Pose Ethical Dilemmas

George J. Annas

George J. Annas is the Utley Professor of Health Law at Boston University School of Medicine. In the following viewpoint, he argues that the human genome project raises serious medical and ethical issues which have not been adequately addressed by the scientific community. Potential health advantages from mapping the human genome, he argues, may be overshadowed by social harms as scientists try to genetically improve humans.

As you read, consider the following questions:

1. What lessons does Annas draw from the Manhattan Project and the Apollo Project concerning science and ethics?
2. What legal and ethical issues does the author see arising from human genetic research?
3. According to Annas, how might the human genome project change the way humans think about themselves?

George J. Annas, "Who's Afraid of the Human Genome?" *Hastings Center Report,* July/August 1989. Reprinted with the author's permission.

In Edward Albee's 1962 play, *Who's Afraid of Virginia Woolf?*, George (a historian) describes the agenda of modern biology to alter chromosomes:

> . . . the genetic makeup of a sperm cell changed, reordered . . . to order, actually . . . for hair and eye color, stature, potency. . . . I imagine . . . hairiness, features, health . . . and *mind*. Most important . . . Mind. All imbalances will be corrected, sifted out . . . propensity for various diseases will be gone, longevity assured. We will have a race of men . . . test-tube-bred . . . incubator-born . . . superb and sublime.

George's view of the future was sinister and threatening in the early '60s. But today these same sentiments seem almost quaint. Mapping and sequencing the estimated 3 billion base pairs of the human genome (the 50,000 to 100,000 genes we are composed of) is "in"; raising serious questions about the project itself is "out." There is money to be made here, and even the "ethicists" are slated to have their share.

The Case for Research

The *Wall Street Journal* summarized the case for the human genome project in early 1989 when it editorialized, "The techniques of gene identification, separation, and splicing now allow us to discover the basic causes of ailments and, thus, to progress toward cures and even precursory treatments that might ward off the onset of illness ranging from cancer to heart disease and AIDS." All that is lacking "is a blueprint—a map of the human genome." Noting that some members of the European Parliament had suggested that ethical questions regarding eugenics should be answered *"before it proceeds,"* the *Journal* opined that "This, of course, is a formula for making no progress at all." The editorial concluded, "The Human Genome Initiative . . . may well invite attack from those who are fearful of or hostile to the future. It should also attract the active support of those willing to defend the future."

The National Institutes of Health have created an Office of Human Genome Research headed by James Watson, and that office has issued a request for funding proposals to study "the ethical, social, and legal issues that may arise from the application of knowledge gained as a result of the Human Genome Initiative." The brief announcement makes it clear that such projects are to be about the "immense potential benefit to mankind" of the project, and focus on "the best way to ensure that the information is used in the most beneficial and responsible manner." Those with less optimism apparently need not apply.

Watson is perhaps the genome project's most prominent cheerleader, having said, among other things, that the project provides "an extraordinary potential for human betterment. . . . We can have at our disposal the ultimate tool for understanding ourselves at the molecular level. . . . The time to act is now." And, "How can we not do it? We used to think our fate is in our stars. Now we know, in large measure, our fate is in our genes."

Are there any difficult legal and ethical problems involved in mapping the human genome, or is everything as straightforward and rosy as the project's advocates paint it? NIH plans to devote only 1 to 3 percent of its genome budget to exploring social, legal, and ethical issues, and James Watson sees no dangers ahead. But Watson himself, reflecting on his own early career, wrote in 1967: "Science seldom proceeds in the straightforward, logical manner . . . its steps are often very human events in which personalities and cultural traditions play major roles."

Simplistic Solutions

The sequencing of the human genome will leave us with a deluge of undigested genetic data. . . .

Because this store of base sequences will represent an incredibly precise inventory of minute, often inconsequential hereditary differences between people, it will be highly vulnerable to abuse. Computerized human gene banks are likely to offer new opportunities for wholesale genetic screening programs—some useful, others of dubious merit—for identifying individuals who harbor genes considered "defective" or "inferior." With such a bounty of unexplored data on the human genome available, there may be a temptation to hastily assign too great a causal role to many freshly mapped genes—simply because of their preliminary statistical associations with perplexing health problems.

As in the past, some people are bound to eagerly exploit such findings by publicly proclaiming that they offer "scientific solutions" for "fixing" everything from alcoholism and mental illness to homosexuality and learning disabilities. In the absence of other, more compelling evidence for links between specific DNA sequences and disease, our swollen DNA data banks could quickly become reservoirs of easy genetic "answers" to complex human problems.

David Suzuki and Peter Knudtson, *Genethics*, 1989.

The human genome project has been frequently compared to both the Manhattan Project and the Apollo Project, and "big biology" is clearly happy to have its own megaproject of a size formerly restricted to physicists and engineers. But the sheer size of these two other projects obscures more important lessons. The Manhattan Project is familiar, but it still teaches us volumes about science and the unforeseen impact of technological "advance." In late 1945, Robert Oppenheimer testified before the U.S. Congress on the role of science in the development of the atomic bomb:

> When you come right down to it, the reason that we did this job is because it was an organic necessity. If you are a scientist, you cannot stop such a thing. If you are a scientist, you believe that it is good to find out how the world works; that it is good to find what the realities are; that it is good to turn over to mankind at large the greatest possible power to control the world. . . .

The striking thing in Oppenheimer's testimony is his emphasis on the notion that science is unstoppable with the simultaneous insistence that its goal is *control* over nature, irreconcilable concepts that seem equally at the heart of the human genome project. Of course, with the atomic bomb, control quickly became illusory. The bomb, which carries with it the promise of the total annihilation of mankind, has made the nation state ultimately unstable and put it at the mercy of every other nation with the bomb. Necessity has forced all nuclear powers to move, however slowly, toward a transnational community.

The Apollo Project

The Apollo Project had its own problems. An engineering exercise, it was about neither the inevitability of scientific advance nor the control of nature. Instead, it was about military advantage and commercialism, disguised as science and hyped as a peace mission. As Walter McDougall has persuasively documented, the plaque Astronaut Neil Armstrong left on the moon, which read, "We came in peace for all mankind," was ironic:

> The moon was not what space was all about. It was about science, sometimes spectacular science, but mostly about spy satellites, comsats, and other orbital systems for military and commercial advantage. "Space for peace" could no more be engineered than social harmony, and the UN Outer Space Treaty . . . drew many nations into the hunt for advantage, not integration, through spaceflight.

The *Wall Street Journal* seems more attuned to the commercial applications of gene mapping and sequencing than NIH, although Congressional support of the project is based primarily on the hope that mapping the genome can help the U.S. maintain its lead in the biotechnology industry. Neither ethicists nor social planners played any real role in the Manhattan or Apollo projects. It appears they will at least play some minor role in the Genome Project. What should the role be, and how should it be structured?

The Legal and Ethical Issues

The basic legal and ethical issues implicit in the human genome project are, on the first level, the same issues involved in current genetic screening for various traits, such as carrier status for sickle cell and Tay-Sachs disease. Mapping and sequencing the human

genome could, of course, lead to screening on an almost unimaginable scale—not only for certain diseases and traits, but also for tendencies toward certain diseases, such as cancer or manic depression. When all genetic traits can be deciphered in a genetic code (something that will require far more than a simple map of location), we will enter a new realm—taking not simply a quantitative step, but a qualitative one. Exactly what the consequences of such a step will be are not entirely foreseeable. Just as it was unforeseeable that the most lasting impact of the Apollo Project would be the photographs of the planet Earth: a fragile blue jewel that helped energize environmental protection on a global scale.

There will be issues of information control and privacy. Employers, insurance companies, the military, and the government, among others, will want to have access to the information contained in our genome. Scientists may want such information restricted, but they will certainly have little influence over its use, as they had little influence over the use of the atomic bomb. Routine genetic screening will be easy to justify under current law (which already mandates newborn screening in most states, for example) in many settings. Although we are utterly unprepared to deal with issues of mandatory screening, confidentiality, privacy, and discrimination, we will likely tell ourselves that we have already dealt with them well, and so the genome project poses no threat there.

The second order of issues relates to what is generally termed "eugenics," the improvement of the species, either by weeding out genetic "undesirables" or by actually using genetic techniques (breeding or genetic engineering) to increase the number of desirable traits in offspring. Given the U.S.'s sad history with involuntary sterilization, and the Nazi campaign on sterilization modeled after it, we are unlikely to engage in a direct program of sterilization. Nonetheless, eugenics has its supporters, and the European Parliament is right to be worried about the dangers of repeating history. It was our own U.S. Supreme Court, after all, that wrote in 1927, approving involuntary sterilization of the mentally retarded:

> We have seen more than once that the public welfare may call upon the best citizens for their lives. It would be strange if it could not call upon those who already sap the strength of the State for these lesser sacrifices often not felt to be such by those concerned, in order to prevent our being swamped with incompetence. It is better for all the world, if instead of waiting to execute degenerate offspring for crime, or to let them starve for their imbecility, society can prevent those who are manifestly unfit from continuing their kind.

That may seem like ancient history, but in 1988 the U.S. Congress's Office of Technology Assessment, in discussing the "Social and Ethical Considerations" raised by the Human Genome Project, used strikingly similar language:

> Human mating that proceeds without the use of genetic data about the risks of transmitting diseases will produce greater mortality and medical costs than if carriers of potentially deleterious genes are alerted to their status and encouraged to mate with noncarriers or to use artificial insemination or other reproductive strategies.

The primary reproductive strategy, mentioned only in passing in the report, will be genetic screening of human embryos—already technically feasible, but not nearly to the extent possible once the genome is understood. Such screening need not be required, people can be made to *want* it, even to insist on it as their right. As OTA notes, "New technologies for identifying traits and altering genes make it possible for eugenic goals to be achieved through technological as opposed to social control."

Pricing Human Attributes

A third level of concern relates to the fact that powerful technologies do not just change what human beings can do, they change the very way we think—especially about ourselves. As one example, the ability to completely screen embryos could lead to a market in "high grade embryos" that could be bought and sold. They could also be gestated by contract or surrogate mothers, and the resulting child delivered to the purchaser of the embryo. This could lead not only to putting a specific price on all human characteristics (such as height, intelligence, race, eye color, etc.), but also to viewing children as commodities that have no rights or interests of their own, but that exist to further the interests of parents and future societies. A map of the human genome could also lead to a more narrowly focused view of a "normal" gene complement, and how much deviation we permit before considering any individual genome "abnormal," deviant, or diseased. We haven't seriously begun to think about *how* to think about this issue, even though we know normalcy will be invented, not discovered.

At a Workshop on International Cooperation for the Human Genome Project held in Valencia in October, 1988, French researcher Jean Dausset suggested that the genome project posed great potential hazards that could open the door to Nazi-like atrocities. To attempt to avoid such results, he suggested that the conferees agree on a moratorium on genetic manipulation of germ line cells, and a ban on gene transfer experiments in early embryos. Reportedly, the proposal won wide agreement among the participants, and was watered down to a resolution calling for "international cooperation" only after American participant Norton Zinder successfully argued that the group had no authority to make such a resolution stick.

Genes and the Handicapped

University of Washington ethicist Albert Jonsen is concerned that people with grave illnesses might be viewed simply as carriers of genetic traits. "Rather than saying 'Isn't that family unfortunate to have a schizophrenic son,' we'll say 'That's a schizophrenia family.'" Advocates for the handicapped fear that in the future the physically afflicted may no longer be seen as unfortunates worthy of special treatment, but as "wrongful births," genetic errors committed by parents who failed to take proper action against a defective gene.

Philip Elmer-Dewitt, *Time*, March 20, 1989.

This listing is neither novel nor complete, but suggests that the legal and ethical issues posed by the human genome project are real and poorly appreciated. Other issues that are currently unanticipated may, of course, even turn out to be more important. Today's fascination, however, is not with substance, but rather with procedure: How should the genome actually be mapped? With today's techniques, it is estimated that it takes forty professional years for a biologist to sequence one gene. Assuming 100,000 genes, it would take 400,000 biologists ten years working full time. This seems an immense waste of time and talent, as much faster methods of sequencing will be available within the coming decade. On the other hand, the U.S. is worried that if it waits to get deeply into this project, other countries, especially Japan, might gain commercial advantage. Thankfully, the scope of the project, as well as the capabilities possessed by other countries, make it impossible for the U.S. to complete the genome project alone. But what form should international cooperation take? . . .

Zinder was, of course, correct, and a moratorium and ban on research that no one wants to do at this point would have only symbolic value—and negative symbolic value at that. It would signal that the scientists could handle the ethical issues alone, and could monitor their own work. It would tend to quiet the discussion of both germ line research and gene transfers in early embryos—both subjects that deserve wide public debate. But Dausset also had a point. The Nazi atrocities grew out of the combination of a public health ethic that saw the abnormal as disposable, and a tyrannical dictatorship that was able to give the physicians and public health authorities unlimited authority to put their program into bestial practice.

An Oversold Endeavor

Ethics is generally taken seriously by physicians and scientists only when it either fosters their agenda or does not interfere with it. If it cautions a slower pace or a more deliberate consideration of science's darker side, it is dismissed as "fearful of the future," anti-intellectual, or simply uninformed. The genome project has been overhyped and oversold. It is the obligation of those who take legal and ethical issues seriously to insure that the dangers, as well as the opportunities, are rigorously and publicly explored. We must get beyond Honey's response to George's musings on our genetic future in Albee's play: "How exciting!"

Distinguishing Bias from Reason

When dealing with controversial subjects, many people allow their feelings to dominate their powers of reason. Thus, one of the most important critical thinking skills is the ability to distinguish between statements based upon emotion and those based upon a rational consideration of the facts.

The following statements are taken from the viewpoints in this chapter. Consider each statement carefully. *Mark R for any statement you believe is based on reason or a rational consideration of the facts. Mark B for any statement you believe is based on bias, prejudice, or emotion. Mark I for any statement you think is impossible to judge.*

If you are doing this activity as a member of a class or group, compare your answers with those of other class or group members. Be able to explain your answers. You may discover that others come to different conclusions than you. Listening to the rationale others present for their answers may give you valuable insights in distinguishing between bias and reason.

> R = *a statement based upon reason*
> B = *a statement based upon bias*
> I = *a statement impossible to judge*

1. Once we decide to begin the process of human genetic engineering, there is no logical place to stop.

2. We are utterly unprepared to deal with issues of mandatory genetic screening, confidentiality, privacy, and discrimination.

3. The genome project has been overhyped and oversold.

4. Given the U.S.'s sad history with involuntary sterilization, and the Nazi campaign on sterilization modeled after it, we are unlikely to engage in a direct program of sterilization.

5. The ever improving ability to read base-pair sequences will enable researchers to speed the discovery of new proteins.

6. Environment and personal habits play key roles in inherited diseases. One form of colon cancer, for example, has been traced to a faulty gene, although eating fatty food may trigger it to begin making tumors.

7. DNA is no more responsible for a cell's activities or traits than a menu is responsible for a meal.

8. Scientists using current techniques cannot select where in a chromosome a particular piece of foreign DNA will be inserted, and thus cannot ensure that it will be active in the cell.

9. Specific removal of defective genes is impossible with current or foreseeable technologies.

10. Genetic engineering promises longer and healthier lives through increased food production and new ways of treating afflictions.

11. Even when not subject to accident or disease, the human body is an imperfect structure made of imperfect materials.

12. Adapting humans to digest cellulose would be a very minor modification in biochemical terms, but it would be of very considerable significance.

13. Powerful technologies do not just change what human beings can do, they change the way we think.

14. The genetic message contained in human genes has been difficult to come by. Most genes consist of between 10,000 and 15,000 code letters, and only a few genes have been completely deciphered.

Periodical Bibliography

The following articles have been selected to supplement the diverse views presented in this chapter.

John W. Anderson — "Scrambling for Biotech Bucks," *The Nation*, April 10, 1989.

David Baltimore — "Conquering the Gene," *Discover*, October 1989.

Jerry E. Bishop — "Biological Weapons: Engineered Antibodies Show Great Promise in Fighting Cancer," *The Wall Street Journal*, July 10, 1989.

Gene Bylinsky — "Bringing Biotech Down to Earth," *Fortune*, November 7, 1988.

Betsy Carpenter — "The New Designer Drugs," *Science Digest*, November 1989.

John Deedy — "Five Medical Dilemmas That Might Scare You to Death," *U.S. Catholic*, April 1988.

Philip Elmer-Dewitt — "The Perils of Treading on Heredity," *Time*, March 20, 1989.

Leroy Hood — "Biotechnology and Medicine of the Future," *Journal of the American Medical Association*, March 25, 1988.

Richard John Neuhaus — "The Return of Eugenics," *Commentary*, April 1988.

Kathleen Nolan and Sara Swenson — "New Tools, New Dilemmas: Genetic Frontiers," *Hastings Center Report*, October/November 1988.

William Saletan — "Genes 'R' Us," *The New Republic*, July 17-24, 1989.

Harold M. Schmeck Jr. — "New Methods Fuel Efforts to Decode Human Genes," *The New York Times*, May 9, 1989.

Robert Steinbrook — "Genetically Engineered Protein Speeds Wound Healing," *Los Angeles Times*, July 13, 1989.

Larry Thompson — "Should the Holy Grail of Biology Get the Green Light?" *The Washington Post National Weekly Edition*, February 22-28, 1988.

Does Genetic Engineering Improve Agriculture?

Chapter Preface

Genetic engineering has potential agricultural applications in two broad areas: farm products—animals and plants—and microbes. Both areas have attracted controversy.

For thousands of years farmers have genetically changed plants and animals through breeding. Many agricultural scientists and farmers now see genetic engineering as a more efficient and precise tool for the same goals. Biotechnology proponents argue that genetic engineering has the potential to produce certain desirable characteristics in plants and animals. These include insect and herbicide resistance in plants and faster growth for animals.

Opposition has come from several quarters. Some critics worry that scientists, in their pursuit of genetically ideal plants and animals, might inadvertently cause negative changes as well, such as leaving crops more vulnerable to pests or bad weather. Author Jack Doyle argues that genetic engineering is designed to bring profits to large corporations at the expense of individual farmers. For example, plants may be genetically engineered by a company so as to need more fertilizers and herbicides sold by the same company. Finally, animal rights activists argue that tampering with an animal's genes is both unethical and harmful to animals.

The genetic engineering of agricultural microbes (bacteria) has progressed faster than that of plants and animals. In 1987 the first sanctioned release of genetically altered organisms occurred in California when a strawberry patch was sprayed with bacteria genetically designed to make the plants resistant to frost. More recently, bovine growth hormone, a chemical produced by cows that stimulates milk production, has been reproduced by genetically altered bacteria. The hormone is then fed back to cows to artificially increase milk production. These experiments have likewise raised controversy as critics have raised environmental and ethical questions.

The authors in this chapter debate the costs and benefits of genetic engineering in agriculture and whether farmers should pursue or avoid this new technology.

"Genetic engineering . . . has many practical applications to the age-old art of farming."

Genetic Engineering Benefits Agriculture

Industrial Biotechnology Association

The Industrial Biotechnology Association is a Washington, D.C.-based coalition of companies that develop products through biotechnology and genetic engineering. In the following viewpoint, the Association argues that genetic engineering can make farming more efficient and environmentally sound. It argues that genetic engineering can make agricultural plants and animals more resistant to disease, less expensive to grow, and more nutritious.

As you read, consider the following questions:

1. What limits of traditional breeding can genetic engineering overcome, according to the author?
2. According to the Association, what goals besides increased yield do researchers hope to attain through genetic engineering?
3. Why does the Association believe genetic engineering is safe?

Industrial Biotechnology Association, *Agriculture and the New Biotechnology*, 1987. Reprinted with permission of the Industrial Biotechnology Association.

115

Stone Age farmers were, in a sense, the first genetic engineers. They started by planting the seeds of wild plants. Later, they selected the most productive of their domesticated plants to provide the next year's seed stock. Over thousands of years, this process gave rise to most of today's crops.

In the early 20th Century, scientists applied Gregor Mendel's classical laws of genetics to quicken the pace of crop improvements. By the 1950s, classical genetics was making enormous contributions in academic research and traditional agriculture, and it was playing a major role in the Green Revolution, which has been responsible for averting starvation in many parts of the developing world.

Limits of Old Techniques

But classical genetic techniques, which involve sexual reproduction of plants and animals, have several limitations.

First, classical techniques are slow, requiring many years to produce a new crop variety. Many biologists believe biotechnology will enable them to develop new varieties more quickly.

Second, only closely related species can mate. For example, primitive alfalfa and modern alfalfa have accumulated so many genetic differences that they are no longer capable of mating with each other. Thus, breeders using classical techniques often cannot transfer a desirable trait from one kind of plant to another.

But recent discoveries in biology have increased scientists' understanding of how genetic information is passed from cell to cell and from generation to generation. With this knowledge, biologists have developed a technique to transfer a gene for a desirable trait from one species to another. This technique is called recombinant DNA technology, or genetic engineering.

Biologists have already used genetic engineering to develop crops that resist disease and insects. Genetic engineering may also yield plants that tolerate cold and drought. "Genetic engineering is going to allow us to take plant breeding to a new level where it has never gone before," says Dr. Richard Meagher, associate professor of genetics at the University of Georgia. . . .

What Is Genetic Engineering?

Among the variety of techniques that fall under the general heading of biotechnology, genetic engineering is one of the most important.

The first genetic engineering experiments were performed in the early 1970s and, since then, the technique has had a major impact on many fields of biology.

Genetic engineering became possible as biologists deepened their understanding of deoxyribonucleic acid, or DNA, the molecule that codes the instructions for growth, maintenance, and reproduction of all living things. Each instruction is called a gene. Many genes—100,000 to 300,000 in a human—make up an organism's entire instruction manual.

In plants and animals, most DNA is generally found in chromosomes, tiny structures in the nucleus of the cell. Each chromosome contains thousands of genes.

Tools of Genetic Engineering

The tools of genetic engineering are certain enzymes—natural substances that control biochemical reactions—that work like chemical scissors and glue, cutting and pasting DNA molecules. Biologists use these enzymes to snip genes out of DNA molecules and stick them into the DNA of microbes.

The microbes with these transplanted genes may be commercially useful because they can produce proteins that cannot be obtained economically from other sources. Or scientists can take advantage of nature's own genetic engineering ability, using the microbes to insert the transplanted genes into plant cells. Genetically engineered microbes and plants express the traits coded in the new genes and pass these traits on to their offspring.

Biologists move a gene from one species of plant into another with the help of a bacterium that naturally performs genetic engineering. Called *Agrobacterium tumefaciens*, the bacterium contains a free-floating ring of DNA, called a plasmid, that can insert some of this DNA into plant chromosomes.

New Crops

The largest agricultural segment to be affected by the adaptation of genetic research is crop production—in particular, major food crops such as fruits, vegetables, and grain. Through recombinant DNA and the less advanced methods of plant tissue culture, protoplast fusion, and hybrid crop variations, new improved characteristics can be conferred to or instilled within crop varieties. These characteristics include higher yields, herbicide-tolerance, disease-resistance, and ability to withstand environmental stress. In addition, quality traits such as taste, freshness, crispness, and solid content can be enhanced through biotechnology.

USA Today, June 1988.

The biologist removes the plasmid from *Agrobacterium*. A desired gene—one that confers viral disease resistance, for example—is removed from the DNA of a donor plant, animal, or microbe and spliced into the plasmid DNA. The plasmid, carrying the gene to be transferred, is put back into *Agrobacterium*, which is placed in a dish with cut leaves of the recipient plant.

Where the leaves are cut, the plasmid can insert the new gene into the plant cells. The gene becomes a permanent part of the recipient plant's DNA.

Many plant cells have the remarkable ability to regenerate an entire new plant. When a whole plant is grown from a cell that contains a new gene from an *Agrobacterium* plasmid, the transplanted gene will have conferred on the plant the desired trait from the donor organism.

Genetic engineering is an invaluable tool for biologists trying to learn more about plant genetics. It also has many practical applications to the age-old art of farming.

Benefits of Genetic Engineering

Farming is civilization's most essential enterprise. The ability to produce food, fiber, and other agricultural products determines, in large measure, the standard of living that people will enjoy. Nations have prospered or perished through the success or failure of their agriculture.

But farming is a risky business. Weeds are always ready to compete with crops for moisture and nutrients. Insects and plant diseases take their toll. A late frost in spring or an early frost in autumn can destroy an entire season's produce. Too much rain can be just as devastating as too little.

Some of the problems faced by farmers require political and economic solutions. Technological changes, however, can alter the forces that make farming an unpredictable and sometimes unprofitable occupation. Many of these changes will arise from the field of biotechnology.

Until recently, agricultural innovation has focused on increasing yield. Today, agricultural researchers have other goals:

• *Reliability.* Genetic engineering has already produced plants that resist viral disease and microbes that may protect crops from frost damage and insect pests. Protecting crops from the vagaries of nature can make farming an even more reliable business.

• *Cost Efficiency.* American farming has become capital intensive, often requiring farmers to incur heavy debt to pay for seed, equipment, and supplies. With genetic engineering, scientists are developing new crops and agricultural products that may reduce farmers' need for costly herbicides and pesticides. Reductions in chemical use will also bring environmental benefits.

• *Crop Quality.* Biotechnology is being used to develop crops that are tastier, more appealing, and more nutritious. Genetic engineering may result in leaner animals that produce meats lower in calories and cholesterol. Research is under way to develop corn that contains higher percentages of important proteins, giving corn protein the nutritional quality of milk protein.

• *Crop Diversity.* Genetic engineering may yield entirely new crops that will open new markets to farmers. For example, farmers may someday grow crops that produce high-value proteins for use in pharmaceuticals. . . .

New Plants for Farmers

Although some years will pass before these goals of agricultural biotechnology can be achieved, scientists have already made substantial progress in the development of genetically engineered crops.

Genetically engineered tomato and tobacco plants have been made resistant to a viral disease that costs farmers as much as $200 million every year. "The farmer has learned to live with between 5 and 30 percent crop loss each year caused by virus infection," says Dr. Roger Beachy, professor of biology at Washington University, who developed the viral-resistant plants.

"Bringing in new sources of disease resistance should make it possible for the farmer to reduce that loss to either nothing or a much smaller level," he says.

In Beachy's research and other genetic engineering experiments, tobacco serves as a model for developing similar genetically engineered traits in food and fiber crops.

Better Products

Biotechnology can provide fresher, better-tasting produce, with lower chemical residues, better storagability, easier processing.

New products mean new market niches and new strains of grain with higher protein content, a quality that suffered in our pursuit of yield. This is what biotechnology pursues in agriculture: Better, not more—unless we need more.

Earle H. Harbison Jr., Speech given at The American Enterprise Institute and The Brookings Institution, Washington, D.C., June 1, 1988.

Other researchers are experimenting with plants that tolerate herbicides and resist bacterial disease. Some biotechnology companies have inserted into tobacco and tomato plants a bacterial gene for a natural, environmentally safe protein that protects the plant from leaf-eating insects. Many of these genetically engineered plants have been successfully field tested. . . .

Helpful Microbes

Plants are not the only inhabitants of agricultural fields. Myriad bacteria and other microbes live on plants and in the soil. Most are harmless, and many are beneficial to crops.

Some microbes, for instance, are natural fertilizer factories. An entire family of soil bacteria, the Rhizobia, convert nitrogen in the air into a form of nitrogen needed for plant growth. For more than 50 years, farmers have inoculated soil with these bacteria to encourage growth of crops like peas, soybeans, and alfalfa. Biologists are using genetic engineering to enhance nitrogen fixation in these bacteria.

Another bacterium—*Bacillus thuringiensis*, or B.t. for short—produces a non-poisonous protein that turns into a poison in the digestive tract of caterpillars. B.t. presents no significant risk to humans, animals, plants, or beneficial insects. The bacterium has been used by home gardeners as a safe, natural pesticide for more than 20 years.

Unfortunately, B.t. is not effective in the soil, where a species of caterpillar feeds on the roots of corn plants. So biologists have transferred the gene for B.t.'s natural pesticide to another bacterium that lives on corn roots. The genetically engineered bacterium is designed to protect the corn roots, without causing environmental damage.

Other kinds of bacteria play a role in frost damage that can ruin crops. These bacteria produce a protein that serves as a nucleus for ice crystal formation when temperatures dip below freezing.

Noting that some forms of the bacteria do not possess this characteristic, biologists have developed a way to remove the gene that produces the ice-nucleating protein. They hope that the resulting non-ice-nucleating bacteria, when spread on crops, will prevent frost from forming on the plants at temperatures several degrees below freezing.

Improving Farm Animals

In addition to developing improved plants and microbes, biologists are using biotechnology in animal husbandry. Many of the achievements of biotechnology in human health care have comparable applications in prevention and treatment of animal disease and in promotion of animal growth and efficiency.

To prevent animal disease, biotechnology is being used to develop safer vaccines. Traditional vaccines are made from weakened or killed disease-causing microbes, which means that a defective batch of vaccine could actually cause disease instead of prevent it. Some veterinarians believe that major outbreaks of hoof-and-mouth disease have been caused by defective vaccines.

With genetic engineering, scientists are better able to disarm the infectious organism used in vaccine production. Genes essential to the disease process can be removed from viruses used in a vaccine, rendering the viruses harmless. . . .

Scientists also use genetic engineering to develop new therapies, as well as promote animal growth and efficiency. In these uses of genetic engineering, the genes for certain animal proteins are spliced into bacteria. The bacteria are grown in fermentation vats, where they produce large quantities of the proteins. The proteins are then purified and administered to animals.

Among the therapeutic animal proteins, scientists are studying genetically engineered bovine interferon and interleukin, natural components in the immune system of cattle. These proteins may prove to be effective against shipping fever, a viral disease that attacks cattle during transport, causing an estimated $250 million in losses each year. . . .

Solving Age-Old Problems

Farm crops today are constantly at risk. Frost, insects, disease, drought and other plant stresses cost billions of dollars every year in lost crops and income—losses which plant breeding and agricultural technology cannot completely eliminate. . . .

Recent developments in molecular biology and genetic engineering, however, promise to provide novel answers to such age-old problems. Scientists have now learned how to transfer single genes from one living organism into another—accomplishing on the molecular level what plant breeders have been doing for over a century with whole plants.

Monsanto Company, *Of the Earth: Agriculture and the New Biology*, 1989.

Scientists are also using genetically engineered bacteria to produce a naturally occurring porcine protein that promotes rapid growth in pigs. The aim is to reduce the time, and thus the cost, of raising pigs until they reach market size. This protein may also lower the fat content of the pork, making the meat more healthful. . . .

The Safety of Biotechnology

Biotechnology companies are regulated by the Environmental Protection Agency, the Department of Agriculture, the Food and Drug Administration, and the Occupational Safety and Health Administration. In 1986, the White House's Office of Science and Technology Policy issued a framework for coordinating the activities of all federal agencies involved in regulating biotechnology.

Under the federal regulations, organisms with new genes from unrelated species must be evaluated for safety before being tested outdoors. Scientists conduct extensive laboratory and greenhouse experiments to determine that test organisms are not toxic to humans, animals, or beneficial plants and insects.

A number of universities and government agencies have convened scientific advisory boards to judge the safety of proposed field tests of genetically engineered plants and microorganisms. These expert panels have recommended approval of the proposed tests. A number of these field tests have been completed, with no evidence of harm to health or the environment.

The scientific evidence indicates that biotechnology is safe. Genetically engineered organisms look and behave much like their non-engineered counterparts, which have been used safely in agriculture for many years.

Conclusion

Biotechnology is a variety of safe techniques for developing new products and improving microbes, plants, and animals. In agriculture, it has the potential to make farming more reliable, produce foods of higher quality, protect the environment through the use of biodegradable agricultural products, and help developing countries feed their people.

"I believe that biotechnology presents to us today opportunities that are so great that we can't conceive what those benefits might be," says Dr. Fred Davison, former president of the University of Georgia. "We only begin to see some of the indications."

Adds Davison: The age of biotechnology "can be the most exciting period, in my estimation, in recorded history. I think, personally, it will be."

"There will be risks and side effects with this new technology, as well as unforeseen consequences."

Genetic Engineering Harms Agriculture

Jack Doyle

Jack Doyle is director of the agriculture and biotechnology project for the Environmental Policy Institute, a nonprofit organization in Washington, D.C. that studies energy and natural resources policy. He has written the book *Altered Harvest* and many articles on agricultural biotechnology and has lectured widely on the subject. In the following viewpoint, he argues that genetic engineering has unknown environmental hazards and may increase the use of chemical pesticides. Doyle further states that because genetic engineering technologies will be under the control of a few large corporations, it will benefit them more than farmers and rural communities.

As you read, consider the following questions:

1. What reasons does Doyle provide for believing that genetic engineering poses significant risks?
2. How will genetic engineering affect the economics of agriculture, according to the author?
3. How does Doyle distinguish between high-tech and low-tech biotechnology? Which does he prefer?

Jack Doyle, "Agricultural Biotechnology: Perils and Promise." Speech delivered to the Fourteenth Annual Maine Biological and Medical Sciences Symposium, May 26, 1988. Reprinted with the author's permission.

There are four general areas that I would like to cover. . . .

First, I will describe some risks and side effects we face with biotechnology. I think it's safe to say that there will be risks and side effects with this new technology, as well as unforeseen consequences. And to deal with these risks and side effects, we need adequate regulation, which we don't have now at any level.

Second, I will look at how biotechnology will affect agriculture and rural America, from farmers and local economies to the changing nature of the food system, as well as the use of rural America as a testing ground for genetically engineered organisms.

Third, I will explore the use of DNA as a special kind of raw material in the larger economy—as "the microchip of biology"; the new premier natural resource that may drive our economy more toward monopoly and centralization than it will economic opportunity and diversity.

And finally, I will discuss research opportunities and public policy choices, and the notion that there are really two kinds of biotechnology out there, but only one kind is getting all the hype. I believe there are crucial choices to be made between high-tech biology and low-tech biology; between biotechnology on the one hand, and "common sense" biology on the other. . . .

Risks of Biotechnology

With biotechnology, I think it's safe to say there will be some risks, and there will be some unforeseen consequences. Some of these consequences will not be cosmetic or trivial, and they could have substantial negative economic and public health effects as well. . . .

I read in the paper that there were 1,000 reported toxic accidents in the State of New York in 1987—in one year. There were 600 such accidents in New York in 1986. That kind of thing makes you wonder about biotechnology. And, unlike a chemical spill that can be cleaned up, or a tragic disaster like a plane crash, a biological accident will not be a one-time occurrence; it won't be a "once-and-done" kind of thing. Rather, a mistake in the biological realm is something that could . . . keep on causing problems. . . .

Unknowns

A second reason why there will be risks with genetically engineered organisms is because of the uncertainties and unknowns—that is, how much we don't know about genes, organisms, and ecosystems.

Take higher plants, for example. They contain upwards of 10 million genes, each one of which holds information or "instructions" governing particular functions and traits. In terms of understanding the plant genome, we are still really at a rudimentary level. We have identified and fully characterized maybe 50 or 100 plant genes at the most. And what do we know about the interaction of genes and gene products in the plant genome? . . .

Another reason why there will likely be some risks with biotechnology is the frequency of mutations. The use of large numbers of genetically altered microorganisms will spawn some unexpected mutations, and possibly greater rates of mutation as well, perhaps then making the introduced organism more fit and more apt to survive in ways that could be damaging.

The New Biotechnology

The new biotechnologies in agriculture will, in some cases, ensure the continued and increased use of herbicides in agriculture: more of the old cycle of chemical-intensive agriculture. In other cases, they will force farmers into high-yield technologies for which farmers, already strapped with surpluses, are not asking. But the choice facing U.S. farmers will be either to use them, or to foreclose on farming. Vertically integrated ownership of agriculture—from seeds, patents on plants, microbes and animals, to fertilizer, herbicides and pesticides, together with the political power that such economic power wields—is shaping and forcing the biotechnology revolution in agriculture.

H. Patricia Hynes, *Reproductive and Genetic Engineering*, vol. 2, no. 1, 1989.

In the past, we have often ventured into the unknown with our new technologies, only to find out later they did have substantial consequences we didn't anticipate. . . .

But even if you assume that the questions of environmental risks and regulation are resolved, there are still other questions raised with biotechnology. Take pesticides, for example.

How will biotechnology affect the present use of chemical pesticides? From the very earliest days of this technology we've heard great promises—about how this technology will do what Rachel Carson wanted to be accomplished with biological controls; and that the new products now made possible with genetic engineering will mean a safe new era of biological pest management in agriculture. And indeed, one of the reasons why the chemical and pharmaceutical industries have invested so heavily in agricultural biotechnology is because they see clearly that the days of hydrocarbon chemistry in agriculture are numbered. But all is not what it appears to be.

First of all, just because something is biological, doesn't necessarily mean it's benign or safe.

Secondly, when you examine how capital and scientific talent are being invested in agricultural research programs for pest and weed management, you find that there may not be a new era coming after all; or at least not coming as fast as suggested by some pronouncements. In fact, much of the money now being spent on biotechnology research in agriculture suggests that the chemical pesticide approach will be *extended* with the use of biotechnology, not ended.

Take, for example, the work now going to make crops herbicide resistant, that is, giving them the genetic wherewithal to tolerate or resist the chemical's toxic killing effects so the herbicide can be used without worry of crop damage. . . .

Such applications of biotechnology are troubling because they suggest a continuation of chemical toxicity in agriculture and for public resources like groundwater, not to mention farmer and farmworker exposures to pesticides or dietary exposures through tainted foodstuffs. Such applications are also troubling because of the new kind of "product synergy" they pose for agriculture, extending the web of integrated products that may increase agriculture's production costs as well as its dependencies and vulnerability.

Agriculture and Rural America

What about agriculture and rural America? How will biotechnology affect the farm system and the larger rural economy?

In the June 5, 1987 issue of *Science*, the Monsanto Company ran the following full page color advertisement:

Farming:
A Picture of the Future

Biotechnology will revolutionize farming . . . but it won't change the ways things look.

The products of biotechnology will be based on nature's own methods, making farming more efficient, more reliable, more environmentally friendly and—important for the farmer—more profitable.

Plants will be given built-in ability to fend off insects and disease, and to resist stress. Animals will be born vaccinated. Pigs will grow faster and produce leaner meat. Cows will produce milk more economically. And food crops will be more nutritious and easier to process.

For the American farmer, biotechnology offers an opportunity to retain the competitive edge by producing higher quality crops and livestock at lower cost.

And because most of these products don't require high technology farming practices, they can be used in the agriculture of the Third World, where starvation is a daily event.

High technology in a familiar package. Monsanto scientists are working with nature to develop innovative products for farmers today, and of the future.

MONSANTO
We challenge tomorrow every day.

126

Now, this is how Monsanto portrays the coming of biotechnology to agriculture. The company suggests that the appearance of the farm won't change.

But there is another way to look at this. While it may be true, perhaps, that the appearance of the farm per se might not change much with biotechnology, the agricultural system as a whole and much of rural America might look very different over time.

In 1950, for example, there were some 2,000 counties spread across the U.S. that had agriculture as the principal source of personal income; at that time, nearly 25% of the U.S. population lived in these counties. By the 1975-77 period the number of such counties had shrunk to 673; in which less than 4% of the U.S. population lived.

The Census Bureau announced on Feb. 10, 1988, that the nation's farm population dropped below 5 million people—4,986,000 to be exact. That's the lowest its been since 1820, when James Monroe was President and the total U.S. population was 9.6 million. Today, our farm population now comprises 2 percent of the nation's total population.

Time will tell what biotechnology will produce in rural America,

© Gibb/Rothco

but the early signs seem to suggest more of the same; more consolidation.

At the farm level we're told there will be more consolidation. The Congressional Office of Technology Assessment (OTA) says that biotechnology will contribute to the demise of approximately 1 million farms between now and the year 2000, mostly moderate-size and small farms. About 50,000 large farms will then account for 75 percent of U.S. agricultural production.

In fact, today, there are as many lawyers, bankers, scientists and accountants involved in the production of food as there are farmers.

In the farm supply industries—seed, feed, fertilizers and agri-chemicals—there is massive restructuring going on, some of which is motivated by what biotechnology will do to traditional farm supplies.

Eight of the world's top ten seed companies are now multinational corporations—nine if you count Pioneer as a multinational. Six of these are chemical, energy or pharmaceutical corporations, including Sandoz, Pfizer, Upjohn, Shell, ICI, and Ciba-Geigy. . . .

In the food processing industry, there is enough activity in biotechnology research and contracting to illustrate the objective of "genetic integration" as well as vertical integration—especially when it comes to capturing the raw material base.

"Of all the technologies coming to agriculture", says the Congressional Office of Technology Assessment, "the biotechnologies will have the greatest impact because they will enable agricultural production to become more centralized and vertically integrated".

On one level, there is no longer a food industry, or an agribusiness industry per se; increasingly they are intertwined with the energy, chemical and pharmaceutical industries. And part of the reason is DNA.

Meanwhile, in biotechnology research reports from the field and the laboratory, we can see what lies ahead. Orange juice from tissue culture in California. Cotton fibers from cultured cotton cells in Texas. And in Australia, work with epidermal growth factor to produce "shearless sheep".

Quite simply, genes are becoming a substitute for labor and resources in agriculture, and thereby, a powerful ingredient for economic consolidation throughout the food system.

Economic Power

In the long run, the big issue in biotechnology, I believe, is going to be about economic power—about who owns and controls this technology; about who owns and controls the genes. The central issue is going to be about who is in a position to dispense biotechnology's miracle cures, or its productive powers in agriculture.

We are in a time of historic consolidation in our society in a number of areas—we can see it all around us—in industry, in government, in science, in our universities. And in part, the shifting nature of our raw materials and natural resource base in some of those areas is playing an important, if not formative role in that restructuring.

Genetic Centralization

Today, agriculture, like other sectors of the economy, is experiencing unprecedented economic consolidation. Farmers are going out of business by the thousands. Mergers, takeovers, and conglomeration in the food and farm-supply industries are occurring worldwide. Such changes are simply the facts of life, we are told. But something else is going on here too. Biotechnology is revolutionizing food production. Suddenly economic consolidation in the food industry is magnified a hundredfold. And genes are the magnifiers. They are now at the center of food production; multinational corporations own them, and nation-states want them. . . .

The genetic centralization of food production *is* something to worry about. The stuff of national sustenance is involved: the sustaining, essential ingredients of life; the most basic components of food-making. These are the food determinants at the innermost sanctum of biology.

Jack Doyle, *Altered Harvest*, 1985.

Winston Churchill once said something about land monopoly being the greatest of monopolies, the most enduring form of monopoly; the mother of all other kinds of monopoly.

Well, when Churchill said this, the resources of economic and political power were in fact found in the land, were on the land, or lay beneath the land. Today, that has changed. If Churchill were alive today, he might see things a bit differently.

Today, the premier raw material is not land or oil; it is DNA. If you are doing business in any of the industries dependent on the workings of biology or genetics, the raw material you want to control is DNA. In one very powerful sense, DNA is the new oil, and it is helping to fundamentally transform our economy. . . .

Let me say that there is another possibility here with biotechnology—and I don't necessarily mean genetic engineering when I say that. I think there are really two kinds of applied biology possible now, but only one kind—the high-tech kind—is getting all the hype. There is also a low-tech, common sense biology that hasn't been explored much in the context of today's "new biology". . . .

In a very general sense, high-tech biology is the province of the

129

genetically engineered solution—i.e., the genetically engineered crop, the genetically engineered microbe, etc.—while low-tech biology might utilize a molecular insight in a more conventional way—say in plant breeding, or in insect behavior—so that a new product or treatment might not be necessary.

Low-tech biology, in this vein, is what I call "common sense" biology, relying less on the gene as the "fix it" solution, and more on understanding how the whole system works.

In agriculture, high-tech biology may look for ways to maximize the number of products used—say to integrate a genetic strategy with a chemical one, so as to multiply product possibilities. In doing this, some labor will be removed—that is, some "management know how"—and some technology substituted. Low-tech biology, on the other hand, might place a higher value on labor's knowledge and on-farm management for pest control.

Smart Biology

The issues here, of course, are not only agricultural in the old high-yield or "maximize efficiency" models; there are also jobs at stake, rural communities at risk, environmental values, and public health issues. But none of these need be sacrificed for advances in agricultural productivity with "smart biology"; that is, low-tech biology. And the same idea applies to biotechnology in medicine, natural resources management, and other fields as well.

But today, high-tech biology is prevailing—in capital, in commerce, in university research, and in scientific orientation. . . .

We need jobs in rural America, we need a healthy farm economy with new opportunities, we need an assured, safe and wholesome food supply, and we need to protect the environment. Certainly, the revolution in biological knowledge that is now before us, offers us some wonderful opportunities in each of these areas. The choices, it seems, are ours to make, but we better make them soon.

"For sheep and swine, chickens and cattle alike, the 21st century looks bright regarding improved knowledge and techniques for fighting disease."

Genetic Engineering Improves Farm Animals

Sandy Miller Hays

Much genetic engineering research has focused on farm animals such as chickens, pigs, and cattle. In the following viewpoint, Sandy Miller Hays describes agricultural research in which genetic engineering is used to make these animals grow faster, resist disease, and have other desirable characteristics. She argues that genetic engineering can improve the health of farm animals and benefit American farmers and consumers. Hays writes for *Agricultural Research*, a magazine published by the Agricultural Research Service of the U.S. Department of Agriculture.

As you read, consider the following questions:

1. How do scientists use diseases to research the genetic information stored in organisms, according to Hays?
2. What are some of the potential genetic improvements in animals that Hays describes?
3. According to the author, what aspect of animal production will not change in the future?

Sandy Miller Hays, "Farm Animals of the Future," *Agricultural Research*, April 1989 and May 1989.

Broilers blooming to market size 40 percent quicker, miniature hens cranking out eggs in double time, a computer "cookbook" of recipes for custom-designed creatures—this could well be the face of animal production in the 21st century.

At least some of the keys to these sorts of scientific miracles are already in the hands of researchers, according to Robert J. Wall, a physiologist with the United States Department of Agriculture's Agricultural Research Service. Wall works at ARS' Reproduction Laboratory at the Beltsville Agricultural Research Center in Beltsville, Maryland.

"We'll analyze the entire genetic composition of the animal and store that information on computers," says Wall. "Then we'll be able to hook up a machine we already have, called a DNA synthesizer, and recreate the genes we want.

The Genetic Alphabet

"Simply put, there are only five letters in the genetic alphabet, and only four occur in DNA—A, T, C, and G. These letters stand for the names of a kind of molecule called a nucleotide base. These bases occur in sequences—say ATCCGATCCG. The particular order of the letters and the length of the sequence, that's basically the recipe for a gene."

The chemicals represented by A, T, C, G, and U are no mystery, Wall says: "I have them in bottles in the refrigerator." But that doesn't mean scientists are ready to start building an animal from scratch.

"We can read the sequence of specific genes, although only in the last 10 years have we had the ability to do this with genes from higher organisms," Wall says. "We know the words, but we don't know the syntax of the sentences. There may be 100 genes involved in eye color. We have to learn not just what they are, but how they work together.

"We've figured out the sequencing on 1,000 genes, but there are probably 50,000 genes in humans or animals. And the ones we know about, we've reached through sort of a back door approach."

This approach is to identify a disease and determine that it's inherited and then to work backwards until researchers find the gene responsible for a disease.

"Right now, without a disease, we don't have any information to work with. We can read a chromosome from start to finish and write down every A, T, C, and G, but we don't know what that sequence is *for*. But someday we will—it will be done." . . .

Scientists in the next century will have fine-tuned the addition of desirable traits in the birds, such as disease resistance, according to Michael D. Ruff, microbiologist at ARS' Protozoan Diseases Laboratory at Beltsville.

"When you select birds for disease resistance, it's hard to get that trait and still keep the production qualities you want," says Ruff. "Say, for example, you want a bird with the genes 1, 2, 3, and 4. But when you add a bird with one of these genes to your breeding line, it may also have a 6 or 8 gene, which you don't want.

"In the 21st century, instead of having to accept the thousands of genes that are in a bird, some of which we want and some we don't, we'll be able to pull out gene 2 and insert it into another bird's genetic material."

Scientists in the future will manipulate not only the birds, but also the diseases that threaten them, Ruff predicts.

"Take Marek's disease, for which we do vaccinate," he says. "We may alter the causative virus by removing the gene for pathogenicity. Or perhaps we will enhance the bird's immune response to the virus. Or we might be able to change the disease organism so it can't withstand the temperature of the bird's body for very long—just long enough to prompt an immune response, but not long enough to let the disease get a good start."

Gene insertion is also on the minds of swine experts. "But after inserting a foreign gene, we'd have to be able to turn it on and off at will," says Norman C. Steele, an animal scientist at ARS' Non-Ruminant Animal Nutrition Laboratory at Beltsville. "For example, too much growth hormone can expose the animal to very bizarre metabolic disorders."

Animal Agriculture

Recombinant DNA techniques also have been used for the production of proteins that enhance animal health and productivity.

Again, using bacteria as factories, scientists have produced vaccines for foot-and-mouth disease and for a diarrhea-causing disease called "scours" that kills young animals.

Proteins that will allow milk and meat to be produced more efficiently are already being tested. These substances may significantly improve farming efficiency and economy.

Monsanto Company, *Genetic Engineering: A Natural Science*, 1984.

"We could insert genes that regulate the pig's immune system or give us females that ovulate more. Either of these could lead to more pigs produced per sow. The national average is now 11-12 pigs born per litter, but because of diseases and other problems only an average of 7.7 of these live to weaning size, the same as 30 years ago." . . .

The pigs of tomorrow will be bigger, but not fatter," says Norman Steele.

"In the very near future we'll be able to control growth through somatotropin," Steele says. "That's a natural growth hormone with tremendous potential to alter not only weight and rate of gain, but body composition. With somatotropin, you can increase the yield of muscle tissue 20 percent and simultaneously reduce the amount of body fat up to 70 percent.

"But it requires a daily dose for about 30 days in the early stages of growth, and it must be administered as an implant. The barrier to using somatotropin is the lack of a feasible delivery system."

Another group of chemicals, called beta-adrenegic agonists, has a major impact on reducing fat on the animal's body and works well in oral doses but leaves the animal in a hyperactive state, Steele says.

"What will happen, in all likelihood, is that drugs will be developed that have no unwanted side effects but will still alter the fat-to-lean ratio.

"Currently, we slaughter pigs at 220 to 240 pounds. The carcass is about 70 percent of the pig's live weight. Of that, the fat-to-lean ratio is now 2-to-1. A ratio of 1-to-1 is easily within our grasp."

The ability to control fat levels will change the market weight of hogs, Steele predicts.

"We slaughter them when we do, mainly because beyond that weight, they become too fat. But if we can control the amount of fat, there's no reason to stop at 240 pounds. We could go to 300 pounds. The key is body composition."

New Food

Steers in the future may find themselves contentedly chomping down all sorts of materials that would hardly qualify as quality forage today, according to Robert R. Oltjen. Oltjen is associate deputy administrator for Animal, Human Nutrition, and Post-harvest Sciences on ARS' National Program Staff.

"I think in the 21st century, we'll be able to economically unlock the energy in lignin, the binder for fibers in wood," says Oltjen. "And through genetic engineering, we'll be able to come up with a microbe that can chew it up. If that happens—if cattle have lignin-digesting microbes in their stomachs—we can feed them all kinds of woody products if we want to.

"We know there are rumen microorganisms that can partially degrade lignin, although not very effectively. Termites, however, are good at it; maybe we can take a gene from them. We could take a microbe that normally lives in the cow's rumen and insert the gene we need."

On a more typical diet, not necessarily one that includes trees or industrial byproducts, "The speed to market size will change a lot," predicts Oltjen. "We'll see cattle grow 50 percent faster. That's because we'll know more about their nutritive requirements and will feed them precisely to those requirements to more fully use their genetic ability for meat production." . . .

The big news in dairy cattle for the 21st century will be output—herds yielding as much as 40,000 pounds of milk per animal per year, according to H. Duane Norman, research leader of ARS' Animal Improvement Programs Laboratory at Beltsville, Maryland.

Improving Animal Husbandry

Biologists are using biotechnology in animal husbandry. Many of the achievements of biotechnology in human health care have comparable applications in prevention and treatment of animal disease and in promotion of animal growth and efficiency.

Industrial Biotechnology Association, *Agriculture and the New Biology*, 1987.

"We've had individual cows already that produced 50,000 pounds," Norman says. "In 1945, we had 25 million dairy cows in the United States; today we have about 10 million. But the milk yield per cow is up from 4,600 pounds to an average of 14,000 pounds today.

"Who would have said, back when we were making 4,600 pounds of milk, that we'd go to 10,000? We've got whole herds now that are producing 25,000 pounds."

The difference, says Norman, is genetic improvement, a steady selection process that sends older cows to slaughter and keeps only the best new animals on the milking line. . . .

Improving Cows

Oddly, for all their gains, the modern dairy cow is still producing only 0.65 calorie of milk for every calorie of useful energy absorbed from the digestive tract, according to Henry F. Tyrrell, a research animal scientist in the Energy Metabolism unit of ARS' Ruminant Nutrition Laboratory at Beltsville.

"You can go back in the scientific literature 80 or 90 years, and the estimates were still 65 percent," says Tyrrell. "This says to me that the modern dairy cow, from a metabolic point of view, is no more or less efficient than the cow of 100 years ago."

Nor is that percentage likely to change on its own, in Tyrrell's opinion.

"That's not to say there won't be some changes in the future," he adds. "When a cow consumes another calorie, she either puts it in milk or in maintaining her body. That's partitioning of energy."

But the use of bovine somatotropin, the so-called bovine growth hormone, would shift the balance in favor of milk production, says Tyrrell.

"BST acts as a repartitioning agent," he explains. "It doesn't change the basic metabolic processes going on; it just repartitions energy toward milk at the expense of body tissue. Typically with BST, you get a 15 percent increase in milk output, and it can be 30 to 50 percent short-term."

Looking ahead, "I'd say we'll see basically a continuation of the same trends of the last 50 years," Tyrrell projects. "What I see is more emphasis on tailoring milk to meet specific product demands. Genetically, you can change the relative proportions of proteins—casein, albumen, globulins—in milk. Part of the reason cheeses are different from each other is the various proteins in the milk. It's in this area, altering the proportions in the milk for specific products, that we'll see a change."

Milk-producing animals might be put to even more exotic use through gene insertion, says Vernon G. Pursel, a reproductive physiologist in ARS' Reproduction Laboratory at Beltsville.

"We've been working on targeting components to the mammary glands of farm animals," explains Pursel. "Depending on what gene you insert, you could have some of the rare medical proteins produced in the mammary gland. These special proteins could be extracted from the milk and purified."

The blood-clotting factor used to treat hemophilia is an example of a rare protein that may someday be extracted from milk, Pursel says.

"We've transferred a gene for a mouse protein into pigs. If the mouse gene functions correctly, the mouse protein will be present in the milk produced by our transgenic pigs.

"The next step will be to connect the regulatory part of the mouse gene to the structural part of a gene for a rare medical protein and thereby produce it in the milk.

"The final step will be to transfer such a gene into the dairy cow. If the regulatory part of the mouse gene works, it could also be used to modify the composition of the milk."

Preventing Poultry Diseases

Although predictions for poultry include the prospect of more disease-free production environments, scientists aren't relaxing when it comes to the future threat of poultry diseases, says Charles W. Beard, veterinary virologist at ARS' Southeast Poultry Research Laboratory at Athens, Georgia.

"We hope to determine the fundamental genetic traits of viruses that will let us predict the behavior of those viruses in poultry," says Beard. "Take avian influenza and Newcastle disease. Both have a range of disease-producing capability, from strains that won't kill any birds to ones that will kill 100 percent.

"Our goal is to come up with a genetic marker whereby we can rapidly and precisely distinguish the mild viruses from those with

136

disastrous potential—in other words, separate the good guys from the bad guys—and relay the information on what we've found to state and federal disease control officials. In the 21st Century, we'll have that capability.

"We're also looking for DNA probes to examine bird tissue and detect minute quantities of infectious agents in chickens. If a flock has survived an infection, you could examine tissues from that flock and determine if some members are carriers.

"The philosophy has been that if the flock becomes infected with certain diseases, you kill and bury them. But that's very expensive for the producer, the government, and ultimately, the consumer.

"With probes, we could check a representative sample of the flock to see if they have any residual virus. If the sample was found to be negative, you could conceivably grow out the rest of that flock."

Fighting Disease

For sheep and swine, chickens and cattle alike, the 21st century looks bright regarding improved knowledge and techniques for fighting disease, says Alex B. Thiermann, former ARS National Program Leader for Domestic Animal Diseases.

"I don't think we'll see animals resistant to everything," Thiermann says. "But we'll be able to develop animal lines with increased resistance to certain diseases."

Improving Livestock Quality

The genetic engineering of chickens, swine and cattle themselves will move forward rapidly. Livestock and poultry will be *born vaccinated* and resistant to diseases. We will also see a rapid acceleration of animal breeding for feed efficiency, disease resistance and other desirable qualities. Biotechnology holds the promise of improving livestock quality enormously.

Howard A. Schneiderman, Speech given at the University of Massachusetts at Amherst, September 30, 1986.

"It's possible that we may end up with certain genetic lines of swine resistant, for example, to African swine fever. Even if it wasn't a pig as efficient as we have today, we'd still be able to use this pig in areas where we're trying to control and eradicate African swine fever."

One of the more hopeful developments in genetic engineering against diseases involves a device Thiermann calls "the nonsense gene."

"Certain viruses, such as African swine fever virus, have the capability to incorporate themselves into the genetic material of an animal, then be carried into the animal's offspring," he explains. "But the virus has to establish itself in a particular spot on the genetic material.

"If we can occupy that 'parking spot' with a nonsense gene, the virus has no place to go. Work has already been done along these lines with avian leukosis, a virus that gets into the genetic material of poultry.

"We've come up with an avian leukosis virus that is modified so it can no longer cause disease, but it can still get into the genetic material of the chicken. The birds infected with this modified virus are resistant to the nasty avian leukosis virus. The parking lot is already full."

The altered avian leukosis virus itself has room for genetic insertions that scientists could put to good use, says Thiermann.

"We'd like to introduce desirable genes in there—production genes, more eggs, less fat, quick growth, whatever, or genes that would produce antigens to allow birds to produce antibodies against other diseases," he says.

"Again, the chickens would pass this on to the next generation, because it's in their genetic material. We're very close to this now. All the pieces are already there."

Vaccines

Along similar lines, scientists have successfully taken the disease-causing power away from vaccinia virus—a relative of smallpox virus—and used vaccinia virus to carry "messages" to protect animals against other diseases.

For example, field tests are underway in Canada and Europe on a vaccinia vector vaccine for rabies. A gene was removed from the rabies virus and put in the vaccinia virus. Animals that get the non-disease-causing vaccinia virus also get the rabies gene that promotes production of antibodies against rabies without actually contracting rabies.

Still, vaccinia virus has its foes, those who worry about vaccinia virus' ability to spread from one species to another, Thiermann notes.

"What I'd like to see is this being done with a host-specific virus that infects only cattle or pigs, for example. You could insert the desirable genes into the virus or bacteria.

"In the next 30 years, we could be engineering viruses by taking disease-causing properties out and putting desirable genes in," he says. "I think we will be dealing a lot more with genetically engineered vector vaccines in the future. Once we get through the preliminary stages, we can mass-produce these at low cost."

But there are still many miles to travel before science reaches that point, Thiermann adds.

"In theory, we can cut the disease information out of any virus.

But it takes a long time to study a virus and map out what each area of genetic material is responsible for. Not every virus has its disease-causing properties in the same place; every one is different."

Making the System Better

Despite all these modern miracles, one aspect of animal production probably won't have changed much 100 years hence, says James W. Deaton, supervisory research animal scientist for ARS' South Central Poultry Research Laboratory at Mississippi State, Mississippi.

"In 100 years, there will still be scientists attempting to make the system better—more efficient, more environmentally sound, with continued good health for the consumer," Deaton says.

"Will genetic engineering of animals cause suffering? The answer is that it already has."

Genetic Engineering Harms Farm Animals

Michael W. Fox

Michael W. Fox is a vice president of the Humane Society of the United States and specializes in farm animals and bioethics. In the following viewpoint, he argues that genetic engineering has caused significant disease and suffering among farm animals and urges that the practice be stopped. He states that most genetic engineering research emphasizes production instead of animal welfare, and that genetic engineering has harmful side-effects.

As you read, consider the following questions:

1. In what ways does genetic engineering cause animal suffering, according to Fox?
2. Why does Fox dispute claims that genetic engineering can help animals fight diseases?
3. What alternative to genetic engineering does the author suggest?

Michael W. Fox, "Genetic Engineering and Animal Welfare," *Applied Animal Behavior Science*, vol. 22, 1989. Reprinted with permission of Elsevier Science Publishers and the author.

Will genetic engineering of animals cause suffering? The answer is that it already has.

A major concern of all humanitarians is whether or not genetic engineering will cause animals to suffer. The answer is being evaded by proponents of biotechnology who claim that "unnecessary" suffering will be avoided and existing Federal animal care guidelines and regulations will take care of the problem. As will be shown, transgenic engineering of animals has already caused animals to suffer and this was not anticipated by the researchers. Federal animal welfare regulations contain no reference to genetically engineered animals and have to do with the care of animals; they have nothing to do with preventing or alleviating animal suffering following genetic reprogramming.

Acknowledging the fact that as more animals are subjected to transgenic intervention (or reprogramming), the probability of animal suffering increases, we should specify what types and sources of suffering we are dealing with. These types are as follows.

Developmental Abnormalities

Following gene insertion into embryos, the embryos often fail to develop and are aborted. Some may develop abnormally and die in utero, being aborted or resorbed, or are born with a variety of developmental defects, some resulting from so-called insertional mutations. These may not be manifested until later in life; hence, there can be no accurate prediction as to whether or not engineered animals are going to suffer and because of the nature of genetic reprogramming, there can be no safeguards to prevent animal suffering. These problems are to be expected in the initial phase of creating transgenic animals and in other genetic manipulations.

W. French Anderson has emphasized that the microinjection of eggs with foreign genes "can produce deleterious results because there is no control over where the injected DNA will re-integrate in the genome." This can mean that a gene, say, for a certain hormone or other protein, expresses itself in an inappropriate tissue. He notes, "There have been several cases reported where integration of microinjected DNA has resulted in a pathological condition." This is one of the major reasons why he is opposed to transgenic germ line therapy in humans and it is a valid reason for concern over the welfare of animals subjected to this kind of treatment in early embryonic life.

Once the anticipated genetic changes have been accomplished and the new animal prototypes developed as foundation breeding stock, additional problems are to be anticipated. These have already been shown to occur in transgenic animals.

These problems are now well recognized by biotechnologists.

The term pleiotropism refers to multiple effects by one or more genes on the animal's phenotype where the phenotype is the entire physical, biochemical and physiological make-up of an individual.

The well publicized health problems of the U.S. Department of Agriculture's (U.S.D.A.'s) transgenic pigs that carry the human growth gene were unexpected, since mice and rabbits reprogrammed with this same gene did not manifest deleterious pleiotropic effects to anywhere near the same degree. These pigs were arthritic, lethargic, had defective vision, arising from abnormal skull growth, and did not grow twice as big or twice as fast, as was anticipated on the basis of the effects of the human growth gene in mice. These pigs had high mortality rates and were especially prone to pneumonia, the conclusion being that the genetic change had seriously impaired their immune systems.

Human Domination

When technologists speak, as they do, of creating 'super animals' what they have in mind is not super lives for animals so that they may be better fed, have more environmentally satisfactory lives, or that they may be more 'humanely' slaughtered, rather what they have in mind is how animals can be originated and exist in ways that are completely subordinate to the demands of the human stomach. In other words, animals become like human slaves, namely 'things'—even more so in a sense since human masters never—to my knowledge—actually consumed human slaves. Biotechnology in animal farming represents the apotheosis of human domination.

Andrew Linzey, *Slavery: Human and Animal*, 1988.

This illustrates that pervasive suffering can arise from genetic engineering. It also demonstrates another principle: that a genetic change in one species may cause little apparent sickness and suffering, as in the case of transgenic mice, but this does not mean that the same genetic change in another species will have comparable consequences (as in the case of the U.S.D.A.'s sickly transgenic pigs). In other words, predictions and assurances as to the safety and humaneness of genetic engineering cannot be generalized from one animal species to other species. . . .

Disease and Genetic Disorders

Biotechnologists contend that through genetic engineering animals can be made disease resistant and this will help reduce animal suffering; shipping fever in cattle, which is a cause of considerable economic loss to the livestock industry, is a commonly used example.

However, the notion that genetically engineered disease resistance will reduce animal suffering is scientifically naive. It is naive because it reflects a single cause (bacteria/virus) approach to disease. Simply endowing an animal with resistance to a particular disease will not protect it from other pathogens or the stress factors and contingent suffering that make it susceptible to disease in the first place, such as transportation stress, overcrowding, etc.

It has been claimed that genetically engineering livestock to be resistant to various tropical diseases (such as sleeping sickness) and to extremes in climate would benefit them as well as the industry, but this would not benefit other animals, i.e., threatened and endangered wildlife species, since they would be displaced and exterminated as their habitats are taken over by the livestock industry.

There are other erroneous claims of the potential benefits of biotechnology to the animals themselves. It has been claimed that genetic engineering could be used to help cure animals of genetic disorders. This claim is made despite the almost 200 diseases of genetic origin that have been identified in highly inbred "purebred" dogs, and there are dozens that afflict other domesticated species. Aside from the fact that it would be a poor investment to correct germ line defects since disease termination in this way is not profitable (and this point is also relevant to corporate investment and involvement in human medicine), simply stopping the practice of inbreeding and breeding defective animals is the best prevention.

One transgenic study designed to cure an inherited disease resulted in animal suffering and death. Following the successful insertion of the gene for human insulin into diabetic mice, their diabetes was cured. However, after several weeks the mice died of an excess of insulin.

Productivity and Suffering

Using genetic engineering biotechnology to increase the productivity and "efficiency" of farm animals (growth rates, milk or egg yield, etc.) will increase the severity and incidence of animal suffering and sickness. It is already extensively documented that farm animals raised under intensive confinement husbandry systems, in order to maximize production and efficiency, suffer from a variety of so-called production-related diseases. The argument that if animals are suffering they will not be productive and farmers will not profit is demolished by the fact that animal scientists, in using the term "production-related diseases", acknowledge that animal sickness and suffering are an unavoidable and integral aspect of modern livestock and poultry farming. Using biotechnology to make animals even more productive and efficient under these conditions will place their overall welfare in greater jeopardy than ever because the severity and incidence of production-related diseases will be increased.

Biotechnologists argue that genetic engineering is simply an extension of selective breeding and that since mutations (spontaneous genetic changes) occur naturally, then there is nothing morally wrong or unethical about altering animals through genetic engineering. In so doing they totally ignore the scientific and medical evidence of the harmful consequences to animals of deliberate genetic manipulation, as witness the wide variety of disorders in purebred dogs.

The domesticated dog, man's closest and oldest animal companion, is afflicted by almost 200 diseases of hereditary origin. These have been produced (like the genetic disorders of farm animals) through traditional selective breeding and inbreeding procedures in order to "fix" various traits for reasons of utility and aesthetics. . . .

Veterinary medical research has only recently begun to recognize that so many of the health problems of companion animals are genetic in origin. Few of the disorders that affect farm animals have been looked at from this perspective, but the research that has been done reveals the same trend: an increasing incidence of health problems, many of them of genetic origin, arising as a consequence of selectively breeding for reasons of utility. The genetic engineering of farm animals for these same

STOP THE MACHINE

Reprinted with permission from SACA NEWS, published by the Student Action Corps for Animals, PO Box 15588, Washington, DC 20003.

144

reasons will, therefore, have similar consequences—an increasing incidence of structural and functional disorders of genetic origin that will be the cause of even more animal suffering. For those animals used in biomedical research that are subjected to genetic engineering to serve as "models" of various human disease conditions and as "tools" to test new diagnostic and treatment procedures, suffering will also be their burden and to what final end or purpose? Surely the betterment of humanity and social progress should not become ever more dependent upon the exploitation and suffering of other sentient, non-human beings. . . .

Many of the health problems that afflict livestock and poultry have been related to selectively breeding for certain utility traits such as rapid rate of growth, which has been shown to be linked with calving difficulties and higher mortality rates. Genetic engineering aimed at increasing the utility of farm animals is thus likely to intensify these already existing problems in livestock and poultry.

Animal Suffering

That biotechnologists promise that genetic engineering will also be used to improve the health/disease resistance as well as the utility of farm animals, and thus actually reduce their overall suffering, is a falsehood of considerable magnitude. The new and profitable vaccines and other biologics that are being developed by the biotech industry will help reduce the incidence of certain diseases and associated secondary suffering in farm animals. The same can be said of genetically engineering the animals themselves to be resistant to specific diseases. However, the stress and primary suffering that arise from the consequences of how they are selectively bred, raised and handled, and which have led to dependence upon vaccines and other biologics to protect their weakened immune systems, will not be eliminated.

In fact, with such artificial supports (vaccines and drugs), primary suffering will increase as producers are able to adopt even more intensive methods of animal production. In other words, the absence of actual disease does not mean an end to animal suffering under current farm animal husbandry conditions. Using biotechnology to control infectious and contagious diseases, even though the animals are chronically stressed under overcrowded confinement conditions (which are standard treatments on large factory-scale commercial livestock and poultry operations) will do little, therefore, to improve the welfare of farm animals and in the final analysis, may actually jeopardize it even more. . . .

There are many alternatives that are already available or could be developed so that animals do not need to be subjected to the risks of genetic engineering.

(1) Improved handling, transportation and housing/husbandry

practices are alternatives to developing genetically engineered disease-resistant animals.

(2) Bacteria can be engineered to produce insulin and other pharmaceuticals. The genetic engineering of farm animals to perform the same task (as by reprogramming cows and sheep to produce such biologics in their milk) is to be questioned. Animals are sentient beings and can suffer, while bacteria are clearly not capable of suffering.

No Need to Alter Genes

On closer examination, it is not mere animal rights sentiment or some spiritual or religious belief that leads to the conclusion that it is wrong to alter an animal's *telos* or intrinsic nature by genetically altering its germline. Beyond the moralist polemics of right and wrong, there is the cold fact that regardless of any purported benefits to animals from such genetic engineering, there are safer, less invasive and more practical alternatives such as changing husbandry practices and the deliberate selection of mutations and other inherited anomalies in domestic animals. . . . In sum, the sanctity of being and the inviolability of the telos of animals are ethical principles that need not be dismissed for utilitarian or quasi eugenics reasons because there are many alternatives to enhancing the welfare and overall well-being of animals without having to resort to genetic engineering biotechnology.

Michael W. Fox, "Animal Welfare Concerns of Genetic Engineering Biotechnology," March 1989.

---

(3) Alternatives to genetically engineering animals as "models" for various human diseases should also be sought, if the application of research findings to human patients are not primarily preventive in nature. Prevention of genetic and developmental disorders in humans includes such non-animal alternatives as genetic screening and counselling, and decontamination of environmental chemical pollutants that are teratogenic and mutagenic (i.e., cause developmental and genetic abnormalities).

Conclusion

In conclusion, we should all ask why we need to genetically engineer farm animals, especially in these times of agricultural surpluses and chronic overproduction. Most of the health problems of farm animals are best addressed by making much needed improvements in overall handling, transportation, housing and husbandry. Are the risks and costs of potential and actual animal suffering worth the benefits, and who will be the primary beneficiaries? The animals will certainly not be the latter. Additionally, the genetic engineering of laboratory animals is more the domain of profitable interventive human medicine. This is surely of lesser importance than public health, environmental and preventive medicine, which no amount of genetic engineering of animals can advance.

In the final analysis, is the public interest and good of society really being served (biotech industry promises aside) by the genetic engineering and patenting of animals? Long-term social and environmental consequences also need to be considered, as well as the ethics of this new technology, but in view of the suffering that will result in animals subjected to certain forms of genetic reprogramming purely for reasons of utility, tighter and more appropriate animal welfare regulations, or better guarantees of corporate responsibility with regard to the animals' wellbeing are not sufficient. The best way to prevent animal suffering and reduce its probability of occurrence before this new industry expands further, is surely to put a moratorium on all animal patenting and to establish an Animal Bioethics Council composed of representatives from government, industry, academia and public interest groups, particularly those involved in animal welfare, rights and conservation, that could give the question of animal genetic engineering and animal patenting the attention and consideration that have been so lacking to date.

"Biotechnology can enormously enhance food
production in developing countries."

Genetic Engineering Will Reduce World Hunger

Howard A. Schneiderman

Hunger is a severe problem in many countries in Africa, Asia, and
Latin America. In the following viewpoint, excerpted from a
speech, Howard A. Schneiderman argues that genetic engineering
can reduce hunger. Genetic engineering, according to Schneiderman, will help Third World nations increase their agricultural output by improving the yield and durability of food crops and plants.
Schneiderman is a senior vice president in charge of research and
development for the Monsanto Company. The St. Louis firm produces herbicides and other agricultural products and is an industry
leader in genetic engineering research.

As you read, consider the following questions:

1. Can genetic engineering by itself solve the problem of
   world hunger, according to Schneiderman?
2. In what respects can plants be improved by genetic
   engineering, according to the author?
3. Why does Schneiderman believe genetic engineering will
   be especially helpful to farmers in developing nations?

Howard A. Schneiderman, "Biotechnology: A Key to America's Economic Health in
Health Care and Agriculture." Speech delivered to the Second Annual American Society
for Microbiology Conference on Biotechnology, San Diego, California, June 25-28, 1987.
Reprinted with permission of Monsanto Company.

Within developing tropical countries, 100,000 people, including 40,000 small children, die each day from conditions related to poverty and malnutrition. We do not yet have a reliable vaccine for some diseases like malaria, AIDS or schistosomiasis. But an effective vaccine for starvation is well known to all of us—food. Starvation is an unnecessary disgrace to our global society. In my brief remarks, I should like to offer evidence that biotechnology provides an opportunity to enhance the food production of developing tropical countries in a safe, clean and ecologically-sound way. But it is important that we place biotechnology in perspective and recognize clearly what it can and cannot do.

Not a Quick Fix

Biotechnology will not solve the problems of world hunger. I hope to show you that it can be a powerful tool in that struggle, and a good case can be made that it is a necessary tool. But in addition to biotechnology we need economic and political reform, education, solutions to the problem of rural landlessness, effective ways to soften the impact of the great international debt which plagues developing countries, new ways to provide farmers in developing nations with the information they need to put in place more sustainable and productive agriculture and forestry, new ways to cultivate trees along with crops to secure durable yields from tropical soils, new ways to limit deforestation, the setting of realistic levels for government-controlled food prices to provide an incentive for farmers to be more productive, population control through family planning . . . and dozens of other matters.

Biotechnology may provide wonderful new seeds which give rise to crops that can grow in salty soils, resist heat, cold, disease, pests and drought. But such seeds will be of limited value in enhancing food production unless their use is accompanied by economic and political changes.

I have made these statements at the outset so that I can proceed with an enthusiastic description of what biotechnology can do. I just want to make certain that no one concludes from my comments that biotechnology can provide a "quick scientific fix" for the problem of world hunger.

Genetic Engineering of Crops

You all know what genetic engineering is and what it can do. It permits genetic recombination between different organisms. It enables scientists to take just one or several genes from one organism—a corn plant or a cow—and insert these genes into a completely different organism such as a bacterium to produce a bacterium with those new genes. Each new gene inserted into the bacterium carries instructions to manufacture a new protein.

It is now commonplace to insert various foreign genes into plant cells as well and to endow plants derived from those cells with desirable new traits. It is important to emphasize that this process of recombining genes is as natural as plant breeding. The plant breeder has a limited menu of useful traits—genes—to put into his crop seeds. The genetic engineer offers a much larger menu of potentially useful traits and can also enormously speed up the process of plant breeding.

The Need for New Technologies

As world population increases and food supplies diminish, the need for new technologies to improve agriculture will become even more apparent. Not only will genetic engineering provide seeds to the world's farmers which can be grown successfully in both mechanized and labor intensive agriculture, it also will provide food of higher quality and with better nutritional value.

Monsanto Company, *Agriculture and the New Biology*, 1989.

The impact of genetic engineering on crop production promises to be enormous. Plant breeding has already provided plants with resistance to major diseases, to some insect pests, and with enhanced yields. But genetic engineers offer new and rapid ways to protect crops and enhance yields. Genetic engineers have the tools to enhance significantly the efficiency of production and to make farming throughout the world a more reliable and profitable business. Plant breeders remain the key agents of change, but their genetic engineering partners increase their effectiveness.

Since 1983, when scientists originally developed the capability of plant transformation for petunia and tobacco which are the *E. coli, Drosophila* and white mice of plant molecular biology, more than a dozen vegetable and commercial crop plants have been transformed in various laboratories. We have already genetically-engineered plants to resist caterpillars and beetles, to resist viruses of all sorts, and to resist an environmentally-friendly herbicide, Roundup®or glyphosate. In the next 5-7 years, genetic engineers will have conferred these and other commercially desirable properties, such as resistance to fungi, to bacterial pathogens, to pests and to stress on many major crops including soybeans, rice, corn, wheat, canola, sorghum, cotton and alfalfa. Various tropical species will soon follow.

Advantages to the Farmer

The advantages to the farmer are manifold. For example, when cotton has been genetically engineered to resist both caterpillars like the pink bollworm and beetles like the boll weevil, it will dramatically impact the growing of cotton. No longer will cotton farmers have to spray their fields six or more times each growing season with a conventional insecticide. The opportunity to reduce the load of conventional insecticides in the environment is tremendous. Rachel Carson would love it. Furthermore, the input cost savings to the farmer should be large.

We are also learning how to make crops grow hardier and have better yields with less use of fertilizer and to grow without the need for tilling. We are learning to increase the range of important food crops and permit marginal acres in many tropical areas to be cultivated productively. We are in a position to improve rapidly and efficiently crops such as millet, cassava and yams with which farmers in developing countries are intimately familiar. Overall, genetic engineering will lower the input required for farming and increase its reliability.

We are also learning how to make foods of higher quality—better taste, better storageability, better processability, better brewability, and more nutritious.

Moreover, unlike conventional plant breeding which narrows diversity, plant genetic engineering can increase the genetic diversity of plants and make crops less vulnerable to disease and stress. Virtually any desirable trait—whether found in a bacterium, another plant or even an animal—can now be used to improve plants. During the next two decades genetic engineering will provide the plant breeder with a precise and powerful tool to improve germ plasm, to introduce quickly important new diversity into key crops and ultimately to introduce new crops.

It is especially attractive for developing countries because it is not capital intensive, does not require high inputs of energy, dollars or chemicals. Genetic engineering provides high-technology seeds that do not require high-technology farming. It could improve the productive efficiency and reliability of farming worldwide by making crops more resistant to diseases, pests and stress.

To make this happen, we must provide opportunities for scientists from developing countries to apply genetic engineering to the key crops of their country, to substitute knowledge and nature for conventional insecticides and fungicides and to develop "seeds of tomorrow" that will reliably produce useful crops on impoverished soils and require less input of fertilizer, other chemicals and energy.

Genetically-Engineered Microorganisms

Another attractive way to improve the efficiency of agricultural production worldwide is the use of genetically-engineered microorganisms to replace many crop chemicals, to extend the range of certain crops and to enhance the productive efficiency of agriculture. . . .

Most plants live in loose association with microorganisms, forming biological partnerships. One partner is the plant itself; the other tiny partners are the root-colonizing bacteria and fungi which may be intimately associated with the root system of the plant and act as "middlemen," transferring nutrients from the soil to the plants. Some of them live near the roots of the plant, others actually invade the roots. The bacteria that invade the roots of soybeans and "fix" nitrogen there to the benefit of the soybean plant are familiar examples. But there are numerous other opportunities to use root-colonizing microorganisms to reduce our current dependence on pesticides and fertilizers. The idea is to genetically-engineer a soil microbe which colonizes the roots of a crop with a trait useful to the crop. For example, one could endow the microbes with the ability to protect the crop from fungal diseases, nematodes or specific insect pests. Such genetically-modified bacteria would be coated on the seeds or added to soil surrounding the seeds at the time of planting. The microbe would provide the crop with natural protection against certain diseases and pests. It might also be engineered to enhance the plant's nutrient uptake from the soil. . . .

Growing Food in Deserts

Tinkering with a plant's genetic information could produce crops that are able to grow in salty environments. That would mean food crops might be raised on currently nonarable land, such as alkaline deserts. Some plants can already live in such deserts, and scientists think that eventually they may be able to splice the genes leading to that ability into food crops. In the nearer term, plants may be engineered to produce natural pesticides, cutting food production costs and eliminating a major health hazard and cause of pollution.

Edward J. Sylvester and Lynn C. Klotz, *The Gene Age*, 1987.

Beyond the direct benefits of applying biotechnology to agriculture, there are important side benefits that should not be forgotten. If we can make each acre of recently deforested farmland in developing countries and each farmer more productive, we can slow the horrendous rate of destruction of tropical forests. Those forests are a vital source of genetic diversity. The plants, trees and microbes that live in them contain a huge variety of traits which will be essential to our efforts to keep pace with the constant evolution of diseases and pests. If we continue to destroy our genetic library—a library as yet largely unread—we are plowing under our future productivity and health.

In thinking about the application of biotechnology to agriculture, it is also important to focus on the increasing demand for food over the next decades. The world's population will almost double by about 2025 and the vast majority of this population growth will occur in developing countries. Where will the food come from? One cannot redesign human beings for greater fuel economy, the way one redesigns cars. Hence, as far as food is concerned, in the long run we have two planetary choices: we either plow up the rest of the planet or increase the productivity and productive efficiency of existing acres.

How does one increase the productive efficiency of existing acres? Biotechnology offers one of the most powerful tools. Because of the problems of food distribution, agricultural productivity must be enhanced most in developing countries, and it is precisely in such areas, where new strains and kinds of plants are needed to cultivate marginal lands, where increased protein must be engineered into root crops, that the contribution of genetic engineering may be the most important. . . .

Helping Developing Countries

If biotechnology is effectively used by developing countries, it can help them secure the sustainable agricultural productivity they need to feed and maintain themselves. It can help them to become contributing partners in the world's economy, and gain purchasing power that they can use for internal development and to purchase products from the United States and other countries.

Once basic hunger is reduced, developing countries can aspire to become NICs, "new industrialized countries," with higher expectations for food and other products, expectations that will increase world trade and promote political stability.

To conclude, biotechnology can enormously enhance food production in developing countries and can enhance the productive efficiency and profitability of American agriculture in an environmentally-friendly way.

And, beyond that, biotechnology offers Nature's own method to protect the Global Commons—the air, the rain forests, the oceans. Unless these and other new methods are applied to halt tropical deforestation, to reduce excess nitrogen fertilizers, to replace many traditional insecticides, fungicides and many other conventional crop chemicals, the Global Commons will undergo what is probably irremediable environmental damage.

"Biotechnology has potential for benefits but also may cause negative economic and social effects."

Genetic Engineering Will Not Reduce World Hunger

Anne K. Hollander

The Green Revolution is a term that describes programs to increase agricultural production in developing countries by using hybrid seeds, fertilizers, and advanced farm technology. Some development experts argue that many Green Revolution changes had negative environmental and social effects, and question whether the new techniques of genetic engineering will work any better. In the following viewpoint, Anne K. Hollander argues that developing countries may be harmed instead of helped by genetic engineering. Hollander is an associate of the Conservation Foundation, an environmentalist research organization in Washington, D.C. She directs the Foundation's Biotechnology Project.

As you read, consider the following questions:

1. What three challenges do developing countries face if they want to use genetic engineering, according to Hollander?
2. What are the economic risks of genetic engineering, according to the author?
3. Does Hollander believe that genetic engineering has any value for developing countries?

Anne K. Hollander, "Biotechnologies Are Tricky to Manage in the Third World," *Conservation Foundation Letter*, no. 6, 1988. Reprinted with permission of the Conservation Foundation.

The possible benefits of biotechnology for the less developed nations of the world are impressive. Increased food production, better disease control, new sources of renewable energy, and new approaches to conservation of genetic resources and the environment—these are among the potential gains that, if realized, could help to solve many of the developing countries' most persistent and severe problems. . . .

Major Challenges

It is important also to acknowledge that some major management challenges face those who would introduce biotechnologies to the Third World. Three challenges in particular deserve attention:

• the need to ensure that important public benefits of biotechnology are realized;

• the need to avoid unexpected environmental harm; and

• the need to channel economic changes in constructive directions so they do not create unintended and unmanageable disruptions within developing countries.

Unfortunately, some of the most significant products of biotechnology envisioned by scientists may not be available for a long time, if ever. Four factors are chiefly responsible for this delay: technical constraints, lack of economic incentives for companies, inadequate infrastructure to disseminate products to those who need them most, and insufficient public sector research.

The technical difficulty of achieving goals in the laboratory and applying the findings to large-scale biotechnical production are well documented. Scientists have barely begun to understand the physiology of plants and microorganisms and their ecological relationships to other organisms. For example, over 90 percent of all soil microorganisms cannot yet be cultured in the laboratory, a prerequisite to identifying and studying them. Thus, technical and scientific constraints certainly hinder the realization of biotechnology's potential. On the other hand, these constraints are being overcome more rapidly than social and political constraints, which seem to present greater challenges.

Political Obstacles

One sociopolitical problem lies in the private sector: Internationally as well as in developing countries, private firms have insufficient economic incentive to develop some of the most promising applications of biotechnology. One example is narrow-spectrum pesticides for crop protection. An important advantage of using genetic engineering to develop such pesticides is that they can be targeted to only one pest and one crop at a time. They therefore are apt to cause limited adverse effects—for example, they would not kill beneficial insect predators or cause toxic effects in mammals. However, narrow-spectrum pesticides tend to be poor business investments. The potential market for a product effective against a single pest is usually too small, especially compared to the market for one that is effective against many pests on multiple crops. The fact that the public derives benefits from a narrow-spectrum pesticide because of its safer characteristics has little economic relevance in the marketplace.

A Double-Edged Sword

Biotechnology is a double-edged sword for the Third World. It has the potential to increase the quality and efficiency of agricultural production, offering a long-awaited answer to malnutrition and foreign food aid dependency. But, it also has the potential to disrupt local agriculture and encourage further dependency on expensive agricultural imports and technology.

In many ways, it depends on who controls and dispenses this new technology. If biotechnology is vested primarily in the hands of advanced nations and major businesses, those interests will be in a position to pull the plug on locally significant kinds of agricultural development in the Third World, possibly with dire consequences for national economies and international trading patterns.

Jack Doyle, *Multinational Monitor*, February 28, 1986.

As another example, human vaccines are critically needed to reduce the endemic diseases of tropical countries—but the attendant liability risks and the inability of users to pay for the products have a dampening effect on their development. When the president of Genentech, a U.S. biotechnology firm, was asked by the World Health Organization to participate in developing a vaccine for malaria, he declined. The potential economic gains were apparently insufficient to justify the cost and the financial risk.

Infrastructure

A third obstacle to achieving the full potential of biotechnology arises because of poor infrastructure. Before benefits can be realized by users, applied research must be integrated with an established infrastructure for marketing, manufacturing, and distributing final products. In developing countries, these factors are in chronically short supply. Other constraints include shortages of experienced researchers, research managers, and senior executives; of production facilities; and of the large injections of risk capital that are needed to finance new businesses.

Private control is widely believed to enhance the dissemination and application of new technologies. Thus, a possible way to overcome the lack of infrastructure in developing countries is for the public sector to conduct research and develop products that otherwise would not be developed, with the private sector engaged to market and distribute them. Collaborations of this nature are, in fact, increasing in popularity. However, such arrangements can lead to the diversion of already limited public research funds to research that has high profit potential, instead of research that meets the most critical needs of developing countries. . . .

Everyone who has studied biotechnology acknowledges that eventually it will bring vast economic and social changes. Some economic development experts have argued that these changes may cause serious economic problems, such as the reduction of developing countries' control over their genetic resources, or crop displacement and lost export markets. Others see biotechnology as the solution to these very same problems. In fact, both groups could be right, for biotechnology has potential both to benefit and harm social and economic systems. The challenge is to manage it so the beneficial uses are predominant.

Rich and Poor

One thing on which all economic development experts agree is that economic development can occur only if the gaps narrow between rich and poor people and between nations. Therefore, a legitimate concern of development economists is whether biotechnology will increase or decrease these economic gaps.

Several types of evidence suggest that gaps may in some cases move in the wrong direction when biotechnological products are introduced. For one thing, benefits of technological change, as they pass through an existing social order, tend to be distributed in rough proportion to the existing distribution of productive assets and power. This phenomenon, the "refraction effect," has occurred throughout history.

A study predicting the economic impact of increased corn production in Mexico is relevant. The study, which analyzes the impacts of nitrogen-fixing biotechnologies on corn production, concluded that the disparity between rich and poor will be reduced only if these production-enhancing technologies are implemented in the poor, rural sector, and not if they are implemented (as we would expect them to be) primarily by wealthier landowners.

Lessons from the Green Revolution

Experience with the Green Revolution also suggests that as new technologies are distributed in a society, the gap between rich and poor can be widened rather than narrowed. Parallels between the Green Revolution and the biotechnology revolution have been drawn by a number of authors in the last few years. All reach the conclusion that biotechnology has potential for benefits but also may cause negative economic and social effects similar to those seen after the Green Revolution—except that biotechnology's ef-

157

fects will be magnified because it will affect many more crops and geographic areas than the Green Revolution.

A second type of economic risk that may be associated with biotechnology involves rapidly shifting export markets. Research is likely to permit industrialists and agriculturalists in the developed countries to produce many raw materials and final products that they formerly purchased chiefly from the tropical developing countries. . . .

"Frostban" is another example. If Frostban succeeds in reducing frost damage on a wide variety of crops, the result may be more tropical fruits grown in regions with temperate climates such as the United States or Europe. The impacts of such a change on the export markets of developing countries, many of which are dependent on exports of tropical fruits and vegetables, are potentially serious. "[The] sad irony," says G. Edward Schuh, "is that the United States government lectures [developing] countries to get their economic houses in order and to strengthen their export sectors . . . only to have their efforts to do this wiped out by [competition from] . . . the same country that is lecturing them so severely."

Increasing Dependence on the West

Genetic engineering proponents say biotechnology will set off a second Green Revolution by enhancing yields and conserving resources in the Third World. But rather than increase Third World farmers' control over production, the agri-genetic revolution may increase those farmers' dependence on the West. For example, seeds for the new high-yielding supercrops will only be available through seed houses, now almost entirely controlled by multinational petroleum and chemical companies such as Shell Oil, British Petroleum and Ciba-Geigy. Only a small percentage of farmers may be able to afford the new seeds or corporate-bred hormones and chemicals.

Kathleen Selvaggio, *Multinational Monitor*, March 1984.

The product substitution process has been going on for many years, of course. What is different about genetic engineering is that it is likely to allow substitutes to be developed and adopted much more quickly than before, leaving less time for national economies to adjust and find new markets in which to compete.

A Technology Treadmill

Two agricultural economists have identified a related risk from biotechnology. Patrick Madden and Paul B. Thompson call it the "technology treadmill." They observe that poor farmers who fail to adopt new innovations will find themselves at an economic disadvantage. Furthermore, late adoption of a technology will not improve their profits because prices will fall as the technology is adopted in other countries and worldwide production expands. The resulting price declines will cause many small farmers to have trouble realizing net benefits over the long term compared with the situation during the period before the technology was introduced. Reduced prices benefit consumers and many national economies, but those farmers who are unable to expand their operations sufficiently to compensate for the reduced profits will be forced to leave their farms and seek other forms of employment.

In the United States, the shrinking agricultural sector is a controversial economic and social issue. In developing countries this trend, particularly if it occurs rapidly, could have significant demographic and environmental implications. Rapid displacement of large numbers of farmers to urban areas could add to already high unemployment, exacerbate environmental stresses and crime, and strain the few existing social services.

Again, it is usually the lack of time and ability to manage displacements, due to their rapid pace, which is a greater cause for concern than simply the effects of displacement themselves.

Conclusion

In conclusion, a variety of policy and social management challenges need to be addressed if society is to succeed in providing sustainable economic opportunity for people in developing countries using biotechnology as part of the strategy. To date, however, very few governments, international research agencies, or multinational companies conducting genetic engineering research have implemented strategies to meet this looming technology management need.

Understanding Words in Context

Readers occasionally come across words which they do not recognize. And frequently, because they do not know a word or words, they will not fully understand the passage being read. Obviously, the reader can look up an unfamiliar word in a dictionary. However, by carefully examining the word in the context in which it is used, the word's meaning can often be determined. A careful reader may find clues to the meaning of the word in surrounding words, ideas, and attitudes.

Below are sentences adapted from the viewpoints in this chapter. In each excerpt one or two words are printed in italicized capital letters. Try to determine the meaning of each word by reading the excerpt. Under each excerpt you will find four definitions for the italicized word. Choose the one that is closest to your understanding of the word.

Finally, use a dictionary to see how well you have understood the words in context. It will be helpful to discuss with others the clues which helped you decide on each word's meaning.

1. Today, the *PREMIER* raw material is not land or oil; it is DNA. If you are doing business in any of the industries dependent on the workings of biology or genetics, the raw material you want to control is DNA.

   PREMIER means:

   a) largest   c) most important
   b) worst   d) cleanest

2. To succeed in American farming requires more and more cash, forcing farmers to *INCUR* heavy debt to pay for seed, equipment, and supplies.

   INCUR means:

   a) ignore   c) take on
   b) wish for   d) refuse

3. When a cow consumes another calorie, she either puts it in the milk she makes or in maintaining her body. That's *PARTITIONING* of energy.

PARTITIONING means:

a) storage
b) creation
c) good use
d) division

4. Farmers who fail to adopt *INNOVATIONS* will find themselves at a disadvantage as they rely on old ways to raise crops.

INNOVATIONS means:

a) new methods
b) debt
c) machinery
d) a good attitude

5. First of all, just because something is biological, doesn't necessarily mean it's *BENIGN* or safe.

BENIGN means:

a) calm
b) serious
c) alive
d) nonthreatening

6. Protecting crops from the *VAGARIES* of nature can make farming a more reliable business.

VAGARIES means:

a) disguises
b) advantages
c) unpredictable actions
d) fatal diseases

7. Simply making an animal resistant to a particular disease will not protect it from other *PATHOGENS* or the stress that can make it weak and then sick.

PATHOGENS means:

a) disease-causing agents
b) problems
c) weather conditions
d) animals

8. Once the genetic changes have been made, the new animal *PROTOTYPES* will be used as foundation breeding stock to produce more animals with the same features.

PROTOTYPES means:

a) technologies
b) original models
c) ideas
d) descriptions

Periodical Bibliography

The following articles have been selected to supplement the diverse views presented in this chapter.

Sharon Begley   "Putting Crops on the Wagon," *Time*, August 8, 1988.

Samuel S. Epstein   "Growth Hormones Would Endanger Milk," *Los Angeles Times*, July 27, 1989.

H. Patricia Hynes   "Biotechnology in Agriculture: An Analysis of Selected Technologies and Policy in the United States," *Reproductive and Genetic Engineering*, vol. 2, no. 1, 1989.

Thomas Kiely   "Appropriate Biotech," *Technology Review*, August/September 1989.

Constance Matthiessen and Howard Kohn   "Ice Minus and Beyond," *Science for the People*, May/June 1985.

Dale A. Miller   "The Biological Future of Pest Control," *Vital Speeches of the Day*, March 15, 1989.

Wayne Pacelle   "Bio-Machines: Life on the Farm Ain't What It Used to Be," *Vegetarian Times*, January 1989.

David Pimental   "Down on the Farm: Genetic Engineering Meets Ecology," *Technology Review*, January 1987.

Keith Schneider   "Biotechnology's Cash Cow," *The New York Times Magazine*, June 12, 1988.

Keith Schneider   "Building a Better Tomato: New Era in Biotechnology," *The New York Times*, September 18, 1989.

George E. Seidel Jr.   "Geneticists in the Pasture," *Technology Review*, April 1989.

Ward Sinclair   "Invasion of the Square Tomatoes," *The Washington Post National Weekly Edition*, April 11-17, 1988.

Adam Smith   "Does More Food Mean Less Famine?" *Esquire*, July 1987.

Dennis Wyss   "A Furious Battle over Milk," *Time*, May 29, 1989.

Is Genetic Engineering Adequately Regulated?

GENETIC ENGINEERING

Chapter Preface

In 1974 scientists took the virtually unprecedented step of voluntarily halting an area of scientific research in order to evaluate its long-term effects. The new technology placed on hold was genetic engineering. The following year in Asilomar, California, scientists gathered at a conference to discuss such questions as the safety of genetic experiments, the protection of the environment, the ethics of genetic engineering, and its social ramifications. At that conference and over the next several years, scientists developed guidelines and procedures for genetic engineering research in order to deal with these questions. They have worked closely with the federal government to develop regulations for genetic engineering. Many researchers now point to the 1975 Asilomar Conference as a good example of how scientists can responsibly regulate themselves.

Since 1975, however, a whole new biotechnology industry has developed around genetic engineering, and many people wonder whether current regulation of genetic engineering is adequate. Critics such as philosopher Sheldon Krimsky argue that scientists cannot regulate themselves anymore. He contends that many of those researching genetic engineering now work for private companies or otherwise have a direct financial stake in the development of biotechnology. Krimsky and others argue that the public and the government should have a greater say in monitoring genetic engineering research.

How should genetic engineering be regulated? Who should have the final say in how it is used? The viewpoints in this chapter debate these questions.

"The existing statutes are adequate for regulating the products of agricultural biotechnology."

Government Regulation of Genetic Engineering Is Adequate

John A. Moore and Kenneth A. Gilles

Several federal government agencies are involved in the regulation of genetic engineering, including the Environmental Protection Agency (EPA) and the U.S. Department of Agriculture (USDA). In the following two-part viewpoint, government officials representing these two departments describe the laws and procedures being used to regulate genetic engineering. Both officials assert that government regulation successfully protects the environment and public health. Part I of the viewpoint is by John A. Moore, an assistant administrator for the EPA. Part II is by Kenneth A. Gilles, an assistant secretary in the USDA.

As you read, consider the following questions:

1. What laws form the basis for the Environmental Protection Agency's jurisdiction over genetic engineering, according to Moore?
2. How does Moore describe the process by which the EPA evaluates genetic engineering experiments?
3. What are the three main elements of USDA policy towards regulating genetic engineering, according to Gilles?

John A. Moore and Kenneth A. Gilles. Testimonies before the U.S. House of Representatives Science, Space, and Technology Subcommittee on Natural Resources, Agricultural Research, and Environment, May 5, 1988.

I

The Environmental Protection Agency [EPA] is one of several Federal agencies involved in regulating biotechnology products. To present the context in which EPA regulates products of biotechnology, I would like to describe the Federal Coordinated Framework for the regulation of biotechnology and the philosophy which led to its adoption.

In 1984, the U.S. government, recognizing its responsibility to address issues raised by the use of biotechnology, formed an interagency working group under the White House Cabinet Council on Natural Resources and the Environment. This group examined existing laws and concluded that, for the most part, these laws would adequately address regulatory needs in biotechnology.

The Coordinated Framework

The federal approach to regulating biotechnology recognizes that biotechnology encompasses a large and varied collection of techniques and activities, and that the products potentially resulting from this technology will cover a wide spectrum of uses. The Coordinated Framework provides that biotechnology products will be regulated in the U.S. as are products of other technologies, i.e., by the various regulatory agencies on the basis of *use*.

Thus, many agricultural uses of microorganisms, plants and animals are regulated by the U.S. Department of Agriculture [USDA] under a variety of statutory authorities; foods, drugs and related items are regulated by the Food and Drug Administration [FDA] under its authorities; microorganisms used as pesticides are regulated by EPA under Federal Insecticide, Fungicide, and Rodenticide Control Act [FIFRA], and commercial uses of microorganisms not covered by other existing authorities are regulated by EPA under Toxic Substances Control Act [TSCA]. Examples of the types of uses covered by TSCA include microorganisms used in metal mining, degrading wastes, conversion of biomass for energy, production of proteins and enzymes for non-pharmaceutical purposes, and non-pesticidal agricultural applications such as nitrogen fixation.

A policy statement appearing in the June 26, 1986 *Federal Register* described the comprehensive federal framework for regulating biotechnology. This comprehensive framework provides a basic network of agency jurisdiction over both research and commercial products.

Two Laws

As part of the coordinated framework described in the June 1986 *Federal Register*, EPA is regulating certain products of biotechnology under two laws, TSCA and FIFRA.

TSCA authorizes EPA to acquire information on chemical

166

substances and mixtures of chemical substances to identify and regulate potential hazards and exposures. TSCA's applicability to the regulation of microbial biotechnology products is based on the interpretation that microbes are chemical substances under TSCA. The simplified basis for this interpretation is that all substances, living and non-living, have a chemical foundation at the most fundamental molecular level. As a result of this interpretation, microorganisms are subject to all provisions of TSCA, except for categories of organisms explicitly excluded under Section 3 of TSCA, i.e., those covered by other statutes such as microorganisms processed or distributed in commerce for use as pesticides, foods, food additives, drugs, cosmetics, or other related items.

No New Regulations Needed

One question in particular arose early on as the Food and Drug Administration prepared to confront the explosion of new products derived through biotechnology: Were new regulations needed? We soon concluded that the answer was no—that the products of biotechnology are fundamentally similar to those produced by conventional techniques, and they are adequately controlled by existing regulations. We do not need new rules. The best course is to judge each product on its own merits.

Frank E. Young, *The Saturday Evening Post*, October 1988.

FIFRA establishes EPA's authority over the distribution, sale, and use of all pesticide products, including microbial pesticides. FIFRA authorizes EPA to regulate pesticides through a registration process. Microbial pesticides have been registered for almost 20 years, and the Agency was able to draw on this experience in developing its policy for regulating microbial products of biotechnology.

FIFRA specifies that a pesticide can be registered for use only if the pesticide will not cause unreasonable adverse effects to humans or the environment. In order to register a pesticide, an applicant must submit or cite data on subjects such as product composition, human health effects, environmental fate, and effects on nontarget organisms.

The Review Process

I would now like to briefly describe the Agency review process for products of biotechnology that are to be tested or used in the environment. . . .

The Agency is dedicated to using a comparable review process under TSCA and FIFRA. At this time, reviews are conducted on a case-by-case basis.

When a submission for small-scale field testing is received under FIFRA, EPA staff evaluate the submission and develop a scientific position. During this process, any potential problems, issues, or significant unanswered questions are identified and the likelihood of significant risk from the proposed field testing is addressed.

Similarly, for a submission involving small-scale field testing received under the TSCA provisions, EPA staff groups assess hazard and exposure, and integrate their conclusions in a coordinated risk assessment.

Under both TSCA and FIFRA, intra-Agency workgroups then comment on the positions developed by staff. If appropriate, the submission and EPA's scientific position are sent to other Federal agencies for comment. Appropriate State regulatory agencies are also contacted to alert them to the submission, to discuss EPA's assessments, and to ensure that the Federal and State positions are as consistent as possible.

A Careful Process

In some cases, to obtain an independent peer review of the Agency's scientific position, to address specific scientific questions raised by the Agency, or to identify any additional data that may be needed to complete the risk assessment, the submission and the Agency's scientific evaluations are sent to a group of independent scientists constituted as a subcommittee of an Agency advisory group. The Agency has established a specific advisory committee, the Biotechnology Science Advisory Committee (BSAC) for these independent peer reviews. Prior to the establishment of BSAC, the FIFRA Scientific Advisory Panel (SAP) performed this function for genetically engineered and nonindigenous microbial pesticides. Several proposed field trials have been reviewed by either BSAC or SAP subcommittees and these groups have endorsed EPA assessments.

Public comment is considered an important aspect of reviews, and for many proposals the public is provided several opportunities to comment during the review process.

At the conclusion of a review, the Agency determines whether the microorganism may be released into the environment. Under both TSCA and FIFRA, this decision is based on an assessment of both the potential risks and the potential benefits of the proposed use of the microorganism. Should the analysis indicate that use of the microorganism may pose unreasonable risks, the Agency has authority under either statute to impose restrictions on its use.

I believe that EPA's scientific review process is credible, sound and respected by the scientific community, while assuring that potential human or environmental impacts have been addressed.

In addition, I feel confident that EPA's regulatory programs will protect the public health and the environment from unreasonable risks while allowing all of us to reap the benefits of scientific and technological innovations.

II

Biotechnology offers great potential in many areas, particularly in continuing improvement of our capacity to develop products that are of critical importance to the future of American agriculture. It is vital that products of biotechnology be regulated based on firm scientific principles and meet the same high standards of safety and efficacy as do those products made through conventional technology. Thus, we seek to foster a regulatory climate that encourages innovation, development, and commercialization of beneficial new agricultural products derived from biotechnology, while implementing a responsible policy that limits potential of real risks.

Sufficient Protection

Existing federal regulatory apparatus provides sufficient protection for all parties including the American public and the environment. Additional reviews, unless prompted by scientific concerns, should be avoided.

American Council on Science and Health, *Biotechnology: An Introduction*, 1988.

USDA, along with other Federal agencies, stated its policy for regulating biotechnology in December 1984, and June 1986, as part of the "Coordinated Framework for Regulation of Biotechnology." The USDA policy is based on three main elements:
• the existing statutes are adequate for regulating the products of agricultural biotechnology;
• USDA does not anticipate that such products would differ fundamentally from those produced by conventional methods;
• the product and the risk should be regulated, rather than the technology.
These elements are consistent with the National Academy of Sciences report that was issued in 1987. . . .

Regulation

Statutes administered by USDA and applicable to the regulation of biotechnology were listed in the final USDA policy statement, which was published in the Federal Register on June 26, 1986. The USDA regulatory agencies administering these statutes are the Animal and Plant Health Inspection Service (APHIS), the

Food Safety and Inspection Service, and the Agricultural Marketing Service. Because APHIS has been actively involved in regulating the testing and development of genetically engineered organisms, I will focus my comments on the APHIS effort.

Through a variety of statutes, APHIS has authority to regulate organisms and vectors which may spread or cause diseases of livestock or poultry; veterinary biological products; and plants, plant products or plant pests which may cause injury, disease, or damage to plants. . . .

APHIS issues U.S. Veterinary Biological Product Licenses after a manufacturer satisfactorily completes all requirements, which are designed to ensure that the product is pure, safe, potent, and efficacious. Veterinary biological products produced by recombinant methods are evaluated on a case-by-case basis using the same stringent standards for licensing employed for conventionally produced biologics. . . .

Plant Pests

The Agency has used its existing statutory authority under the Federal Plant Pest Act and the Plant Quarantine Act to issue a new rule for genetically engineered organisms or products which are or may be plant pests. The final rule, which took effect on July 16, 1987, established permit and other requirements for the importation, interstate movement, and release into the environment of genetically engineered organisms and products that are or may be plant pests. A product is regulated for its potential risk if the product consists of or contains an organism listed as a plant pest in the final rule. The rule also gives APHIS authority to regulate any other organism or product produced through genetic engineering when the Agency determines that it is a plant pest or when we have reason to believe it is a plant pest. The rule requires that we notify affected States so that they may review permit applications. We also publish notices describing genetically engineered organisms for which we have received permit applications and which are being reviewed for environmental release. Although the rule was published as a final rule, it is flexible and can be amended. The rule also contains a provision allowing for petitions to amend the list of plant pest organisms. We have recently amended the rule to remove some restrictions pertaining to the interstate movement of certain microorganisms under specified conditions that would provide adequate safeguards to prevent the introduction and dissemination of plant pests.

Since the July 1987 rule took effect, APHIS has received 23 applications for environmental release of genetically engineered plants and microorganisms and [as of May 1988] we have issued 11 permits for release. For each application for release into the environment of an organism deemed to be a regulated article,

APHIS prepares a thorough environmental assessment according to the requirements of the National Environmental Policy Act. Thus far, for each field test that has been approved by APHIS, the Agency has determined that these tests do not present a risk of plant pest introduction or dissemination. The environmental assessments have concluded with findings of no significant impact.

Ample Protection

Fortunately, the environmental legislation passed by Congress in the 1970s, together with other federal laws, provide ample protection of public health and environmental quality. . . .

Under the federal regulations, organisms with new genes from unrelated species must be evaluated for safety before being tested outdoors. Scientists conduct extensive laboratory and greenhouse experiments to determine that test organisms are not toxic to humans, animals, or beneficial plants and insects.

Industrial Biotechnology Association, *Agriculture and the New Biology*, 1987.

Our regulatory actions have made it possible for products of biotechnology to move from the laboratory to the field while retaining safety measures and ensuring continued public confidence in the products. One of the most positive developments in the implementation of Federal biotechnology policy has been the coordination with other Federal agencies through the BSCC [Biotechnology Science Coordinating Committee]. USDA shares jurisdiction with the Environmental Protection Agency (EPA) and the Food and Drug Administration (FDA) in certain areas. Coordination and consultation have been demonstrated through joint reviews of applications between EPA and APHIS, through committee activities, and through individual contacts among scientists and joint reports to the Organization for Economic Cooperation and Development. . . .

Conclusion

We are confident that we are meeting our responsibilities in a way that will make the products of biotechnology available to our agricultural community as quickly as possible while ensuring that full protection is provided to agriculture and the environment.

"The present ambiguous and conflicting state of regulation satisfies no one."

Government Regulation of Genetic Engineering Is Inadequate

Sheldon Krimsky, Kostia Bergman, Nancy Connell, Seth Shulman, and Nachama Wilker

The authors of the following viewpoint are editors of *geneWATCH*, a publication of the Boston-based Council for Responsible Genetics (CRG). CRG is a national group of scientists and environmentalists concerned with the social impact of genetic engineering. In the following viewpoint, the authors argue that existing laws do not adequately regulate the new genetic engineering technology. Potentially dangerous experiments, they assert, are proceeding with little or no federal oversight.

As you read, consider the following questions:

1. What comparisons do the authors draw between past regulation of the chemical industry and today's regulation of biotechnology?
2. According to the authors, what are the disadvantages of having several government agencies regulating genetic engineering?
3. What changes do the authors recommend?

Sheldon Krimsky, Kostia Bergman, Nancy Connell, Seth Shulman, and Nachama Wilker, "Controlling Risk in Biotech," *Technology Review*, July 1989. Originally published in *geneWATCH*, vol. 5, no. 2-3. Reprinted with permission of the Council for Responsible Genetics, 186 South St., Fourth Floor, Boston, MA 02111, (617) 423-0650.

Biotechnology entrepreneurs envision a future where genetically altered bacteria digest oil spills and toxic waste, kill crop pests, and immunize wild animals against rabies. These organisms, say the biotechnologists, pose no unique hazards to health or the environment; they are as safe as their component parts—a natural bacterium and a gene taken from another organism.

This optimism brings to mind the early days of the synthetic-chemical industry. Like biotechnologists, chemical pioneers of the 1940s and 1950s saw great promise in new products that would be released into the environment. But government regulation of these chemicals was based on public health statutes that dated from the turn of the century. These statutes were not suited to deal with the thousands of synthetic chemicals introduced into agriculture and manufacturing. They did not address complex biological effects such as cancer and various chronic illnesses.

Finally, in the 1970s, the government enacted a series of new laws, including the Federal Insecticide, Fungicide, and Rodenticide Act (FIFRA) and the Toxic Substances Control Act (TSCA). Some laws required safety testing for all new chemicals, but exempted the tens of thousands of untested substances already on the market. Now, a generation after the chemical revolution, the country has to contend with 60 million tons of hazardous chemical wastes produced each year.

The Hazards of Biotechnology

Could the biotech revolution prove equally destructive? If ecologists are right, our picture of the risks involved is no more complete than that of chemical risks 30 years ago. They assert that no one can predict the environmental effects of genetically engineered organisms, or GEOs, merely by knowing the host organism and the foreign genes. Before a new organism can be safely released, they say, it must be tested in a microcosm, and the dynamics of the ecosystem for which it is targeted must be carefully modeled. And while the probability of harm is small, the magnitude of any damage could be great. Introductions of GEOs might create new human diseases, spawn new plant or animal pests, or otherwise disrupt delicate ecological balances, just as introductions of exotic species—such as the gypsy moth and the citrus canker—have done in the past.

The risks of releasing new organisms will multiply as the biotech industry grows. Today only a handful of releases, sanctioned or unsanctioned, take place each year. But over the next three to five years, the Department of Agriculture (USDA) expects to receive over 200 applications for release of GEOs, including plants and animals. And the number of releases will skyrocket as small-scale field tests give way to commercial-scale manufacture and dispersion. As ecologist Martin Alexander has cautioned, if an undesirable event has a probability of occurring once in 1,000 uses of a given technology, the risk from a few uses would surely be low. Complacency should disappear, however, if 600 or 1,000 or more uses are envisioned.

As we stand at the threshold of a burgeoning biotechnology industry, it would seem prudent to take the ecologists' concerns seriously. Yet the U.S. regulatory system governing the release of GEOs is anything *but* prudent. It is modeled after the same controls that apply to the chemical industry—just as the first chemical regulations were based on earlier statutes. It does not take into account the unique properties of microorganisms, such as their ability to reproduce and mutate. It spreads oversight too thin and requires too little scientific review of proposed releases. It does not provide adequate safeguards against accidents. And it ignores important social and economic questions raised by environmental releases.

A Bad Start

Adequate safeguards must be created to prevent the release into the environment of genetically engineered material that will unfavorably upset natural systems. Not a simple task because, unlike chemicals, these new life-forms could reproduce—unpredictably, and perhaps without limit.

We are off to a bad start. Four separate federal agencies—the Food and Drug Administration, the Environmental Protection Agency, the National Institutes of Health, and the U.S. Department of Agriculture—have been given jurisdiction over biotechnological products and testing. A regulatory process based on a patchwork of statutes that were not originally designed to deal with genetically engineered organisms is producing confusion and contempt.

Peter A.A. Berle, *Audubon*, January 1988.

To prevent biotechnology from going down the same dangerous path as the chemical industry, we need a set of coherent, forward-looking regulations. Among other things, that will mean creating a single lead agency and making sure it has the technical and financial resources to do its job.

A Patchwork of Policies

The current federal system for regulating environmental release is a loose patchwork of policies spread over five different agencies and at least ten different laws. The Food and Drug Administration regulates organisms intended for use in drugs, food additives, and medical devices. The National Institutes of Health (NIH) regulates the use of recombinant-DNA molecules developed with its funding. Workplace hazards connected with genetically engineered organisms come under the purview of the Occupational Safety and Health Administration. Veterinary products and organisms that could harm plants are governed by the USDA. Meanwhile, the Environmental Protection Agency (EPA) covers pesticides and new microbes not falling into other categories.

An interagency Biotechnology Science Coordinating Committee is supposed to tie the various threads of policy together, but so far it has been largely ineffective. With authority for regulating GEOs distributed among various agencies and covered by widely disparate laws, agencies use different definitions and risk assessment criteria, and confusion can arise over who regulates what product.

All the statutes under which new organisms have been lumped predate genetic engineering. For example, EPA regulates releases through FIFRA and TSCA. Both laws, particularly the latter, were intended for chemical substances, not self-replicating organisms. The laws neither address the special environmental and public health risks raised by the new industrial and agricultural uses for GEOs nor establish a program for better identifying those risks.

Current System Weak

Some of the most glaring weaknesses of current regulation stem from TSCA. Unlike FIFRA, which requires that a firm obtain a license to manufacture a substance, TSCA is a notification statute. All a company has to do is inform EPA that it plans to manufacture a certain chemical or biological. Since the manufacturer does not even have to provide data attesting to the safety of its products, a notification system places the burden of proof on the regulator.

EPA has 90 days to review a TSCA submission. If it determines that a substance might pose an unacceptable risk, the agency may issue a set of rules applying only to that product. This rulemaking process is cumbersome and laborious, and it injects considerable discretion into regulatory decisions.

As more and more companies notify EPA that they intend to release organisms, the system will undoubtedly break down. The overburdened agency will be forced to use a "triage" system to determine which organisms deserve more careful scrutiny, and will be unable to review them on a case-by-case basis when the pace of submissions reaches 30 or 50 a year.

The role of the USDA presents another serious problem. No agency that is supposed to promote biotechnology in industry, commerce, and agriculture should be responsible for regulating its use in those sectors. Yet this is exactly the position that the USDA is in. The agency also lacks a coherent policy on engineered plants and organisms. And it has a poor record of encouraging citizens to participate in its decision making on biotechnology and

175

of informing the scientific community how it plans to evaluate new products. . . .

Even if the regulatory system were to do an adequate job of determining the safety of GEOs, its efforts would be meaningless without some guarantee that only safe organisms would reach the environment. Unsanctioned releases have already taken place in Montana, Nebraska, South Dakota, Texas, and California.

In addition, whole classes of release experiments are regulated inadequately or not at all. These include experiments in the private sector, university research, and large-scale fermentation. Some of these settings are inherently unsafe. In August 1987, for example, a biochemist working in his beachfront home in Kingston, Mass., was recombining the genes of sea organisms to create a new type of building material, when his house collapsed. Microorganisms, which the scientist maintained were not dangerous, escaped from his home. The investigator violated no law; private funds were involved, so he was not obligated to follow any guidelines. Since

© 1989 Jon McIntosh. Used with permission.

a harmful microbe can multiply and spread regardless of the type or size of organization conducting the test—or the source of funding—exemptions from the regulatory process make little sense. . . .

Lack of Plans

If an organism did escape, the current regulatory regime would be unprepared to deal with the ecological upset that might ensue. No plans have been developed for containing damage. Nor are any serious research programs under way in this area.

While the regulation of GEOs during research and testing is merely inadequate, the regulatory framework for dealing with biogenetic waste is virtually nonexistent. The biotechnology industry brings with it a new form of waste that can live and multiply in the environment. Because it consists of living organisms, biological waste has the potential to spread disease. It could also transfer genetic material to organisms of different species, genera, and even families, fostering the creation of new pathogenic strains or compromising the ability of humans, animals, or ecosystems to protect themselves. The rapid spread of antibiotic resistance among bacteria in clinical settings is an obvious example of the ease with which certain kinds of genetic exchange take place.

However, the only regulations for treating biogenetic waste are NIH guidelines, which have no legal authority over industry, and FDA rules for sterilizing bioreactors. Most industrial fermentation plants may simply dispose of spent GEOs along with other untreated effluent. . . .

What Do We Gain?

When an industry designs a new product for release into an environment where it will pose discernible risks, we must ask: What do we gain? What could we lose? What are we displacing? Does the new product fill real social needs? We cannot rely on industry to answer these questions for us. Advanced Genetic Sciences, for example, promoted ice minus as a substitute for chemical pesticides, even though pesticides have never been the method of choice for preventing frost damage. Meanwhile, other agrochemical and biotechnology companies are genetically engineering crops resistant to harmful side effects of pesticides—a practice that will expand and prolong the chemicals' use. Pesticides are the most profitable products of some of these corporations. Yet biotechnology could also be used to develop non-pesticide alternatives that would lessen farmers' dependence on a few big agrichemical companies.

With a powerful emerging technology, especially one with potential risks and large amounts of public funding, we cannot assume that the market will operate in the interest of the public without social guidance. The public sector should actively shape public policy, not allow it to be created by default. If weaning agriculture from chemical pesticides is a desirable goal, then public policies should help realize it.

In deciding what degree of risk is acceptable, regulators must begin to weigh the interests of industry against those of society at large. If the overall social and economic effects of a product are negative, any environmental risk that accompanies its testing or use should be deemed unacceptable. At present, no regulatory mechanisms exist for making such judgments or for answering communities' questions about social and economic impacts.

Inadequate Protection

The current Federal regulatory system is inadequate to assure protection of health and the environment. The Federal policies are confusing, duplicative, and operating without clear Congressional sanction. The current controls are a loose patchwork, pieced together across five agencies and at least ten different laws, all of which predate genetic engineering. They are not equipped with the authority, the coordination or the resources to adequately address the upcoming boom in genetically engineered organism releases.

National Center for Policy Alternatives, "Regulating Environmental Release of Genetically Engineered Organisms: The State Perspective," June 1, 1988.

The present ambiguous and conflicting state of regulation satisfies no one. It creates confusion in the biotechnology industry, it does not adequately safeguard public health and the environment, and it largely excludes the public from the decision making. To deal with the coming wave of genetically engineered organisms, the system needs a top-to-bottom overhaul. The following proposals would help create a rational regulatory process:

Make EPA the lead agency. Designating one agency to oversee all environmental releases of genetically engineered organisms would help ensure careful review of the risks before a release was authorized. EPA should also be given greater authority over all large-scale uses of GEOs and empowered to regulate and inspect facilities to reduce the danger of accidental releases.

Amend TSCA. As applied to new organisms, the Toxic Substances Control Act is cleary inadequate. Instead of merely notifying EPA of a planned release, companies should be required to obtain licenses. As a prerequisite, the manufacturers—not EPA—should have to demonstrate an organism's safety and efficacy, as well as show that they are prepared to stem the worst impacts of a release. When a new technology is replacing an established one, the law should require end users to choose the least risky available technology to do a job. EPA should also have the latitude to request further information and testing on comparative risks.

Regulators also need to be able to penalize wrongdoers quickly and effectively—and the penalties should be high enough to discourage even small unauthorized releases. EPA should have the power to assess fines for violations without taking companies to court. This would shift the burden of bringing suit onto violators.

Give regulators more resources. The expansion of industry's genetic experimentation will place tremendous economic pressure on regulators to act quickly and without due care. With more funding, regulators would be able to provide better oversight within a timeframe that industry could live with. They would also be able to hire the necessary range of professionals—including soil ecologists and microbiologists—and keep them up to date on the latest developments in the field and techniques for evaluating them. . . .

Public Involvement

Involve the public. A public voice in the regulatory process is vital, since the experts' assessment of "acceptable" risks may differ dramatically from the views of the public that bears those risks. Such involvement can also benefit industry. For one thing, communities may be able to contribute useful information in the deliberations. For another, communities left out of the process are likely to oppose, and even obstruct, local releases. . . .

Monitor released organisms. EPA should carefully monitor the survival rate and dispersion of modified organisms in the environment. This monitoring would be both a precaution, in case the organism did harm, and a research tool to strengthen future risk assessments.

Increase safeguards. Because even a small release of a harmful organism could be devastating, regulators and biotech firms must do their utmost to prevent GEOs from escaping accidentally. Waste streams should be carefully regulated and monitored, and labs required to have barriers such as secondary containment chambers. Measures such as protective clothing and standardized lab practices can help prevent workers from unknowingly carrying GEOs out of their laboratories.

If we fail to move on these fronts, or if we move too slowly, there is every danger that the painful history of the synthetic-chemical industry will repeat itself in the realm of biotechnology. The public became aware of chemical hazards—and the government responded to them—only after substantial damage to health and the environment had occurred. Regulators tried frantically to catch up after decades of neglect. But the nation's economy was already dependent on the firmly established industry.

It is too late to undo all the damage done by synthetic chemicals. But if we can introduce some foresight into the regulatory system, it is not too late to avert disasters from genetic engineering.

179

"We need to control what the biotechnology industry produces."

Genetic Engineering Should Be Publicly Controlled

Barry Commoner

Barry Commoner directs the Center for the Biology of Natural Systems at Queens College at the City University of New York. A well-known environmentalist, Commoner ran for president of the United States in 1980 as a Citizen's Party candidate. He has written extensively on the social and environmental impact of new technologies. In the following viewpoint, Commoner argues that private corporations have exploited genetic engineering to create products of little social value that risk harm to the environment. He asserts that the public should have a greater say in determining how genetic engineering will be used.

As you read, consider the following questions:

1. In what aspects does the petrochemical industry foreshadow the biotechnology industry, according to Commoner?
2. Why does Commoner believe it is important to begin regulating the biotechnology industry now?
3. Why has the biotechnology industry produced items of little social value, according to the author?

Barry Commoner, "Bringing Up Biotechnology," *Science for the People*, March/April 1987. Reprinted with permission.

A fundamental question that any of us concerned with biotechnology have to deal with is the problem of governing the development of a new industry. I'm not talking about regulating its impact on the environment. I'm talking about the social governance of the means of production. That's the fundamental issue. There's no way of working on the industry's regulation without dealing with the decisions that determine what the industry produces and how it produces it. This introduces the whole question of social intervention in the infant industry itself.

Since this is such a taboo subject, I need to mention two justifications for raising it. The first is a very simple one. Most of the basic research information comes from the public domain. We paid for it. I well remember the debate years ago on the structure of the National Science Foundation when practically every senator said, "You know, if we pay for this work, the results should be owned by the people and there should be no way of making private profits out of any research sponsored by the NSF." Well, you know what happened to that idea, but I remember very well when this was a serious issue to debate. Now if ever there was a new industry created by public money, biotechnology is it. So it's worth thinking about public control of publicly funded research in this industry.

The Petrochemical Industry Example

The other reason is that we have before us the example of the petrochemical industry which, in an amazing way, foreshadows what is happening in the biotechnology industry. The lesson from the petrochemical industry is that environmental regulation has become essentially impossible. The only thing you can do is to roll back the industry if you're concerned with its impact on the environment. . . .

Changing Evolution

The petrochemical industry is very much like biotechnology. It was also a rapid conversion of academic research into commercial use: what the organic chemists learned was converted into chemical engineering. Previously, organic carbon compounds on the earth occurred only in living things or in their products. Along came an industry that produced enormous amounts of man-made organic compounds, nearly all of which do not occur in living organisms. . . .

Organic chemistry in life is the outcome of a very long evolution, and it represents a highly restricted assemblage of compounds; incompatible compounds have been eliminated. In my opinion, an organic compound which does not now occur in living things has to be regarded as an evolutionary reject.

Simply put, somewhere down the line a few billion years ago, perhaps some living cell got it into its head to synthesize dioxin and has never been heard from since. You need to regard the products of the petrochemical industry as evolutionary misfits and therefore very likely to be incompatible with the chemistry of living things. The failure to understand this basic fact has caused the whole problem in chemical pollution. We keep being surprised that chemicals which were perfectly nice and simple to make turn out to have very serious biological consequences. . . .

A Look at Biotechnology

Now let's look at biotechnology. My first point is that you have to regard the bioengineered organisms as evolutionary rejects. By that I mean—in parallel with my argument about petrochemical products which do not occur in living things—that the new organisms created by genetic engineering are likely to contain genetic combinations that were, so to speak, once tried out during the course of evolution and rejected. Such a rejected genotype should, I believe, be regarded as inherently dangerous to existing organisms.

Consider, for example, the appearance during the course of evolution of a pathogenic bacterial genotype which is so virulent that it completely wipes out a host species—thus eliminating the bacterium itself from the evolutionary stream. If this organism were to be reinvented by the biotechnology industry, it would be likely to cause considerable damage, especially if the host species has itself evolved in such a way as to facilitate the ongoing propagation of the disease.

Who Should Have Power?

The corporate establishment is quick to point out the potential benefits but steadfastly refuses to acknowledge the grave ethical and environmental risks. . . .

Genetic engineering is the most powerful tool ever invented to control life. To whom do we entrust the power to determine which genes should be engineered and recombined in and between microbes, plants, animals and humans? Who should have ultimate authority over the genetic blueprint of living creatures?

Jeremy Rifkin, *USA Today*, October 6, 1988.

I realize that the industry has often argued that its new organisms ought to be regarded as harmless because all of the genetic combinations have been tried out in the evolutionary past and, in that sense, the industry's creations are not really "new". But that approach fails to take into account—in keeping with the foregoing example—that the reinvented organism now enters into a greatly changed biosphere.

Does that mean we shouldn't use genetically engineered organisms? No; I think you have to ask whether the value of using an organism or a product is so great as to override the inherent dangers. Unfortunately, that is not the way the industry has decided what to produce.

How Private Industry Works

Let me give you a couple of examples: Human insulin was the first genetically engineered product, at least in this country. Genentech developed it, and then made a deal with Eli Lilly, which has an 85 percent monopoly on pig insulin, giving Lilly the exclusive right to human insulin production in the United States.

What's the purpose of producing human insulin? At first it was thought that it would be less immunologically reactive than pig insulin. In fact, both pig and human insulin have about the same positive and deleterious effects, so there is no medical value in human insulin. Eli Lilly's ads say that the purpose of producing human insulin is to be prepared for a shortage of pig insulin. Under what circumstances would that happen? I suppose if religious objectors to pigs take over the world, then we'll be short of pigs. When that happens, we'll need human insulin.

In reality, human insulin has been produced for a very simple purpose: to maintain Eli Lilly's monopoly on insulin. Suppose some other company got the Genentech contract. Eli Lilly would suddenly have a competitor in producing insulin. I have to conclude that this arrangement was not governed by the social need for human insulin; it was governed by the age-old notion of maintaining a monopoly.

Now let's look at human growth hormone. The supply of growth hormone from the human pituitary, as far as I can tell, comes totally from a Swedish company. That company owns fifty percent of another Swedish company. The second firm has the exclusive world contract, outside of the United States, for using Genentech's genetically engineered process for making synthetic bacterial human growth hormone. In other words, this is a system for controlling the market rather than for producing something for human needs.

An Unprofitable Vaccine

Everyone agrees that the most important use of genetic engineering would be to produce vaccines, particularly for malaria. The World Health Organization supported this research at New York University. They got to the point of producing the sporozoite vaccine, and said to Genentech, "OK, how about you making it?" Genentech said, "Well, we want exclusive rights." So the World Health Organization, being a very old-fashioned and un-American organization, said, "We don't work that way. We want this vaccine widely available." And Genentech said, "No thanks."

183

"We've finally developed a scientist who can perform independent research for both the University and private industry without any conflict of interest."

Here was something really needed, unlike human insulin, and it wasn't produced. Quoting from one of the vice presidents of Genentech, "We are forced at this stage in our corporate development to compare vaccines with other opportunities. The company does not have resources such that it can afford to take extraordinary risks. Thus it seems apparent that the development of a malaria vaccine would not be compatible with Genentech business strategy." It is not sufficiently profitable to give them the income they need, and for *that reason* they won't produce it.

Among the products of the biotechnology industry, pharmaceutical products outweigh all others. Sixty-two percent of the companies involved produce pharmaceutical products, and the majority are for diagnosis rather than treatment. What's so important about diagnosis? Did the medical profession hold a meeting and say, "You know, we're short of diagnostic techniques, so please work on that"? The reason is very simple: only sick people get treated, but a lot of healthy people get diagnosed. In other words, the market for diagnostic products is inherently much larger than the market for treatment products because people as a whole, sick and well, outnumber sick people.

In the commodity chemicals sector, most of the chemicals that are being produced by genetic engineering are flavors and perfumes. That's because they're much more expensive than a chemical like ethyl alcohol, which would have a much greater social value as a solar fuel. In pesticides, genetic engineering could be used to introduce pest resistance in plants, but it isn't. Instead, they are working on introducing resistance to herbicides, so that plants could be exposed to more and more herbicides without suffering.

Industry Structure

This brings us to the question of the control of the development of the biotechnology industry itself. The biotechnology industry has repeated, step for step, what has happened in the petrochemical industry. If it is allowed to go much further, like the petrochemical industry, it will become invulnerable to control. For example, fifteen million pounds of vinyl chloride—a powerful carcinogen—are produced in the United States today, chiefly to make polyvinyl chloride. Suppose you say, "This is just too risky. Let's stop making polyvinyl chloride." By this time, it has become so embedded in the industry and represents such a large investment and so many workers' jobs that it becomes socially impossible to quit making polyvinyl chloride. That's why we ought to focus on the industry's structure.

Now, at this early stage (if, in fact, it is not already too late) we need to control what the biotechnology industry produces. A major test is to show that the product is so socially important as to outweigh the inherent risks. This means that a trivial product—with no social value at all—is worth no risk at all and simply should not be produced. The most trivial research I know of comes from Frito-Lay, which makes potato chips. They wanted to genetically engineer a potato that had much less water, so it wouldn't cost as much to ship the potato. I don't know how that would affect potatoes or the viruses in potatoes, or what other impacts there might be. But the point is that biotechnology is an inherently dangerous industry and therefore should not make products which are trivial and have no real social purpose.

The only way to make a proper balance between risks and benefits is to have some say about what is produced, so that at the very least it will maximize the benefits to society. That introduces the question of social control of the choices made by the industry and social governance of the means of production.

People Can Learn

The position that non-scientists couldn't master enough of the complexities of DNA and monoclonal antibodies and bioprocessing to do a competent job of assessing the risks—a claim sometimes made by the experts—isn't borne out by events. When people feel threatened, they manage to learn a great deal. "My point of departure is medicine," says Halstead Holman [an M.D. who teaches internal medicine at Stanford]. "I have the privilege of seeing real people of all backgrounds addressing themselves to the intrusion of technology into their lives and making decisions about whether they will allow a test, allow a treatment, and so on. There's no question in my mind that average citizens deal with these problems very well."

Gina Maranto, *Discover*, June 1986.

In the Office of Technology Assessment's book *Commercial Biotechnology: An International Analysis*, there's a very interesting comparison between the semiconductor chip industry and biotechnology. It points out very clearly that the structure of the semiconductor industry in the United States was dictated by the U.S. government. The Department of Defense insisted on having a system of production that met their needs, since defense is a social need. As a result, legal steps were taken, tax incentives were put in place, and a production system was developed which determined what the new industry produced.

This example shows that it is possible, within our political framework, for the government to intervene in establishing the structure of an industry and its choice of products. Returning to the malaria example, I don't know why the National Institutes for Health couldn't be ordered by the President to set up a laboratory to develop an effective way of producing a malaria vaccine and, when that is done, to find a commercial company which will produce it, under a subsidy if necessary.

There is a legal mechanism built into the Environmental Protection Act, Section 102, which deals with environmental impact statements. That section says that whenever there is a process that has a hazardous environmental impact that can't be avoided, then alternative processes must be considered.

186

For example, in theory you could hold a hearing on plastic chairs, and toxicologists could come in and say that the phthalate emitted from the plasticizer is toxic. Or they might say that a fire in this room would poison everybody before they had a chance to get out; that's an unavoidable hazard of this kind of upholstery. Then a manufacturer of wooden chairs might testify that the function of a chair is for somebody to sit on it, and that their firm can make a chair that avoids the toxic hazards inherent in plastic chairs. Instead of saying, "This plastic is terrible; get rid of it," we have to say, "We want to intervene in the decisions about how chairs are made."

Let's consider Frostban, the bacteria manufactured to protect strawberry plants from frost at lower temperatures. I believe that ice-minus bacteria actually exist as a natural mutant. This raises a very interesting question: why do we have to do the genetic engineering at all? Or let's say someone shows that instead of making a genetically engineered nitrogen-fixing corn plant, there is a way of culturing Azotobacter and giving it enough mannitol so that it works very effectively in increasing the nitrogen content of soil. You can then debate whether this particular piece of genetic engineering is necessary or not. With respect to manufactured insulin, there should have been a debate as to whether genetic engineering should be used to produce insulin when pig insulin is perfectly satisfactory.

A Taboo Idea

We simply have to face an ideological issue which, in this country, is politically taboo. One doesn't raise the issue of society determining what the owners of capital can do. . . .

We have to ask ourselves about the morality of allowing publicly produced knowledge to be taken over by the owners of capital. Or, in the case of our fellow scientists who have become entrepreneurs, they must consider the morality of using their knowledge to create a huge, new, and growing industry which is governed not by the needs of the society which has supported them, but by the principle of maximizing private profit. If every time Genentech makes a decision it is done in their own profit-maximizing interest, it would be a miracle if some of those decisions were also in the social interest. This is exactly what has happened in the petrochemical industry.

We have to raise these moral and political questions and break the taboo. . . . Otherwise, we're going to see very quickly an industry which is too large and powerful, and economically entrenched, to be controlled in the interest of the people.

"The trend toward political control of biotechnology creates serious safety and economic problems."

Genetic Engineering Should Be Privately Controlled

Fred L. Smith Jr.

Fred L. Smith Jr. is president of the Competitive Enterprise Institute, a Washington, D.C. public interest group which advocates market-oriented approaches to public policy issues. He is a former senior policy analyst for the Environmental Protection Agency. In the following viewpoint, Smith argues that government regulation of biotechnology would stifle the biotechnology industry and harm society by preventing the introduction of beneficial products. He argues that private entrepreneurs can better weigh the costs and benefits of genetic engineering than public regulators.

As you read, consider the following questions:

1. What does the author say are the important lessons of the Prometheus myth?
2. Why does Smith oppose public participation in biotechnology regulation decisions?
3. What are the advantages of private regulation of genetic engineering, according to Smith?

Fred L. Smith Jr., "Managing Biotechnology: The Risks of Political Control of Technology." A 1989 speech revised by the author explicitly for use in *Genetic Engineering: Opposing Viewpoints*.

Biotechnology, the controlled design of biological organisms, is one of the most promising technological breakthroughs in mankind's history. Our new understanding of the life sciences makes it possible to more accurately and rapidly upgrade the valuable properties of our basic foodstuffs and animals, activities in which mankind has been engaged for tens of thousands of years. Genetic engineering offers the hope of making tomatoes again tasty, as well as reducing crop losses from spoilage, climate damage and pests. Already experiments have demonstrated the value of biotech products in reducing frost damages and increasing dairy output. Biotechnology has revolutionized the biomedical industry yielding a whole new class of diagnostic tools and production technologies, enhancing our ability to improve human health at lower costs. Genetic engineering may well yield new environmental cleanup tools for oil spills and hazardous wastes. In brief, biotechnology offers new hope of progress against the basic problems of famine, disease and pollution.

Gains Are Threatened

Unfortunately, these potential genetic engineering gains are threatened by those fearful of this new technology. A powerful and persuasive group of modern day Luddites have succeeded in enacting a wide array of political restrictions that shackle biotechnology. In essence, those seeking to promote this new technology must first satisfy one or more political authorities that the product will have no harmful consequences. The classical liberal tradition in which this decision was left to the individual entrepreneur has fallen into disfavor. Politics now holds hostage the future of biotechnology! . . .

We have come to believe that scientists are less responsible, that politicians are better trusted to judge the wisdom of technology. Scientists have become feared rather than respected, brilliant but like Dr. Frankenstein, a threat to the established order. Clearly society must determine how and whether a new technology should be permitted or not. The Frankenstein myth provides one way of viewing that question and its acceptance provides the logical basis for much modern regulation.

A Tutorial Myth: Prometheus and Fire

To critique that myth, this paper reviews in detail another myth, that of Prometheus and fire. The issue, you may recall, was whether the new technology of fire should or should not be shared with mankind. Zeus and most of the political leaders on Olympus thought not. The gods liked their monopoly privileges and were not eager to give them up. Moreover, they argued that fire was inherently risky and that too little was known about its long run health or environmental effects. Moreover, they viewed mankind as uninformed, as indeed the illiterate, cave-dwellers of the time surely were, and thus unable to manage this risky technology safely. Children, the gods believed, shouldn't play with matches!

Prometheus—the archetypical scientist, entrepreneur and innovator—disagreed with this decision. Unable to sway the political majority, Prometheus decided to defy the divine regulatory authorities and brought fire to man. The record suggests that Prometheus did not act hastily (indeed, the myth emphasizes that fact in the use of "Prometheus" which in Greek means "foresight"), but rather carefully assessed the risks associated with fire and, instructed mankind accordingly. Prometheus knew well that safety rests not in the technology itself but rather in its use or misuse. Mankind shared responsibility for managing this new technology safely.

As fire became more widely used, mankind did indeed learn. Fires were banked, flammables were kept separate from open flames, and voluntary fire brigades were soon organized. Moreover, recognizing that technology did not make man more virtuous or wise, rules evolved to limit arson and careless combustion practices. Finally, fire made mankind wealthier by improving his ability to perform many critical functions more efficiently. This additional wealth made it possible to help those less fortunate survive.

Individuals Develop Technology

The idea that society should "have a say" in how science is developed, if in force 100 years ago, would have prevented such modern necessities as electricity, automobiles, telephones, and medicine. Individual minds, not society, discover new knowledge and develop new technology.

Kurt Leininger, *The American Spectator*, April 1989.

What was the net result? Were Zeus and his crowd correct? Of course not. The new technology was certainly risky, fire killed individuals in horrible ways never before experienced. . . .

Fire was risky, but fire reduced far more risks than it created. Fire allowed man to conquer climate and to fend off wild animals. . . . Even more importantly, fire vastly increased man's wealth, making it possible for individuals themselves to take steps for their own safety. Wealthier is healthier even in primitive societies. Prometheus was correct: mankind was benefitted by fire. . . .

Lessons of Prometheus

There are important lessons to be learned from the myth of Prometheus. First, mankind faces a series of choices as to whether a new technology should or should not be adopted. That decision can be relegated to godlike regulators or left to the individual entrepreneur. Errors, of course, will be made in either case. In principle, the choice is best made by weighing carefully the risks of approving the new technology against the risks that this new technology might reduce (including the risks associated with poverty). . . .

A second lesson is that safety is not a descriptor of technology but rather a description of the interaction of man and technology. Misused, almost any advance can create harm; used wisely, even extremely dangerous techniques can make the world a safer place. Fire still kills and maims many thousands of individuals annually. Yet, individuals are far better informed on these risks than in years past; they recognize that safety is everybody's business and the safety statistics are improving. Third, the risks associated with a new technology and the appropriate responses to these risks are not—and indeed cannot—be known in advance. A new technology will be used in ways not anticipated by its inventors and the risks that result will accordingly differ from those anticipated. Safety is discovered rather than designed. Fourth, a new technology will reduce risks in unanticipated ways both directly (the reduction of the risk of starvation via improvements in food preservation) and indirectly, by increasing the wealth of society and thus allowing individuals to better protect themselves and others.

The last lesson—the resistance of political authorities to change—is perhaps the most important. Those promoting technology can expect major resistance from established groups and severe punishment when, and if, such groups gain the power to restrict their activities. All of these factors relate directly to the modern regulation of biotechnology.

The Flawed Incentives of Political Regulation

Safety consists of balancing old risks vs. new ones to determine whether an innovation should be approved or rejected. We wish to avoid thalidomide disasters (a drug whose use as an anti-nausea treatment for pregnant women resulted in a wave of birth defects in Europe) while avoiding the equally serious risk of delaying the availability of beta blockers for individuals prone to heart attacks (an anti-heart attack drug that reached the American population long after it had been in use in Europe). Let us review the implications of a political approach to this problem.

Politicians have neither the time nor the knowledge needed to judge the risks associated with a product, and thus delegate that task to some bureaucratic agency. That agency will then make such decisions but will, of course, be influenced by the reactions of its political overseers. The agency can make mistakes of two types: it may falsely approve a product that later proves dangerous or it may falsely reject a product that would have proved beneficial. How will the agency view these two types of risks?

Consider first the risks associated with false approval. Is a safety agency likely to concern itself with a thalidomide-type incident? The answer is obvious: politicians are quick to delegate but even quicker to condemn bureaucratic incompetency. Any indication that an agency might have erred by approving something harmful will trigger a political uproar, congressional hearings, banner headlines—all castigating the agency and its personnel, condemning its disregard for the safety of the American people. Charges of corruption are likely as are charges of professional incompetence. An agency and its employees are likely to weigh very heavily the risks associated with false approval.

A Regulatory Morass

Scientists have extended their genetic-engineering skills to the molecular level, producing a variety of organisms that promise to be beneficial to humanity. Study after study by reputable and conscientious researchers have concluded that these altered organisms pose no new threat to the environment or to other life on Earth. Nonetheless, a regulatory morass has developed around genetic engineering that at best delays the use of these organisms and could threaten the financial viability of the nascent biotechnology industry that is creating them.

Los Angeles Times, June 13, 1988.

If going too fast is troublesome, what about going too slowly? How concerned are politically responsive regulators to the possibility that they may unwisely delay or reject a promising technology? Unfortunately, not very. Bureaucrats are all too aware that the political process responds only to organized interests and that victims of technological stagnation are muted in the political process. The Ethiopian dying of malnutrition, the heart attack victim denied TPA, the unvaccinated child—all are statistical victims of the healthier, technologically advanced world that might have been. Moreover, these possible benefits may never be realized—at least within the United States—because the approval of the agency will prohibit that knowledge from ever developing. Only the records of other countries provide any check on such mistakes and such foreign lessons are often missed by the American media. Yet, if there is no media outrage, no headlines, there are unlikely to be hearings and pressures to accelerate the approval process. The result is foreordained: Bureaucrats, like others, respond to the incentives they face and these incentives lead to technology lags.

In the U.S. today, a growing array of Zeus-like bodies has been granted the power to determine when, if ever, any biotechnology product will ever be legal. The biotech regulatory establishment resembles the Hydra of legend, a multi-headed monster which devours everything in its sight. Increasingly, nothing can advance in the biotech arena until someone at the National Institutes of Health, the Food and Drug Adminsitration, the Department of Agriculture, or the Environmental Protection Agency (or sometimes until individuals at all these agencies) approve the product. And, as noted, the incentives of these institutions are heavily biased toward delay or rejection. . . .

Public Participation?

The widespread call for greater "public participation" in the technology approval process is only likely to make a bad situation worse. Most people are far too busy and uninterested to invest the time and energy required to become expert in the nuances of any specific technology. Those who do come forward are certainly unusual. In practice, in America today, these groups will often be self-appointed representatives of the "public," holding a skeptical if not hostile view toward the value of technological change. Their values argue that no technology should be approved until it has demonstrated its social value. Fire, it should be clear, would not easily have survived that test.

There remains one final problem with our obsession with political control of technology: its impact on our competitiveness in the world. Not all nations are as quick to reject or curb innovations. Some still believe that technical progress can make the world a better place. Americans, after all, once did. Such countries may well welcome biotechnology and capture its benefits more completely and more swiftly than we. They may not be so quick to strangle this infant industry in its crib. Nations that stick with Prometheus are certain to leave behind those that side with Zeus. America has done well historically economically, but that past success offers no surety of future gains. . . .

What Can Be Done

If biotechnology is to realize its promise, then we must find some way of addressing the problems now posed by political regulation. . . .

The first step is to recognize that the plight of Prometheus has been repeated many times historically. Galileo and Copernicus were both scientists castigated in their day. Their stories are repeated today but have largely gone untold. Biotechnology proponents have failed to humanize the tragedy of the shackled scientist hampered in advancing human welfare. That failure must be corrected. . . .

Needed also is a program that would educate the American people of the stakes involved if biotechnology remains subject to political control. For many reasons, we modern Americans no longer view science and technology as favorably as did our grandparents. Technological changes have brought us great health and safety benefits, but these now are taken for granted. Individually comfortable, many Americans look with disfavor on any changes that might disrupt their lifestyle, even if such changes made gains possible for others. Politics, the process of redistributing wealth already created, is increasingly seen as preferred to the growth resulting from private action. But stability is not really an option. Nature is not a benevolent force. Soils gradually become less productive, pests more resistant to existing techniques, new bacterial and viral infections are continuously evolving—mankind will either become more proficient, more technologically adept, or we will gradually find our living standard falling. The world in which we live resembles all too well the world described by the Red Queen in *Alice in Wonderland*: to stay in one spot, one must run; to get ahead, one must run even faster. . . .

Individual Innovators

The contemporary belief that individual market decisions are inferior to politically determined decisions is surprising. Only a few years ago, Americans had far more respect for individual innovators. Johnny Appleseed wandered about America dispersing selected genetic material without once filing an environmental impact statement. Henry Ford moved rapidly to democratize car ownership in America without ever being challenged by highway safety proponents. Scientists and engineers advanced numerous innovations, many of which failed, and mankind benefited immensely. Then, the presumption was that the scientist entrepreneur was the best judge of when and whether a given product should reach the market.

Fred L. Smith Jr., "Managing Biotechnology: The Risks of Political Control of Technology," 1989.

A public education program should not focus on the details of biotechnology, not become a series of "ten things you always wanted to know about biotech" lectures. Few people will ever become expert in this field. Our goal rather must be to persuade people that their interests lie in freeing the forces of change rather than regulating them. This requires that we humanize the risk-reduction benefits of biotechnology, while at the same time seeking to restore trust in the legitimacy of market-mediated regulation. We must clarify the ways government regulation fails to advance human safety and welfare, while at the same time developing greater faith in the ability of the private sector to control such risks. That is, we must both provide a realistic appraisal of the dangers inherent in political risk management and also restore trust in private risk management. . . .

Conceptually, the argument favoring private regulation is straightforward. Companies don't benefit from injuring their customers or even of appearing to do so. Private parties are likely to better balance the various risks involved in technological change. A company that produces a product which proves faulty faces major losses. Customers will lose confidence in the company (sales may well decline across the company's whole product line), insurance premiums will increase, and numerous damage suits will be filed. Moreover, there are many other risks, save safety, associated with the introduction of a new product and the firm will have many individuals arguing against hasty approval. A firm considers carefully the downside risks of a product before introducing it.

On the other hand, a company will also consider the risks of rejecting a useful product. A company operates in a competitive environment where the possibility that its products will fall to a superior competitor is always present. Firms are forced constantly to upgrade their products, to lower prices, to avoid the loss of markets. A firm is thus forced to consider the risks of approval and rejection and is thus more likely to arrive at a more balanced decision regarding a new technology. . . .

Debate Must Be Shifted

If reform is to succeed, the debate must be shifted from questions of which agency should control which technologies and what specific types of controls are most effective to the more basic question of whether politics should control biotechnology at all. Most people in this nation now view "regulation" as synonymous with "political regulation." Market-mediated regulation is considered no regulation at all! Yet, if our goal is to advance the interest of society, we must ask whether that regulation is best conducted by those most knowledgeable and most concerned or by politically responsive bureaucrats who have far less information and interest in the potential of this new technology. If we can persuade that question to be addressed, we have an excellent chance of achieving substantive reform.

This paper has argued three major points: (1) that today's politically responsive risk regulation agencies are biased and tend to view change as inherently threatening; (2) that the trend toward political control of biotechnology creates serious safety and economic problems; and (3) that this regulatory structure can and should be reformed.

"The patent office's decision to patent novel animals . . . constitutes sound public policy."

Animal Patents Should Be Allowed

Lisa J. Raines

Lisa J. Raines is director of government relations for the Industrial Biotechnology Association, a Washington, D.C. organization, and a former study director in the Office of Technology Assessment's Biological Applications Program. In the following viewpoint, she argues that patent protection for genetically engineered animals is a legally and morally sound policy. Raines states that banning animal patents would inhibit U.S. genetic engineering research, thus placing the U.S. in danger of falling behind other countries in developing biotechnology.

As you read, consider the following questions:

1. What is the purpose of patents, according to Raines? What lies outside their scope?
2. How does the author respond to arguments that animal patents devalue animal life?
3. What steps have other countries taken with respect to animal patents, according to Raines?

Reprinted with permission from Lisa J. Raines, "The Mouse That Roared," ISSUES IN SCIENCE AND TECHNOLOGY, Volume IV, Number 4, Summer 1988. Copyright 1988, by the National Academy of Sciences, Washington, D.C.

In April 1988, the U.S. Patent and Trademark Office awarded Harvard University the world's first patent for an animal, a mouse whose cells have been genetically engineered to carry a cancer-promoting gene. Although the man-made rodent may prove invaluable in cancer research, its place in history will likely stem more from its role as the symbol of a heated national debate.

Simmering for several years, the controversy began to boil in the spring of 1987, when the patent office announced its intention to award patents for "transgenic" animals—that is, animals created with genes from nonparent animals. Animal rights advocates claimed the new policy would increase animal suffering. Farm groups charged that it would hurt the family farm. Environmental activists said that it would upset the laws of nature. Religious leaders maintained that such patents violated divine law. And Jeremy Rifkin of the Foundation on Economic Trends, the perennial foe of biotechnology, expressed concern about all of the above. . . .

The Nature of Patents

Opponents of animal biotechnology are using the patent issue as a way to focus public attention on matters unrelated to the patent office's mandate. They are, in effect, demanding that patent law be revised to address concerns about product regulation, animal welfare, and morality. Many of the critics fail to understand what a patent is—and what it is not.

The government's authority to issue patents is derived from a provision in the Constitution that states, "The Congress shall have the power . . . to promote the progress of Science and the Useful Arts by securing for limited times to Authors and Inventors the exclusive right to their respective writings and discoveries." The first Congress ruled that patents should be granted for a nonrenewable term of 14 years. This law has been revised periodically and today patents are issued for a 17-year term.

Congress and the Supreme Court have repeatedly underscored the purpose of the patent system as promoting progress. An inventor, in return for the right to exclude others from profiting from his creativity for a limited time, must disclose to the world how to make and use the invention. Exclusivity is offered as an incentive to risk the often enormous cost of research and development. And by making details of the invention public, other people benefit intellectually from the achievement, thereby advancing the state of the technology. Conversely, the inability to obtain patent protection is a significant disincentive for both investment and publication. Trade secrecy is the only avenue of protection for the inventor of an unpatented product, and this is often insufficient to prevent a competitor from pirating the technology. The competitor, who has no R&D investment to recoup, can then market generic versions of the product at a lower price.

However, a patent does not automatically grant an inventor the right to commercialize his or her product. Rather, it only prevents others from commercializing the invention without the inventor's permission. Thus, a patentee may not make, use, or sell his invention if legal restrictions exist or until any required premarket regulatory approval is obtained. For instance, a patented drug may not be sold until it is approved by the Food and Drug Administration, and a patented gun may under some circumstances be prohibited from sale.

Improving Human Health Care

The development of transgenic animals for the large-scale, inexpensive production of pharmaceutical proteins will have a beneficial impact on the health care of people in the United States and around the world. Transgenic animals are manmade and as such are patentable. Transgenic animals for production of pharmaceutical protein production will have negligible impact on the environment.

There are few if any new safety issues, and the ethical ones, though genuinely held, are not new. Neither are they relevant. The patent system is not the place to address such concerns.

Alan E. Smith, Testimony before the U.S. House of Representatives, November 5, 1987.

But the patent system was not created to be a substitute for regulatory authority, which falls clearly within the domains of the various federal and state regulatory agencies. If existing regulations are inadequate to protect public health, the environment, and animal welfare, let them be changed. Indeed, proponents of animal biotechnology acknowledge that some applications should be regulated. For example, transgenic animals designed to carry pathogenic material, such as a mouse that has viral genes added to its genetic code, must be very carefully controlled if there is a risk of the infection spreading.

Philosophical Arguments

Yet, critics persist in offering a number of philosophical arguments against patenting animals. For example, Jeremy Rifkin originated the claim that transgenic animals violate "species integrity." This he defines as the "right" of an animal "to exist as a separate identifiable creature." The concept has been echoed by the National Council of Churches, which objected to violating "creation's inherent structures and boundaries."

However, the concept of species integrity, like "creation science," runs counter to what is known about biology. As stated by the congressional Office of Technology Assessment, which has studied animal bioengineering, "There is no consistent or absolute rule that species are discretely bounded in any generally applicable manner." In the wild, species repeatedly recombine their genes through sexual reproduction. Individual genes are constantly being altered by mutation and natural selection. Viruses insert foreign genes into animal genomes. Occasionally, new species arise from old, or two related species interbreed to form a third species. And for domestic animals, the notion of species integrity is even less meaningful. Traditional crossbreeding has transformed species enormously over many centuries. With each new cross, thousands of genes are mixed. . . .

Current techniques of genetic engineering are capable of inserting only a handful of genes into an animal with 50,000 to 100,000 or more genes. Such manipulations would not disrupt anything fundamental in the animal's architecture. A mouse with a human growth hormone gene is still fundamentally a mouse, though its growth characteristics may be enhanced.

Animals as Tennis Balls?

Critics also argue that animal patents devalue animal life. "The patenting of life reflects a dominionistic and materialistic attitude toward living beings that precludes a proper regard for their inherent nature," says John Hoyt, president of the Humane Society of the United States. And according to Rifkin, patenting animals "reduces the entire animal kingdom of this planet to the lowly status of commercial commodity, a technological product indistinguishable from electric toasters, automobiles, tennis balls, or any other patented product."

Such statements are no more or less true for patenting animals than they are for domesticating animals. Owning animals is legitimate and traditional in our culture, and human dominion over the animal kingdom is even a common biblical theme. Animals are bought and sold daily, valued in the marketplace on the basis of their rarity and utility. We eat them, wear them, perform biomedical research on them, put them on leashes. As bioethicist LeRoy Walters of Georgetown University's Kennedy Institute for Bioethics has suggested, patenting them "seems relatively benign." Of course, patented animals should be treated with care and compassion. Nevertheless, nobody has yet explained how owning a patented animal meaningfully differs from owning an unpatented animal.

The Humane Society argues, too, that transgenic animal research will result in what it calls a "dramatic increase in the suffering of animals." Certainly, it is possible for genetic engineering to produce an animal with characteristics that interfere with its normal functioning. But it is equally possible to create dysfunctional animals through traditional cross-breeding activities. For example, modern turkeys have been bred with breasts so large that it is impossible for them to mate, and numerous breeds of dogs now possess inbred health problems ranging from arthritis to kidney failure.

In fact, genetic engineering may ultimately lead to less animal suffering. One of the most promising areas of research is the development of farm animals that resist disease. For example, scientists may be able to create cattle that are resistant to a disease called shipping fever. This would reduce the chances of their suffering while being transported to feedlots or to market, as well as diminish a major source of economic loss for ranchers. . . .

Patents Will Not Harm Animals

The fact that modern techniques of biotechnology permit the practice of agriculture to be more productive, and to offer improvements in safety and reductions in cost do not mean that novel social issues are presented. The social policy objections to animal patenting should be recognized for what they are: objections to improvements in agricultural practices. Precise and minimal alteration of the genetic material of a plant or an animal cannot possibly raise issues more troubling and different in kind than those already presented by traditional breeding practices, which, for example, result in turkeys with breasts so large that they cannot mate. The irony of the objections to modern biotechnology is apparent. In the words of one European, ''If you don't know what you're doing in changing an organism's genes, then that is allowed. If you *do* know precisely what you're doing, it isn't.''

The plain, but unsensational, facts are that the patenting of animals will not increase the suffering of animals and will not alter the economic realities of modern agriculture and that genetic engineering of agricultural organisms does not present any unique ecological hazards.

Michael S. Ostrach, Statement before the House Judiciary Subcommittee on Courts, Civil Liberties, and the Administration of Justice, August 22, 1987.

But perhaps the most common argument offered by critics of patenting animals is that producing new life forms for profit ''strikes many as morally offensive,'' in the words of the National Council of Churches. However, 68 percent of the American public and 81 percent of college graduates believe that it is *not* morally wrong to genetically engineer plants and animals, according to a Louis Harris survey. Most people, in fact, want to see the technology advance.

Of course, the government should not turn a deaf ear to ethical concerns simply because the views are held by a minority. But neither should the government deny protection to an entire class of intellectual property simply because some people find certain potential applications morally objectionable. Should the government forbid patenting of contraceptives because some people believe artificial birth control is immoral, or deny copyrights for books that some readers judge to be pornographic? . . .

Time to Decide

Although the United States is the first country to patent a transgenic animal, it is not the only nation that recognizes the patentability of transgenic animals. A 1987 survey by the World Intellectual Property Organization shows that 53 countries have not expressly excluded animals from patent protection, and patents are already permitted in 10 of these countries—Japan, Canada, Australia, Argentina, New Zealand, Turkey, Brazil, Greece, Hungary, and the Netherlands. . . .

Even without a moratorium, Congress will always be free to place restrictions on animal biotechnology at any time and by a variety of methods. Congress may place a heavy tax on the sales of patented animals, revise regulatory laws to impede or prohibit sales of transgenic animals, or even modify patent law to reduce the rights of certain patent holders. But unless Congress can find a good reason to ban all forms of transgenic animals, a patent moratorium will be a mistake, discouraging American companies from investing in animal biotechnology while foreign competitors push forward. . . .

The arguments against patentability are for the most part thinly veiled objections from a small number of groups opposed to biotechnology and large-scale commercial farming. On the other hand, the patent office's decision to patent novel animals is consistent with Supreme Court rulings regarding the scope of patentable subject matter and reflects the general opinion of the scientific and legal communities. And given the need to enhance U.S. industrial competitiveness, it constitutes sound public policy.

"The patenting of animals should be prohibited."

Animals Should Not Be Patented

John A. Hoyt

In April 1988 the U.S. Patent and Trademark Office awarded Harvard University a patent for a mouse whose cells had been genetically engineered. This controversial decision marked the first time an animal had been patented and led to calls for legislation to ban such patents. In the following viewpoint, taken from testimony before Congress, John A. Hoyt argues that patents should not be granted for new forms of animal life created by genetic engineering. He asserts that patenting animals is unethical and leads to animal abuse. Hoyt is president of The Humane Society of the United States, the nation's largest animal protection organization.

As you read, consider the following questions:

1. What is the difference between genetic engineering and the traditional breeding of animals, according to Hoyt?
2. According to the author, what are the effects of patenting animals?
3. Does Hoyt believe that patenting animals is fundamentally an ethical or legal issue? What reasons does he give for his belief?

John A. Hoyt. Testimony before U.S. House of Representatives Subcommittee on Courts, Civil Liberties, and the Administration of Justice, June 11, 1987.

On April 17, 1987, the United States Patent and Trademark Office announced its decision to consider nonnaturally occurring organisms, "including animals, to be patentable subject matter." The PTO derived its position from a Supreme Court decision on microorganisms. The Supreme Court in Diamond V. Chakrabarty ruled that Congress intended to allow the patenting of "anything under the sun that is made by man." . . .

A Question of Ethics

Let us assume, for the sake of argument, that from a purely legalistic and technical viewpoint the United States Patent Office is able to justify its pronouncement that it will now issue patents for new forms of animal life created through advances in genetic engineering. This decision, it would seem, is based on a strained reading of a 1980 high court decision concerned only with microorganisms, which opined that it was Congress' "intent" to allow patenting of "anything under the sun that is made by man." However, these legal niceties miss the point completely. For the issue is much more than a question of presumed legal authority to issue such patents. It is, rather, a question of ethics, morality and, finally, a question of a proper regard for the very essence of life itself.

Accordingly, on behalf of The Humane Society of the United States, I must express our strong and concerted opposition to this proposal. As I elaborate more fully in the following pages, I believe that implementing such a proposal is inappropriate, violates the basic ethical precepts of civilized society and unleashes the potential for uncontrollable and unjustified animal suffering.

Proponents of genetic engineering and of the patenting of genetically altered animals are quick to state that humans have been altering animals genetically for thousands of years through the relatively slow process of selective breeding and cross-breeding. Yet both ethically and scientifically speaking, this is not a valid historical precedent for the acceptance of the genetic engineering of animals. Clearly, genetic engineering is of a wholly different order of magnitude, in that in traditional breeding practices, genes cannot be exchanged between unrelated species. Furthermore, genetic changes can be wrought very rapidly through genetic engineering, while in selective breeding such changes occur over a long period of time.

The potential risks to animals, human beings, and society generally in permitting and encouraging this kind of man-made created order are not to be dismissed lightly. My detailed concerns and objections follow.

a. If the patenting of animals is permitted, there will surely be a dramatic increase in the suffering of animals resulting from agricultural, biomedical, and other industrial research. This for the reason that the outcome of many genetic experiments cannot be predicted in relation to the animals' health and welfare or in relation to their long-term social, economic, and environmental impact. Furthermore, many animals will undoubtedly be abnormal at birth and generations will suffer until techniques for treating these deformed and defective creatures are perfected and regulated. And who, may I ask, will be the guardians and protectors of these animals? For it is surely to be expected that such experiments and their consequences will be cloaked in secrecy and deliberately hidden from the eyes of the public.

b. Patenting of animals will also create new health problems. Can we rest assured that those so experimenting will be concerned or able to correct or treat these man-made disorders?

c. Patenting of animals would also result in a monopoly of genetic stock resulting in a predominance of certain genetic lines of animals over others, with an ultimate loss of genetic diversity within a species. This could have a negative economic impact on many farmers as well as adverse social, ecological, and economic consequences for society in general.

d. Patenting of animals is unnecessary. Scientific advances, including those in the field of medicine, have been made in the past without the patenting of genetic engineering techniques involving animals. Moreover, patenting in this area could actually inhibit

scientific progress since, for proprietary reasons, research findings between privately funded laboratories and university research would not be shared. And there would also be considerable unnecessary and costly duplication of research because the patenting of animal models would encourage a competitive rather than a collaborative research atmosphere to the ultimate detriment of the public's best interests.

e. Patenting would also cloud the ownership of wild animals. Wildlife in the United States is held as a public trust by both state and federal governments. If but one gene is altered, can a deer then be patented? Is the public, then, to be disenfranchised from ownership of wild animals? The concept that wild animals belong to all the people is much too ingrained within our cultural and societal mores to now be subject to such a debate.

Ethical Concerns

Even more important are our ethical concerns. From an ethical perspective, the patenting of animals reflects a human arrogance toward other living creatures that is contrary to the concept of the inherent sanctity of every unique being and the recognition of the ecological and spiritual interconnectedness of all life. The patenting of life reflects a dominionistic and materialistic attitude toward living beings that precludes a proper regard for their inherent nature.

The patenting of animals, if permitted, will result in a radical alteration of life as a creative process of nature. And animal life will become little more than another new invention. What, then, of the sanctity of life as we have come to regard it? What, then, of the integrity of unique and diverse species and of the integrity and future of creation itself?

Clearly, there are and must be ethical constraints to protect the sanctity and dignity of life. People cannot be allowed to patent life by reason of altering genes. To do otherwise would be to potentially enslave all species, including our own. To permit the patenting of just one animal will effectively eliminate all constraints—both ethical and social—against genetically altering all other animals, including human beings.

Conclusion

In conclusion, the patenting of animals should be prohibited through congressional legislation. The greatest good can only be assured if we, as a society, continue to hold to the principles of democracy, which, in the context of genetic engineering, amounts to a respect for the rights and sanctity of all sentient beings who are part of the same creation and ecological community as we, and who should, therefore, be part of the same community of moral consideration and ethical concern.

Recognizing Statements That Are Provable

From various sources of information we are constantly confronted with statements and generalizations about social and moral problems. In order to think clearly about these problems, it is useful if one can make a basic distinction between statements for which evidence can be found and other statements which cannot be verified or proved because evidence is not available, or the issue is so controversial that it cannot be definitely proved.

Readers should constantly be aware that magazines, newspapers, and other sources often contain statements of a controversial nature. The following activity is designed to allow experimentation with statements that are provable and those that are not.

The following statements are taken from the viewpoints in this chapter. Consider each statement carefully. *Mark P for any statement you believe is provable. Mark U for any statement you feel is unprovable because of the lack of evidence. Mark C for any statements you think are too controversial to be proved to everyone's satisfaction.*

If you are doing this activity as a member of a class or group, compare your answers with those of other class or group members. Be able to defend your answers. You may discover that others will come to different conclusions than you. Listening to the reasons others present for their answers may give you valuable insights in recognizing statements that are provable.

> P = *provable*
> U = *unprovable*
> C = *too controversial*

1. The first patent for an animal was issued in April 1988.

2. Animal patenting is unethical.

3. Genetic engineering is one of the most promising technological breakthroughs in history.

4. Many studies have concluded that genetic engineering poses an environmental threat.

5. Under federal regulations, organisms with new genes from unrelated species must be evaluated for safety before being tested outdoors.

6. The products of biotechnology are fundamentally similar to those produced by conventional techniques.

7. An interagency working group established by the U.S. government concluded in 1984 that current genetic engineering regulations are adequate.

8. Four separate federal agencies have jurisdiction over genetic engineering regulation.

9. We cannot assume that the market will operate in the interest of the public without social guidance.

10. The regulation of genetic engineering experiments is inadequate.

11. The Environmental Protection Agency has 90 days to review genetic engineering experiment proposals submitted under the Toxic Substances Control Act.

12. If the patenting of animals is permitted, there will surely be a dramatic increase in the suffering of animals in scientific experiments.

13. Genetic engineering may reduce animal suffering by developing animals resistant to disease.

14. The United States is not the only country that allows animal patenting.

15. Genentech, a biotechnology company, turned down the World Health Organization's request to develop a malaria vaccine because it wouldn't get exclusive rights to it.

16. Biotechnology is an inherently safe industry.

17. The majority of biotechnology companies make pharmaceutical products.

Periodical Bibliography

The following articles have been selected to supplement the diverse views presented in this chapter.

Ronald Bailey	"Ministry of Fear," *Forbes*, June 27, 1988.
Michael W. Fox	"Biotechnology: Keeping the Lid on Pandora's Box," *Business and Society Review*, Summer 1987.
Malcolm Gladwell	"Risk, Regulation, and Biotechnology," *The American Spectator*, January 1989.
David J. Glass	"Regulating Biotech: A Case Study," *Forum for Applied Research and Public Policy*, Fall 1989.
Christine Gorman	"A Mouse That Roared," *Time*, April 25, 1988.
Tom Jenn	"Local Grass-Roots Opposition Thwarts Biotech Test in Wisconsin," *Utne Reader*, March/April 1988.
Sheldon Krimsky	"The Corporate Capture of Genetic Technologies," *Science for the People*, May/June 1985.
Patrick J. Leahy	"Toward a National Biotechnology Policy," *Issues in Science and Technology*, Fall 1988.
Los Angeles Times	"Genetic Engineering's Morass," June 13, 1988.
The New Republic	"What Price Mighty Mouse?" May 23, 1988.
Fred L. Smith Jr.	"Biotechnology Flirts with the Regulators," *Bio/Technology*, November 1988.
Gary Strobel, interviewed by Kathleen Stein	"Interview," *Omni*, August 1988.
Shawna Vogel	"Patented Animals," *Technology Review*, October 1988.
John Yoo	"Biotech Patents Become Snarled in Bureaucracy," *The Wall Street Journal*, July 16, 1989.
Frank E. Young	"The Gene Revolution," *The Saturday Evening Post*, October 1988.

Will Genetic Engineering Lead to a Biological Arms Race?

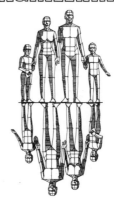

Chapter Preface

Biological weapons are living organisms, germs, used for military purposes.

The use of biological weapons raises many of the same issues that were raised about the chemical gas weapons first used in World War I. Like chemical weapons, biological weapons have the potential for mass and indiscriminate killing. This prompts profound moral questions about their use. And like the poison gas used in World War I, the unpredictability of biological weapons once released makes them as dangerous to the attacker as to the attacked. For both of these reasons, moral and practical, biological weapons have been used very rarely. In 1969 the U.S. unilaterally renounced the development and stockpiling of biological weapons, and in 1972 over one hundred nations agreed to do the same. They signed a United Nations treaty, the Biological and Toxin Weapons Convention, which many people hailed as a deterrent to a biological arms race.

The international community's resolve to ban biological weapons has been severely tested, however, by dramatic breakthroughs in genetic engineering. Since the signing of the 1972 treaty, improved techniques in the genetic alteration of microorganisms have made biological weapons more practical. Despite the 1972 treaty, both the U.S. and the Soviet Union continue to work on "defensive" biological weapons research. While genetic engineering might solve the practical problems of developing and using biological weapons, the moral and strategic questions remain. The viewpoints in this chapter debate the impact of genetic engineering on biological weapons and how the U.S. should respond.

"The new biotechnologies promise to 'improve' CBW [chemical biological warfare] agents and enhance their utility."

Genetic Engineering Will Lead to a Biological Arms Race

Charles Piller and Keith R. Yamamoto

Many people have speculated on how genetic engineering can be used to create biological weapons. In the following viewpoint, Charles Piller and Keith R. Yamamoto argue that advances in genetic engineering make biological weapons a tempting alternative for military planners. They assert that the U.S. and the Soviet Union are on the verge of a biological arms race. Piller is an investigative journalist who has written extensively on chemical and biological warfare, and has served as a consultant for the U.S. Senate. Yamamoto is a molecular biologist at the University of California in San Francisco.

As you read, consider the following questions:

1. What was the conventional wisdom concerning biological weapons, according to Piller and Yamamoto?
2. What three types of unconventional weapons do the authors describe?
3. According to the authors, in what ways does genetic engineering make biological weapons more usable?

Charles Piller and Keith R. Yamamoto, *Gene Wars*. New York: Beech Tree Books, 1988. Copyright 1988 by William Morrow and Company, Inc. Reprinted by permission.

The use of biological weapons has been viewed as a minor issue effectively neutralized by the 1972 biological disarmament treaty. Conventional wisdom has held that such agents are dangerous to develop and handle, hard to disseminate effectively, and impossible to control. Widespread public revulsion against germ warfare has made the potential political and diplomatic risks associated with using these weapons unacceptably high. They have rarely seen action in modern military history.

This may soon change.

Stunning Advances

"The stunning advances over the last five to ten years in the field of biotechnology . . . mean more than new foods, pharmaceuticals and fertilizers. They mean new and better biological weapons. . . . It is now possible to synthesize BW agents tailored to military specifications. The technology that makes possible so called 'designer drugs' also makes possible designer BW," said Douglas J. Feith, deputy assistant secretary of defense for negotiations policy, in 1986 testimony before a congressional committee. "New agents can be produced in hours; antidotes may take years," he continued. "The major arms control implication of the new biotechnology is that the [BW treaty] must be recognized as critically deficient and unfixable."

Feith's assertions are far from proved. In fact, some leading scientists and arms control experts consider the statements naive, irresponsible exaggerations. Does genetic engineering have the power to alter the fundamental strategic or tactical utility of BW? Not immediately. In the long term, though, the answer is less certain. But this may be the wrong question. The way the superpowers perceive BW is the best barometer of whether biotechnology will send the arms race off into a bizarre and dangerous spiral. And superpower perceptions have already recalculated the germ warfare equation. . . .

Chemical and Biological Warfare Defined

This viewpoint is concerned with three types of unconventional weapons: biological weapons (BW), toxin weapons (TW), and chemical weapons (CW).

BW are "living organisms, whatever their nature . . . which are intended to cause disease or death in man, animals and plants, and which depend for their effects on the ability to multiply in the person, animal or plant attacked," according to a United Nations definition. The major forms of BW—each potentially deadly—are bacteria, viruses, rickettsia and fungi. . . .

Chemical weapons are chemical substances in gaseous, liquid, or solid form that could be used with hostile intent because of their direct toxic effects on animals, plants, and human beings. Like all chemical agents, CW are inanimate and incapable of self-reproduction. Many potent industrial chemicals could be used, perhaps crudely, as weapons, but we are concerned only with the relatively limited number of chemicals that have strong practical potential in warfare, terrorism, or sabotage. . . .

In general, toxins are poisons produced by living organisms— from shellfish to fungi. They occupy a middle ground between chemicals and organisms. The active ingredient in poison mushrooms is a toxin. Botulinum toxin, a chief cause of food poisoning (botulism), is produced by a bacterium. Snake venom is also a toxin. Because many toxins have legitimate medical uses, their definition as a weapon is based on clear hostile intent. . . .

Improving Biological Weapons

The new biotechnologies promise to "improve" CBW agents and enhance their utility far beyond the capacity of classical biochemistry, both qualitatively and quantitatively. Whether this potential can be decisively exploited has yet to be determined in definitive examples whose results are available to the general public. But the following applications of the new biotechnologies have pushed CBW to the foreground of arms control concerns:

• Drug resistance. The genetic basis for bacterial resistance to antibiotics and viral resistance to other drugs is well understood. Genes that confer such resistance can be transferred to a BW agent to thwart medical countermeasures.

Cloning Biological Toxins

The most practical strategy for biological weapons may prove to be the use of existing gene-cloning techniques to mass-produce biological poisons inside bacteria or yeast host cells cultivated in huge vats in much the same way biotechnologists already clone human proteins such as insulin or interferon. This procedure would allow military scientists to produce enormous quantities of deadly poisons—such as snake venoms, shellfish toxins or bacterial toxins—that are otherwsie extremely difficult to harvest from organisms in nature.

David Suzuki and Peter Knudtson, *Genethics*, 1989.

• Increased hardiness. Finding a way to keep aerosolized microorganisms from dying once they are sprayed from aircraft or exploded from bombs has been one of the most vexing questions for BW planners. Solar radiation, drying, and temperature fluctuation easily kill most agents adapted to live within humans or animals. But microencapsulation—a novel method of protecting individual BW organisms within organic compounds—has already extended the range of agents that can be weaponized effectively.

• Defeating vaccines, natural resistance, and diagnosis. Our immune system's antibodies overcome a virus or other BW antigen by targeting the organism's specific surface structure. Using rDNA to make minute changes in this antigenic surface could render antibodies ineffective. . . .

Scientists could learn which genes to alter in order to create a new surface structure, unrecognized by antibodies produced in people who have been infected by any of the naturally occurring strains. Virtually anyone exposed would contract the new disease. Through rDNA methods a form of the virus could be created that would frequently mutate—in essence making many "mistakes" as it self-replicates. This would lead to a disease of longer duration because the body's defenses would have to learn to recognize each of the various forms of the new dengue virus.

Similarly, many diagnostic methods are based on the detection of certain sites on a disease organism's surface. Altering these sites could render a BW agent "invisible," thereby frustrating appropriate treatment.

Vaccine Research

• Unlimited vaccine development and new biodetection abilities. A nation probably would not use a BW agent unless it could protect its own people from infection. Only a handful of organisms—for which vaccines or other proved protective measures exist—have ever been standardized and manufactured as weapons.

Just as they have become tools to thwart vaccines, . . . rDNA technologies have revolutionized vaccine research. Under modern bioprocess methods vaccines are simple to mass-produce, and in the foreseeable future they will be created for nearly all known potential BW agents. . . . These developments may reduce an aggressor's fears of backfire and retaliation.

• Increased virulence. Disease symptoms often stem directly from toxins secreted by a pathogen. Anthrax toxin, for example, is the active ingredient of the anthrax bacterium. The genes that regulate toxin production may be manipualted to enhance an organism's virulence. The result would be a more powerful, faster-acting, and invasive weapon, one that would infect and kill more reliably.

• Weaponization of innocuous organisms. Certain harmless microorganisms, such as *E. coli*, are a normal part of the body's ecology. By the transfer of genes that regulate the production of disease-causing toxins to these helpful microbes, they may become lethal toxin factories, already well adapted for survival inside the human body.

It is technically and economically unfeasible to extract militarily significant quantities of many potent toxins, such as shellfish toxin, from their natural sources. But prolific microorganisms fitted with toxin-producing genes can easily and cheaply mass-produce many of them. Further genetic manipulation could yield more efficient toxins—stable under a range of temperatures and resistant to degradation in the body.

Easier Production

• Safer experimentation. Improvements in physical and biological containment since the advent of rDNA technology have made the potentially grave dangers of BW experimentation far less daunting.

Military Applications

In examining the potential impact of genetic engineering on biological warfare research, it is important to recognize the parallels between present bioengineering research and nuclear research in the 1940s and 1950s. The data base developed from nuclear technology was convertible to both military and industrial purposes. Similarly, the data base being developed for the commercial uses of genetic engineering in the fields of agriculture, animal husbandry, and human medicine is potentially convertible to the development of a wide range of novel microorganisms that can attack plant, animal, and human populations.

Jeremy Rifkin, Prepared testimony before Congress, May 3, 1988.

• Enhanced production efficiency. In the past a genuinely military BW production capability required massive, dangerous facilities and storage tanks that were difficult to conceal and maintain. New bioprocess technologies have drastically slashed the minimum size required for a BW production plant. And the time for the manufacturing process has been reduced by several thousandfold over earlier methods, according to the U.S. Army. They have eliminated the need for long-term maintenance of large, deadly stockpiles.

• Ethnic weapons. BW planners have dreamed for decades about precisely targetable weapons that would devastate the enemy but could never backfire or be used in retaliation. Since the advent of rDNA this fantasy has entered the realm of possibility. Specific ethnic or racial groups are susceptible to certain diseases or chemical poisoning, as a result of variations in natural resistance in the human gene pool. One example is valley fever, a fungal disease that has been closely studied by the U.S. Navy for decades. Certain studies suggest that blacks are far more susceptible to valley fever than whites. It may be possible to prey on such ethnic or racial groups by targeting a combination of these genetic factors.

215

• Biochemical weapons. The body produces tiny amounts of hormones and other substances that exert profound regulatory influence over moods, perceptions, organ function, temperature, and other essential physiological processes. The smallest imbalance can lead to severe illness, even death. Genetic engineering methods have made possible the manufacture of nearly unlimited quantities of these rapidly acting substances. This capacity has led to speculation about the weaponization of our own biochemical endowment. . . .

A Dangerous Road

The mere feasibility of these technologies does not make their implementation inevitable or logistically viable. Indeed, genetic engineering cannot "perfect" chemical and biological warfare, and the development of a genetically engineered arsenal would likely prove self-defeating—a destabilizing act with unpredictable and possibly dire consequences. But speculations on potential novel CBW applications are more than paranoia. The United States and possibly the Soviet Union are already traveling this dangerous road.

"World War Three seems most unlikely to be a biological war."

Genetic Engineering Will Not Lead to a Biological Arms Race

William Bains

William Bains is a lecturer in biochemistry at the University of Bath in Great Britain and has done research in molecular genetics. In the following viewpoint, he argues that advances in genetic engineering have not solved any of the obstacles which make biological warfare an impractical military option. Biological weapons remain inefficient and dangerous for whomever uses them, he states.

As you read, consider the following questions:

1. Why are biological weapons militarily useless, according to Bains?
2. What natural barriers in organisms prevent the development of biological weapons, according to the author?
3. What conclusion does Bains draw from his picture of the ideal biological weapon?

GENETIC ENGINEERING FOR ALMOST EVERYBODY by William Bains (Penguin Books, 1987), copyright © William Bains, 1987, pp 193-7. Reproduced by permission of Penguin Books Ltd.

It is very unlikely that the genetic engineering which is being carried out today or is likely to be carried out in the foreseeable future will add any significant problems to those which the bacterial world already cause us. But a grimmer spectre is raised by the related possibility that a harmful bacterium could be released not by accident but by design, as a weapon of biological warfare.

Useless Weapons

In the 1960s, when a biological warfare program was part of every self-respecting nation's defence budget, scientists pointed out just how useless a biological weapon would be if they ever succeeded in making one. The most advanced biological weapons then available, mostly either versions of highly infectious viruses which affected the blood or of anthrax bacteria, had two drawbacks: they did not kill the enemy and they did kill you. They were dangerous, certainly, but never lethal enough to knock out more than 20 to 30 per cent of even an unprepared enemy, compared with the much greater efficiency of atomic bombs, bullets or clubs. They also did not act quickly enough. Even the fastest-acting diseases take more than a day to begin to affect their victims, and in modern warfare entire countries can be laid waste in a day. So the weapons would be pretty useless against any modern army, although they might be quite efficient in killing citizens of Third World countries which lack Western medical facilities. And after the battle the bacteria and their spores would remain on the battlefield for weeks, would drift in the wind and would end up by causing as many casualties among the side that launched them as among the enemy, and many more among the civilians who had to clean up the mess afterwards.

Added to this was the difficulty of producing weapons that did not 'leak', and the problem that is very difficult to find any disease-causing organism that is strong enough to withstand being fired from a gun or exploded out of a bomb—out of 100 of even the toughest bacteria, less than one would be likely to survive delivery to the target. Thus biological weapons would be the opposite of modern nerve gases. 'Binary' nerve gases are mixes of relatively safe materials which react after they have left the gun to form a deadly poison; biological weapons would be lethal when they were being made, but largely harmless by the time they reached their target.

Given these objections, it is not surprising that those people who are for ever searching for new weapons gave up on biological warfare by the end of the 1960s.

The same problems apply today. A few bacteria and their poisons have been studied in much more detail so that we have a better idea how they work, but this has not encouraged the arms merchants. Some exotic uses of bacterial poisons have hit the headlines, as when the Hungarian defector Georgiou Markov was killed by a small pellet loaded with a bacterial toxin, fired from the tip of an umbrella. Delightful as the image of the British Army marching into battle with shrapnel-proof bowler hats, exploding briefcases and poison umbrellas may be, this does not seem a very realistic weapon for anyone other than a terrorist.

Bioweapons Impractical

The claim that exotic bioweaponry is immediately within reach is not borne out by most responsible evaluations of the present state of the biological sciences. Advances in biotechnology have been impressive since the early 1970s—and its industrial application must certainly have reinforced perceptions of its military utility. The new biogenetic technologies make it feasible to change the characteristics of living things, produce novel toxins, and greatly increase the efficiency of production of biological agents. But none of these developments greatly alter the characteristics of biological weapons that have made them unattractive to military establishments in the past: their delayed action, uncertain impact, lack of specificity, and potential to rebound on the user.

Susan Wright, *Bulletin of the Atomic Scientists*, January/February 1989.

The molecular structure of some of these toxins is quite well known. Botulinus toxin, for example, is a protein. In principle we could genetically engineer an *E. coli* to make lots of botulinus toxin, and then use that in a large-scale terrorist campaign, dropping a few grams in a barrel of beer, for example (how terrorists could do this without poisoning themselves is another matter). But that sort of genetic engineering requires a great deal of technology, and any nation with that much expertise would want a far more useful weapon than one which could be used only to put a pub out of business.

Thus the barriers to the use of genetically engineered bacteria as biological weapons are probably greater than those which would militate against the use of 'wild' bacteria. The bacteria which cause disease are highly specialized for their role, and rely on very complex tricks to evade the defences of their victims. Anthrax or plague are not just *E. coli* with a poison added: they are carefully crafted invasion machines, and medical scientists still cannot explain why they cause disease while other bacteria live in or on us and cause no disease, and yet others would die within minutes of landing on our skins or in our stomachs. No one knows why an infection by rabies virus is 100 per cent fatal, while infection by rhinoviruses only gives you a cold. Until someone finds out, we are never going to be able to genetically engineer a 'new' disease even as effective as those that already exist, let alone one which is more lethal.

In short, World War Three seems most unlikely to be a biological war. Nature puts numerous obstacles in the way of those of her children who want to use her resources for killing each other.

Such are the facts. Every year or so, microbiologists and genetic engineers recite them in an almost ritualistic way to counter new suggestions by the more fanatical anti-science groups that we are on the brink of a biological Armageddon, or by political extremists that 'they' are using biological weapons against 'our' allies. The facts are also pointed out to the military planners every time they start to dream of weapons that will strike down the enemy but leave *our* side unaffected. There is no scientific disagreement about the inefficiency and undesirability of biological warfare. And yet the United States and the USSR are once again moving into this field with typical military myopia, each claiming that their growing research programs are purely defensive, a protection against the other's threat. The US Defense Department has openly advertised for scientists to work in its laboratories on aspects of biological warfare; the USSR is less candid, but has increasingly taken to declaring that work on recombinant DNA is secret (as nearly everything is secret in the USSR, it is hard to know what to make of this). In 1980, near Sverdlovsk in the northwestern USSR, an 'explosion' was alleged to have occurred at a germ warfare production plant making anthrax bombs. The impact of the story was rather lost when the real source of the anthrax outbreak was revealed to be contaminated sheep: wool production is a major industry in the area, and sheep are the main carriers of anthrax. Clouds of 'yellow rain' were taken as evidence of the next supposed USSR biological weapon, a horrible spray which sent villagers in South-East Asia running for sanctuary to the CIA. Professor Matthew Meselson of Harvard showed rather convincingly that this dreaded weapon was actually bee faeces. The USSR regularly accuses the United States or Britain of researching, making or actually using biological weapons, as do left-wing groups in Europe. Again, proof is sadly lagging behind accusation.

The Threat of Military Propaganda

This would be an excellent plot for a farcical film were it not for the scale on which these dramas are played. There is a real possibility that the military planners will come to believe their own propaganda and decide that biological warfare really *is* being waged against them—that a biological attack is actually a sensible option—and will load up a bomber with anthrax bacteria and spread it all over Poland or Nicaragua as a substitute for negotiation. Although anthrax is a useless weapon, it is a very dangerous disease. And if 'they' have used biological weapons, what is to stop 'us' from using anything else, maybe chemical or even nuclear weapons? Which, sadly, are much more effective. Thus the fear of biological warfare could generate as much destruction as the weapons themselves are meant to do, but cannot. The military threat from biological warfare is very small. But the threat from fear and misunderstanding of what biology can give the weapons-makers is real, and appears to be growing. It is ironical that this fear should be the most dangerous product of the recombinant DNA revolution, when that revolution has shown us many of the reasons why the fear is groundless in the first place.

The technical obstacles can be overcome, of course. Given enough knowledge, all dreams—even nightmares—become reasonable. In theory we could imagine a weapon which not only killed quickly and efficiently but also discriminated between friend and foe, as gas or nuclear fall-out never could. By turning the body's own defences against itself, a virus could, in principle, kill 70 per cent of orientals but only 25 per cent of occidentals, or be entirely specific for caucasians or negroes. Mercifully, such ideas are only at the science-fiction stage at the moment. However, it is the sort of science fiction which encourages professional doomsters to write headlines of the 'Science Dooms Globe!' type, because they are so much more eye-catching than the correct version, which would read: 'Science might doom globe in 100 years if we let the army get away with it'.

We Can Do It Already

But the pace of research is frantic, and the desire of people to kill other people seems almost unlimited; so someone, somewhere, is bound to try out a biological weapon one day. Such a project could well abandon unreliable viruses or bacteria entirely, and switch instead to engineering a weapon based on a more discriminating organism like the mosquito. Indeed, the biological weapon would be one with enough intelligence to be 'pro-grammed' with a complex battle plan and then to modify the plan if it went wrong, to be extremely tough and flexible, to be able to discriminate friend from foe even in the absence of obvious physical differences, and to be quite safe in between wars but to be so enthusiastic about killing the enemy in wartime that it would die itself for the chance. If that sounds to you more like a religious fanatic than a product of genetic engineering, it demonstrates the last reason why biological warfare is useless: we can do it already.

"Any nation . . . that does not appraise itself of the potentials [of biological weapons] and their consequences only increases its vulnerabilities and risks."

Biological Weapons Research Should Continue

Joseph D. Douglass Jr.

The United States has officially renounced the stockpiling and use of biological weapons, but continues to research these weapons. In the following viewpoint, Joseph D. Douglass Jr. argues that despite the revulsion most people feel about biological weapons, the U.S. should continue to research them. He argues that U.S. security is threatened by the Soviet Union and developing countries that are pursuing biological weapons. Douglass is a defense analyst who has written many books on national security issues.

As you read, consider the following questions:

1. What four principal concerns does Douglass have about biological weapons?
2. Why does Douglass believe biological weapons cannot be controlled by negotiations?
3. What recommendations does the author make concerning biological weapons research?

Joseph D. Douglass Jr., "The Challenges of Biochemical Warfare," *Global Affairs*, vol. 3, no. 1, Winter 1988. Reprinted with permission.

While the world has directed its attention to nuclear warfare, another even more dangerous and sinister form of warfare has arisen: specifically, modern-day biochem warfare.

In 1975, U.S. national security authorities hoped that the threat of chemical and biological warfare was ending when the U.S. Senate ratified the Biological and Toxin Weapons Convention of 1972 and the 1925 Geneva Protocol that banned the use of poisonous and asphyxiating gases and biological agents in war. Much to their dismay, however, even as the ratification was taking place, defense and intelligence analysts were identifying expanding Soviet and East European chemical and biological warfare programs.

The problems presented by the Warsaw Pact programs became especially troublesome as defense and intelligence analysts began to recognize the tremendous potential for new biological and chemical weapons that was contained in the new genetic engineering and biotechnologies. This, coupled with Soviet chemical warfare activities in Afghanistan and Southeast Asia and a wide variety of Warsaw Pact intelligence operations utilizing chemical agents, led these analysts to the unpleasant conclusion that the threat of biological and chemical warfare had not diminished. Rather, the threat had grown in frightening ways the West had not contemplated when the United States unilaterally began disarming in biological, toxin, and chemical warfare in 1970.

Four Areas of Concern

Today, in reviewing the current and future prospects for this most heinous form of warfare, four principal areas of concern emerge that, when melded together, explain why the problem is real, is here today, and deserves immediate and special attention.

First, technology has enabled a wide range of qualitative and quantitative improvements that make possible the development of weapons that are far more flexible, efficient, effective, and desirable than even nuclear weapons in most applications. Indeed, to the extent nuclear weapons are to be rendered "obsolete," modern chemical and biological weapons at present appear to be the most likely reason and substitute.

Second, unlike nuclear weapons, which increasing numbers of people regard as unusable (perhaps erroneously so), chemical and biological weapons are not only usable in a wide-ranging variety of applications, they are being used.

Third, the technology is relatively cheap and accessible to all. Most Third World nations, including those throughout the Middle East, have adequate technology to develop and produce extremely effective chemical and biological weapons. There are levels of technology readily available to all, including terrorists and extortionists, that can immediately capture the attention of even the superpowers.

Fourth, the Soviets and their highly skilled satellites have had high priority efforts to develop new generations of chemical and biological weapons since the early 1960s. While direct evidence is sparse, it is unwise not to recognize that the Soviets and East Europeans have been working hard over the past two decades to develop the most effective arsenal of modern biochem warfare capabilities and are unlikely not to have achieved significant progress.

Technology Base

Beginning with the successful insertion of a gene from one organism into the DNA of another organism in 1973, there emerged a revolution in the life and biotechnology sciences. Not only is this revolution spectacular in terms of both its promises and accomplishments, it is equally fascinating in terms of the speed with which the latest research is commercialized and proliferated to different nations and lower educational levels.

This revolution has greatly increased our understanding of the life processes and our ability to interact with and modify or engineer these processes. The potential of the new science is so tremendous and wide ranging that, at this juncture, it is generally considered unlimited, with consequences that are expected to surpass even those of the industrial revolution. And, while the attention of Western scientists, businessmen, and news media has focused on the beneficial side of the expanding technology, the impact on the dark side, chemical and biological warfare, is equally significant.

National Security

Maintaining a strong program to provide for defense against biological and toxin weapons is essential to our national security and to protecting the lives of U.S. servicemen.

Lynn M. Hansen, Testimony before Congress, May 3, 1988.

A very rough impression of the consequences of the new technology on chemical and biological warfare is not too difficult to convey. Consider toxicity or "effectiveness," in a rough sense of the word. In discussing the effectiveness of classical nerve agents, milligram quantities are most often used to describe lethality or toxicity. As one progresses to toxins, the quantities shrink to micrograms. Still further, the new technology enables the development and manufacture of small molecular weight chemicals (where "toxicity" might be measured in nanograms) and the design of organisms that themselves produce desired debilitating chemicals, where sensitivities on the order of picograms are not uncommon; that is, a factor of ten to the ninth power more potent than nerve agents.

These tremendous increases in potency are why new concepts of use, of delivery, and new measures of effectiveness are required. The classic approaches simply lose their meaning and applicability when the potential of existing technology is examined. . . .

Soviet Interests

The base of Soviet interest that is important in assessing the current and future threat was provided by the high-ranking defector from Czechoslovakia, Gen. Maj. Jan Sejna. Sejna, as secretary of the Defense Council, chief of cabinet at the Ministry of Defense and member of the Minister's Collegium, was privy to most Soviet planning as it affected Czechoslovakia and the Warsaw Pact in general. He has explained how chemical and biological agent development was made a high-priority activity in the early 1960s and how the Soviet interests encompassed tactical, strategic, political, and intelligence applications, as discussed earlier. He identified research and development plans and facilities, test ranges, factories, storage facilities, plans for use in the event of war, actual use in intelligence missions, and top-secret R&D programs that were carried out in direct violation of various arms control agreements. . . .

It would seem that one would have to be politically naive not to conclude that the Soviet program has continued and has been actively incorporating all the useful science and technology to achieve solid advancements in biochem agents and weapons for the full spectrum of political, military, economic, and intelligence applications. . . .

Other Nations

Estimates on the countries that now possess offensive chemical capabilities range from a low of fifteen to twenty-five or thirty-five, depending on criteria and source access. Independent of which figure is the better estimate, the more important observation is that the number is steadily increasing.

Beliefs that chemical or biological warfare can be negotiated out of existence or "controlled" are increasingly being recognized as unrealistic. The problems are simply insurmountable. There is no defining what constitutes a "weapon" or even biological or chemical "agent." Incapacitants have become more effective than classic lethal agents in most applications. Even drugs are extremely effective weapons. There is no distinguishing research quantities from war-reserve stockpiles. Medical research is indistinguishable from offensive-agent research. There are no prospects for effective verification, even with so-called on-site inspection.

Increasing numbers of nations have begun to recognize the vast potential of modern biochemistry, micro, and molecular biology and are beginning to build their own defense and offense programs. The potential of the new agents is so significant that any nation, large or small, backward or advanced, that does not appraise itself of the potentials and their consequences only increases its vulnerabilities and risks.

Where the Road Leads

Following World War I, numerous observers expressed their concern that chemical weapons would become the "ultimate weapons." Fifty years later, the revolution in life sciences that emerged from the advances in biochemistry and molecular biology has provided the technology base that makes the prediction not only realizable but intuitively evident to all who make a cursory examination of the facts.

The only issue in contention concerns what we should assume the Soviet Union and its satellite nations are doing. If one accepts their ideology and political philosophy, as is clearly stated and as many high-ranking defectors have advised we should do, then one has to assume the worst—not to err on the conservative side, but simply because the most likely is the worst. Alternatively, one can continue to hold out hope that arms control will work and not necessarily "deny" that the Soviets are active in the field, but

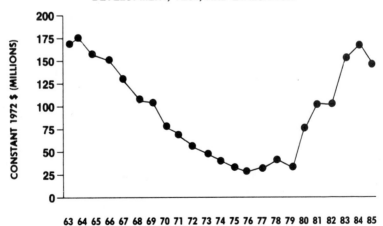

DEPARTMENT OF DEFENSE SUPPORT FOR CHEMICAL BIOLOGICAL WEAPONS RESEARCH, DEVELOPMENT, TEST, AND EVALUATION

Source: U.S. Department of Defense.

rather challenge the notion that the Soviets are active by disputing the evidence. This is the principal tack taken by most arms control enthusiasts. Additionally, it should not go unnoticed that one of the stronger motivations for adopting the latter position is the unpleasant conclusions one must reach if one acknowledges who and what the Soviets really are, simply because the potential of the new technology when applied to modern biochem weapons is so frightening—especially as described by Soviet bloc scientists in the early 1970s.

The threat of modern biochem weapons is with us and will continue to get worse, if for no other reason than as a mere byproduct of the continuing revolution in the biotechnology and life sciences. Accordingly, rather than waste time arguing how bad the Soviets are, or how important it is to trust them so that détente and arms control can proceed, certain actions are imperative. These actions are called for independent of how one judges the morality of the Soviet Union or the viability of arms control.

What Should Be Done

First, and most important, intelligence directed to understand better the range and degree of various threats needs to be steadily and forcefully expanded. It is not unreasonable to ask that the intelligence effort be placed on a 30 to 50 percent yearly growth curve for the next five years. This really indicates how small the current effort is, especially when judged in light of the magnitude and seriousness of the problem. While there have been notable improvements in the intelligence effort since 1983, it is important to recognize that the base was close to zero when the improvements began and that the current effort remains minuscule when compared with the efforts directed to, for example, the nuclear threat. And, it does not appear unreasonable to view the chemical and biological threat as becoming at least as serious as the nuclear threat, if not more serious.

Second, a long-term multidisciplinary effort is required to study developments in the basic biotechnology and life sciences, assess their national security implications, and provide program recommendations to the National Security Council. . . .

These are proposed as the two most important and basic actions. They are both long-term, preparatory and position-formulation actions. That is, they are designed to support the decision process for other actions that are anticipated and will need to follow. Certain of these follow-on actions are almost certain to the extent that they, too, could be initiated immediately, but at the same time should benefit greatly from the first two actions and thus have a direct relationship to them.

One such action is the creation of the capability to detect and respond to crises of a biological or chemical warfare (including terrorism) nature. This action recognizes that the answer to the threat problem is most likely to require a fast-response capability as opposed to defenses in place. That is, in examining the nature of the possible threat, it is clear that it is unreasonable to expect in advance to know what precise form it will take. Thus, it is impossible to specify what specific defenses will be necessary. What will be critical is our ability to respond quickly and efficiently, which will need to be well-planned and supported in advance. . . .

The Political Challenge

Biological and chemical warfare were cast aside by the United States in the early 1970s with the justification that they were not "strategically significant." Today, a continuation of this practice does not appear to be wise because of 1) the major advances in technology since the early 1970s, 2) the highly credible reports on Soviet interests in such weapons, and 3) the growing awareness of the potentials of biological and chemical warfare in many other unfriendly quarters. The political challenge will be to confront the problem, in all its dimensions, and identify and take effective countermeasures.

But chemical and biological warfare are the most distasteful, heinous subjects imaginable. This makes them politically unpalatable. The natural tendency of decision-makers and their advisers is to avoid these subjects because of their perceived politically risky nature.

Moreover, there has developed a small but effective lobby whose goal is to prevent the United States from entering the new world of chemical and biological warfare, independent of how serious the threat may be. To this end, they refuse to see the Soviet Union for what it is, to acknowledge the rampant failure of arms control, or understand how serious terrorism might become should the political situation become ripe for such activities. The result is a mentality, supported by extremely influential segments of the news media, which seems destined to fight for the unilateral disarmament of the West and trust the Russians to follow suit.

"Biological warfare research . . . is expensive, probably illegal, futile, unnecessary, dangerous, and necessarily secret."

Biological Weapons Research Should End

Jay A. Jacobson

Jay A. Jacobson is an associate professor of internal medicine in the Division of Infectious Diseases at the University of Utah School of Medicine in Salt Lake City. In the following viewpoint, taken from prepared testimony before Congress, he argues that biological weapons research is dangerous, expensive, and has no practical benefits. He asserts no sure defense can be created against all the organisms made possible by genetic engineering.

As you read, consider the following questions:

1. What does Jacobson assert about the risks and benefits of biological warfare research?
2. Why does the author believe that defenses against biological weapons are unnecessary?
3. What lesson does Jacobson draw from the AIDS epidemic?

Jay A. Jacobson, Testimony before U.S. House of Representatives subcommittees, May 3, 1988.

My infectious disease colleagues and I are actively engaged in biological warfare. Since the mid-19th Century when Louis Pasteur, Robert Koch and others first identified some of our microbial enemies, we have engaged in a continuing struggle. Our weapons have been improved sanitation, aseptic technique, antibiotics and vaccines. We have won several battles. We have vanquished smallpox and nearly eliminated measles, polio, diphtheria, tetanus and whooping cough in our country and some parts of the world, but we have not won the war. Some agents have eluded our surveillance until very recently when we recognized their role in Legionnaires Disease and Toxic Shock Syndrome. Some such as HIV, the cause of AIDS, have only recently emerged as major threats to public health. Our biological enemies are highly adaptable, seemingly able to parry when we thrust our chemical swords at them. Staphylococci, initially vulnerable to treatment with penicillin became resistant to it and are now becoming resistant to more potent agents necessitating the use of very expensive and potentially dangerous antibiotics. Some bacteria have appeared which are resistant to virtually all of our antimicrobial drugs.

Natural Enemies

The enemy with which we are engaged is our natural enemy. It consists of viruses, bacteria, fungi, and parasites living out their life cycles which sometimes require injury to man and sometimes accidentally result in great harm to the human host as he or she attempts to imprison or repel these invaders.

The great havoc that infectious diseases can wreak and the fear that they engender has not gone unnoticed by military weapons strategists. New techniques in molecular biology and recombinant DNA technology now make it possible not only to use existing pathogens, our natural enemies, but also to create an infinite variety of new and tailor-made microbes, for the purpose of deliberately infecting, disabling or killing soldiers and civilians.

I will speak about six reasons why our defense department should not participate in efforts which increase the likelihood of deliberate biological warfare or an accidental biological attack on our own population or innocent global bystanders.

A theme that will permeate my remarks is that of risk and benefit. In the context of biological warfare research, the risk of a particular adverse event occurring may be small, but the consequences catastrophic. The benefits achieved may be theoretically very appealing, but the likelihood of achieving them is abysmally small.

First, biological warfare research is inappropriately expensive. According to one source (*The New York Times*) the budget for chemical and biological warfare research has risen from $18 million in 1980 to $90 million in 1986 and according to another

(Cole, L. *Clouds of Secrecy*), it rose from $160 million to $1 billion in the same period. The proposed five-year modernization program at Dugway, Utah alone is to cost more than $300 million.

It is not at all clear to me what significant advances have been made as a result of this enormous expense. If all that is forthcoming is an improved mask or protective clothing which cannot be worn longer than several hours, I believe the investment has been a poor one and would predict no better return on the millions yet to be spent.

The risk is diversion of support from other more important, more worthy, and more solvable problems. The benefits to date have been trivial.

Illegal Research

Second, proposed biological warfare research may be illegal. We signed a 1972 treaty which bans the development or stockpiling of biological warfare agents. Senator James Sasser has written to former Secretary of Defense Caspar Weinberger that the expanded facility at Dugway could be used "to test offensive biological and toxin weapons, a capability which is prohibited by the 1972 treaty." The military describes their research program on biological warfare as defensive and compatible with our obligations under the treaty. The projects are offensive to those of us who work toward the elimination rather than the creation of infectious diseases. They are likely to be construed as offensive by our political enemies and for understandable reasons.

No Soviet Threat

U.S. statements about the applications of genetic engineering to biological warfare paint a vivid picture of ominous, growing Soviet technological superiority. Nothing could be further from the truth. Any molecular biologist who has visited Soviet labs can attest to this.

Charles Piller and Keith R. Yamamoto, *Gene Wars*, 1988.

In order to evaluate the efficacy of defensive equipment, be it surveillance or protective devices, the Army has insisted that it will be necessary to use real, virulent, microorganisms under field conditions. They are stating essentially that you can't test a bullet-proof vest without firing a real bullet at it. This means they must test the enemies' present weapons, future weapons and anticipated weapons. This logically leads to the need to actually develop these biological weapons, use them and study their success or failure in overcoming defensive equipment. This weapons development is certainly in violation of the spirit if not the letter of the 1972 treaty and will inevitably lead to an escalation of overt or clandestine offensive research by others.

The risks here are to increase rather than decrease the development of biological warfare agents and to promote the creation of those that are harder to detect, harder to protect against and harder to treat.

The benefits are inapparent. No adequate specific or general defense has yet been developed despite more than 40 years of effort on this problem and none seems likely now—in fact, useful defenses seem less likely.

No Defense

Third, the plethora of real and constructible microbial pathogens and the numerous ways in which exposure to them can occur makes development of agent and route specific defenses foolish and futile. For example, infection can be acquired through the air, from water and food, from animals, insects, and even other people. It can result from contamination of the soil. The microbes that can be used as weapons are not just the hundreds that are known to produce serious disease but uncountable numbers that can be constructed to live longer, to be more lethal, to be resistant to conventional treatment, to be more transmissible or even to wear microbial camouflage. This wolf in sheep's clothing concept is now feasible by inserting a lethal toxin-producing gene into otherwise harmless bacteria. This same technology has already been used for our benefit by having a yeast genetically reprogrammed to manufacture a part of the hepatitis B virus which is used in a vaccine.

Any surveillance device which has the ostensible advantage of detecting a specific biological agent has the real disadvantage of not being able to detect thousands or millions of others. Any device that protects against acquisition through the air will not protect against exposure via water or food. A very grim scenario, indeed, would occur whereby individuals infected by any route could at least temporarily serve as asymptomatic transmitters of infection to companions or health care personnel. No one device or reasonable combination of devices is likely to detect and protect against all the various threats that can be mounted. The protective benefits of biological warfare defensive research are unlikely to be realized.

Fourth, developing so-called defenses against biological warfare seems not only expensive, politically dangerous and futile, but also unnecessary. Once man had the rifle, a leather shield against arrows became obsolete. There is no requirement that a defense must be specific or somehow symmetrical with an offensive weapon. There are, in fact, many weapons for which we have no specific individual defenses such as hand grenades or napalm. What we attempt to do is thwart their delivery by attacking

"And if one green bottle should accidentally fall . . ."

soldiers and destroying airplanes. We have no lack of anti-personnel, anti-battalion, anti-airbase or anti-city weapons of the so-called conventional or nuclear type. Our ability to prevent the launching of a biological attack is extensive and our means for retaliating overwhelming. There is no particular advantage in biological warfare parity since the threat of biological counter-attack is no greater than that of nuclear devastation or conventional conflict. If potential benefits are unnecessary or redundant, no cost and no level of risk is justified.

Dangers of Research

Fifth, biological warfare research is dangerous. It is hazardous to the health of those who do it, those who live with them, and potentially to all of us. Pathogenic microbes are dangerous. They produce disease and death. Those who work with them are exposed to risk just as those who work with explosives and radioactive material are. Accidents happen despite the most well-meaning, most conscientious, most well-monitored, most expensive and extensive precautions that can be taken. Witness, in our country, the space shuttle disaster, the accident at Three Mile Island. Witness, in the Soviet Union, the Chernobyl catastrophe. You realize that accident prevention and risk control programs were operating in all of those cases and you know that the planners calculated the risk of such accidents to be negligible. We continue to pursue development in nuclear power and space exploration because we believe the benefits outweigh the risks.

The risks in biological warfare research are also real. Islands have been contaminated by anthrax spores, laboratory employees have become ill and died even in the most sophisticated "containment facilities." Thousands of sheep were killed in 1968 within 70 miles of Salt Lake County, where nearly 500,000 people live, by an accidental release of a biological nerve agent. The military has charged that hundreds or thousands of people recently died in the Soviet Union in an epidemic of anthrax related to a biological warfare facility. The Soviets have denied this, but even if it is so, don't you believe they would have taken every conceivable precaution to prevent it?

A Possible Accident

As long as the Army insists on using pathogens, agents that cause disease, in their research a serious accident or even an epidemic remains possible. Some of the pathogens they acknowledge testing, the agents of tularemia, anthrax, and Q fever, so-called level 3 pathogens, can all produce pneumonia and death. They are especially lethal when infection follows exposure via aerosol, the very route the military is testing. For these pathogens there is at least some treatment although it is not always effective and the complications of infection may not be reversible. These infections are uncommon, however, and not necessarily distinctive. Though many of us are likely to see laboratory workers or other inadvertently infected individuals as patients, we fear that we will not immediately recognize the nature of the infection and we may not provide appropriate or effective treatment. We believe that for compelling security reasons, the military may not reveal the nature of the organisms to which these people have been exposed, effectively precluding us from treating them quickly and correctly. The Army plans to evacuate and care for employees who become recognizably ill or who have an observed exposure. However, infectious diseases have variable incubation periods and an employee may be well at work only to become ill later off site and possibly even in another city. No provisions are made for the diagnosis and care of household contacts or nonemployees that may become infected as a consequence of a recognized or unrecognized accident. . . .

We need only think for a moment about the AIDS epidemic to envision some of the awful consequences of an accident at a facility or site where untreatable, deadly pathogens are stored, grown, and aerosolized. The event could be observed or unrecognized, unintentional or deliberate, but if a new necessarily secret communicable disease is established in man or animals what can we expect? It took us three years to isolate and identify the agent of AIDS; after seven years we still have no cure and the

234

prospects for a vaccine are slim while the number of deaths approaches 50,000 and the number of HIV-infected patients exceeds 1 million in our country alone. The risk of an accident may be small, but real; the benefits to the military seem illusory.

Secrecy

Sixth, can the Army be relied on to keep their promises to perform only the tests they outline, to test only the pathogens they list in public documents. Historically, they have done little to inform the public about potentially dangerous tests and when testing went awry or the unexpected happened, they have been obstinate in releasing facts or acknowledging responsibility. Witness the fallout, radioactive and medical, from atomic bomb testing in Nevada and the massive sheep kill in Utah. In fairness, can we ask them to be honest with us when we mandate them to develop devices which necessitate the use of new deadly biological agents and acknowledge that their efforts can only be successful if they maintain complete secrecy from our enemies. I don't expect truth or open disclosure.

To summarize my concerns about biological warfare research, even "defensive" research: it is expensive, probably illegal, futile, unnecessary, dangerous, and necessarily secret.

My suggestion is to set aside biological warfare research, negotiate an even stronger treaty which is more comprehensive and which includes inspection and verification. . . .

I would urge the Congress to act in the national and international interest and proscribe all military research associated with biological warfare and direct its attention, emphasis, and financial support to our biological welfare.

"We must continue to strive to prevent biological weapons proliferation by reinforcing the moral, legal, and political constraints against biological weapons."

The Biological Weapons Convention Can End Proliferation

H. Allen Holmes

H. Allen Holmes serves in the U.S. State Department as assistant secretary for politico-military affairs. In the following viewpoint, taken from congressional testimony, he supports the 1972 Biological Weapons Convention, which prohibited the development and testing of biological weapons. He argues that the U.S. should work to strengthen the Convention by holding nations accountable for violations, persuading more nations to sign the treaty, and developing greater international openness in biological research.

As you read, consider the following questions:

1. What is the U.S. position regarding the use and research of biological weapons, according to the author?
2. According to Holmes, why must the U.S. pay special attention to weapons development in the Middle East?
3. What new approaches to eliminating biological weapons does Holmes suggest?

H. Allen Holmes, "Biological Weapons Proliferation," *Department of State Bulletin*, July 1989.

I am pleased to appear before you today to discuss the foreign policy implications of the problem of biological weapons proliferation. These hearings are coming at an opportune time. We are presently witnessing a disturbing and dangerous trend in the increasing efforts by states to acquire biological weapons. The technology to produce them is improving, and the agents themselves are becoming ever more threatening.

I should like to state from the outset that the United States is adamantly opposed to the development, production, or use of biological weapons, and we are committed to doing all we can to eliminate them from the world's arsenals.

I would like first to give you some background on the development of U.S. policy on biological weapons and on the present state of play in this area. I will then describe how we are working to achieve our goal of eliminating these weapons.

Background

There are, in fact, two relevant international agreements, both of which have proven inadequate to prevent the proliferation of biological and toxin weapons.

The 1925 Geneva protocol prohibits the first use in war of chemical and biological weapons but not their development, production, possession, or transfer. The 1972 Biological and Toxin Weapons Convention prohibits the development, production, stockpiling, acquisition, retention, and transfer of biological and toxin weapons.

The United States itself unconditionally renounced all aspects of biological warfare in 1969. President Nixon ordered the Department of Defense to draw up a plan for the disposal of existing stocks of biological agents and weapons. In 1970 this unilateral ban was extended also to cover toxins; that is, poisonous chemicals produced by living organisms. All research in the area of biological warfare has since been confined to the development of strictly defined defensive measures; for example, development of vaccines.

Biological and Toxin Weapons Convention

The United States followed up these unilateral actions by leading the fight for an international ban—the 1972 Biological and Toxin Weapons Convention. Article I of the convention and the treaty's negotiating record make clear, however, that protective and prophylactic activities are permitted.

The Biological and Toxin Weapons Convention was approved by the U.S. Senate on December 16, 1974, and entered into force on March 26, 1975. All U.S. military stocks of biological and toxin agents, weapons, equipment, or means of delivery prohibited by the convention had already been destroyed unilaterally. Facilities in the United States which had been built and used for biological or toxin weapons purposes were converted to other use. For example, military facilities at Ft. Detrick, Maryland, and Pine Bluff, Arkansas, previously used for biological weapons activities, are now the property of the U.S. Department of Health and Human Services and are used by the National Cancer Institute and the National Center for Toxicological Research.

Single Best Hope

Supporters of the biological weapons treaty insist that it remains our single best hope for continued global biological disarmament. . . . That optimism has been borne out to some extent by efforts on the part of the United States, the Soviet Union and other parties to reduce the possibility that genetic engineering techniques will be used to forge new generations of biological weapons. These measures include the exchange of information concerning each nation's special, high-containment laboratory facilities where hazardous genetic engineering experiments are carried out; the reporting of unusual outbreaks of diseases that might be associated with biological weapons research; increased sharing of research findings concerning protection against biological warfare agents; and annual meetings by parties to the treaty. These and other developments suggest that our most effective response to the prospect of genetically enhanced biological weapons may be to work constructively with existing international agreements rather than to hastily discount them or to request additional funding for "defensive" biological weapons research programs.

David Suzuki and Peter Knudtson, *Genethics*, 1989.

After the Biological and Toxin Weapons Convention was completed, many thought that the security problem posed by biological and toxin weapons had been solved. However, this clearly is not the case. Despite the limitations of the convention, which has no verification provisions, we have identified a number of compliance problems. In previous years and again in 1988, President Reagan reported to the Congress that the Soviet Union had continued to maintain an offensive biological warfare program and accompanying capability and that the Soviet Union has been involved in the production, transfer, and use of mycotoxins for hostile purposes in Laos, Cambodia, and Afghanistan in violation of the 1972 Biological and Toxin Weapons Convention. Furthermore we have yet to receive a satisfactory official explanation of the unprecedented outbreak of anthrax at Sverdlovsk in the Soviet Union in 1979.

Two review conferences for the Biological and Toxin Weapons Convention have been held—in 1980 and 1986—with the next scheduled for 1991. At the two review conferences, the United

States confirmed that it is in full compliance with the convention.

At the second review conference, the United States expressed its concern that the Soviet Union, Laos, and Vietnam had violated the convention. Several other states party to the convention also expressed concern about compliance. These concerns are reflected in the final declaration of the 1986 review conference, which notes statements that compliance with Articles I, II, and III of the Biological and Toxin Weapons Convention was "subject to grave doubt" and that efforts to resolve the concerns expressed had not been successful. Since then our concerns have intensified as evidence mounts of biological weapons proliferation, especially in areas of particular concern to us.

In addition the rapid advance of technology in the biological field has led to another set of problems for the convention. In many ways, recent progress in biological technology increases the ease of concealment of illicit manufacturing plants, particularly for biologically derived chemicals such as toxins. Verification of the Biological and Toxin Weapons Convention, always a difficult task, has been significantly complicated by the new technology. The ease and rapidity of genetic manipulation, the ready availability of a variety of production equipment, and the proliferation of safety and environmental equipment and health procedures to numerous laboratories and production facilities throughout the world are signs of the growing role of biotechnology in the world's economy. They also make it easier for nations to produce the lethal agents banned by the convention.

As advances are made in the field of biotechnology, the potential for using this technology for biological and toxin weapons increases commensurately. Not only has the time from basic research to mass production of lethal weapons decreased but the ability to create agents and toxins with more optimal weapons potential has increased. Simply put the potential for undetected breakout from treaty constraints has increased significantly.

Growth of Biological Weapons Capability

When the Biological and Toxin Weapons Convention was negotiated, only the United States acknowledged having biological weapons. In contrast to the openness we have practiced regarding our military programs, the Soviets, to date, have never officially acknowledged having a biological weapons program and, in fact, admitted only in 1987 to having a chemical weapons program.

Today a number of countries are estimated to be working to achieve a biological weapons capability. Our information on which states are involved in biological weapons programs is based on extremely sensitive intelligence sources and methods, and I would defer to the intelligence community to provide you a fuller description of these programs in closed session.

We are especially concerned about the spread of biological weapons in unstable areas and about the prospects of biological and toxin weapons falling into the hands of terrorists or into the arsenals of those states which actively support terrorist organizations. To date we have no evidence that any known terrorist organization has the capability to employ such weapons nor that states supporting terrorism have supplied such weapons. However, we cannot dismiss these possibilities. If the proliferation of biological weapons continues, it may be only a matter of time before terrorists do acquire and use these weapons.

A Model Arms Treaty

The sweeping prohibitions of the Biological Weapons Convention make it a model for other arms treaties. It prohibits not only the use of biological weapons, which was previously outlawed by the Geneva Protocol of 1925, but also their production, possession or transfer, and even their development, thus removing the military temptation to resort to materials at hand in times of crisis.

Barbara Hatch Rosenberg, *Bulletin of the Atomic Scientists*, January/February 1987.

The unilateral U.S. renunciation of biological weapons in 1969 was accompanied by the recognition that maintaining a strong program to provide for defense against biological weapons is essential for national security. That requirement is reflected in Article I of the convention which permits production of biological agents and toxins in quantities required to develop protective measures. In today's circumstances, with the concerns about compliance, proliferation, and rapid advances in biotechnology, the requirement for defensive measures is even greater than in 1969.

The Biological and Toxin Weapons Convention clearly permits research and development for protection against biological and toxin weapons. The U.S. biological defense research program is in full compliance with the provisions of the convention. It is also open to public scrutiny. No other country even comes close in its openness.

Eliminating Biological Weapons

Vigorous action is needed to deal with the problems that I have just outlined. These problems are tough ones that will not be resolved easily or quickly. But we are determined to deal with them.

What do we need to do? We need to persuade states that are not parties to the Biological and Toxin Weapons Convention, particularly states in the Middle East, to renounce the option of possessing biological and toxin weapons. We have expressed our desire to have consultations with the Soviets under Article V of the convention, and this continues to be our position. We also need to explore possible means for strengthening the international norms against biological weapons.

With respect to the Soviet Union, we have repeatedly raised our concerns about noncompliance both through diplomatic channels and at the 1980 and 1986 review conferences. Fortunately the use of "yellow rain" appears to have stopped several years ago. However, the Soviet response to our compliance concerns has not been satisfactory. I might add that it is not primarily a matter of explaining the anthrax outbreak at Sverdlovsk in 1979. After 10 years, we can probably never know with certainty what happened. At this stage, it is more important to resolve our concerns about the very unusual military biological facility in Sverdlovsk that was reportedly the source of the outbreak. That facility still exists and raises serious apprehensions.

We continue to believe that the Soviet Union must deal seriously with our concerns and resolve them. We urge the new Soviet leadership to demonstrate some "new thinking" in this important arms control area.

The Middle East

In addition to ensuring that states fulfill their commitments not to possess biological or toxin weapons, we must persuade additional states to make that important commitment. Currently more than 110 states have renounced the option of possession of biological and toxin weapons by becoming parties to the Biological and Toxin Weapons Convention. Unfortunately, while most states in the Middle East have signed or acceded to the convention, only about half have ratified it and deposited their instruments of ratification, the legal steps necessary to become full parties to the convention. A number of these states have said that they will not take these actions until their neighbors do so. We need to break this vicious circle.

We believe that it would be in the interests of all states in the Middle East to eliminate the spectre of biological warfare from this already very volatile region. For that reason, we have recently renewed our effort to bring all states in the Middle East into the convention. We will persist in this attempt to break the vicious circle. . . .

New Approaches

In addition to resolving compliance issues and promoting broader adherence to the Biological and Toxin Weapons Convention, we should consider new and innovative approaches to making the international arms control regime for biological weapons more effective.

One way to strengthen the regime is to strengthen international reaction to deal effectively with proven violations of the ban on use embodied in the 1925 Geneva protocol. The Paris Conference on Chemical Weapons Use could be a good example of an initial step to build an international consensus. But there must be concrete actions, including international sanctions, to put some teeth into the reaction.

Another way to strengthen the regime is through additional confidence-building measures to create greater openness about biological activities. The United States has taken the lead here. I doubt that any other state anywhere can match the openness we already practice with regard to our defensive research. We need to push others, especially the Soviet Union, to match this openness.

We have joined with other states party to the Biological and Toxin Weapons Convention in agreeing that more information should be made available concerning legitimate biological research activities. By creating greater openness in these areas, we hope that the norm against biological weapons created by the convention can be strengthened. The United States joined with others at the second review conference in calling for an annual exchange of information on each party's research activities using the U.S. policies on program openness as the standard.

Furthermore we should continue programs where researchers from different countries work for extended periods in each other's laboratories. It would be more difficult to conceal signficant research programs of intentions from qualified exchange scientists than it would be to fool inspectors making a brief, one-time visit.

A Difficult Task

We must continue to strive to prevent biological weapons proliferation by reinforcing the moral, legal, and political constraints against biological weapons and, where feasible, seek to prevent states from obtaining sensitive materials and technology for biological weapons purposes. This will be a particularly difficult task and, quite frankly, we do not have the answers yet on how to achieve this. We do know that we cannot do it alone. Our efforts to constrain biological weapons proliferation will require a sustained multilateral approach, involving both U.S. leadership and cooperation with friends and allies.

"The major arms control implication of the new biotechnology is that the [Biological Weapons Convention] must be recognized as critically deficient and unfixable."

The Biological Weapons Convention Is Useless

Douglas J. Feith

The 1972 Biological Weapons Convention, in which over 100 nations pledged not to develop, test, and stockpile biological weapons, was completed shortly before dramatic advances in genetic engineering technology. In the following viewpoint, Douglas J. Feith argues that genetic engineering has made the 1972 Convention obsolete. He argues that because of the treaty's limitations, and because the Soviet Union has continued developing biological weapons, the U.S. should renew its efforts in biological warfare defense. Feith is an attorney in Washington, D.C., and was deputy assistant secretary of defense for negotiations policy from 1984 to 1986.

As you read, consider the following questions:

1. How have advances in genetic engineering altered the potential capabilities of biological weapons, according to Feith?
2. According to the author, what has the Soviet Union done in the field of biological warfare?
3. What does Feith believe to be the principal failing of the 1972 Biological Weapons Convention?

Douglas J. Feith, "Biological Weapons & the Limits of Arms Control," *The National Interest*, Winter 1986/1987. Reprinted with permission.

The stunning advances over the last five to ten years in the field of biotechnology—the advances that have brought into common parlance such terms as genetic engineering, recombinant DNA techniques, monoclonal antibodies, and Nutrasweet—mean more than new foods, pharmaceuticals, and fertilizers. They mean new and better biological and toxin weapons for any country willing to violate what the U.S. government still insists is an international norm against the possession of such weapons. New technology has exploded the standard ideas about BW [biological weapons] that prevailed ten or more years ago.

Old Ideas

Those old ideas can easily be summarized: BW was thought to be a small problem solved. It was thought small because BW was judged militarily insignificant or, at most, of highly restricted utility. Agents best suited for military use—those, for example, like snail or shellfish toxins, which disseminate well in effective concentrations and work quickly and somewhat controllably—could not be produced affordably in large quantities. Those that could efficiently be produced worked in general less quickly and spread infectious disease, with large attending risk to the attacker as well as the target. BW was deemed a strategic weapon and, from a military point of view, far inferior to other—that is, nuclear—strategic weapons. . . .

The BW problem was thought solved because over a hundred states, including the major powers, have subscribed to the Biological and Toxin Weapons Convention of 1972 (BWC), which makes it illegal to "develop, produce, stockpile or otherwise acquire or retain" or transfer biological or toxin agents or weapons. This prohibition, it should be noted, does not extend to very small quantities of agent, possession of which is necessary for "prophylactic, protective, or other peaceful purposes." It was obvious that a ban on tiny quantities could not be policed effectively and, in any event, substantial stockpiles of agent were believed to be a prerequisite for an offensive BW capability.

The BWC came into being three years after the Nixon administration unilaterally destroyed all U.S. BW stocks, renounced future acquisition of BW, and terminated the U.S. BW program, sparing only the facilities for BW defense. This unilateral U.S. action reflected the judgment that BW lacked military usefulness. Under the circumstances, it was not considered necessary that the treaty afford the parties any means of ascertaining each other's compliance. Accordingly, the BWC included no verification provisions. The U.S. government reasoned that it had already renounced BW unilaterally, so there could be no harm in signing an unverifiable ban.

The BW picture has been radically altered by recent scientific

244

developments. It is now possible to synthesize BW agents tailored to military specifications. The technology that makes possible so-called designer drugs also makes possible designer BW. States unconstrained by their treaty obligations can now produce BW agents of varying effects—different types of fast-acting incapacitants as well as lethal substances. Agents can be developed for various climatic conditions. They can be mixed to complicate identification and their chemical structure can easily be altered to circumvent immunogens or antigens that the other side is suspected to possess.

The Soviet Threat

Beginning with World War I, the Soviets have had significant continuing biological and chemical research, development, test, and evaluation programs. In the Hirsch intelligence report on Soviet activities before and during World War II (perhaps the best study of Soviet activities and capabilities in existence), over sixty installations and test facilities were identified. In this report, and in subsequent data from 1950 through 1980, this Soviet research was described as including the use of human guinea pigs as experimental subjects—POWs, political prisoners and dissidents, and even unsuspecting college students. At no time, including the present, has there been any indication that chemical and biological weapons were considered as anything other than effective weapons to be developed and used in the conduct of political, military, and intelligence warfare.

Joseph D. Douglass Jr., *Global Affairs*, Winter 1988.

The BW field favors offense over defense. It is a technologically simple matter to produce new agents but a problem to develop antidotes. New agents can be produced in hours; antidotes may take years. To gauge the magnitude of the antidote problem, consider the many years and millions of dollars that have thus far been invested, as yet without success, in developing a means of countering a single biological agent outside the BW field—the AIDS virus. Such an investment far surpasses the resources available for BW defense work.

New technology can yield BW agents against which a state could immunize its own forces. A state could therefore employ BW without having to require all its own troops in the area to don cumbersome protective clothing. This would enhance BW's military advantage over chemical weapons, such as nerve agent, against which no reliable prophylaxis is available. . . .

Bio-engineered substances are now produced around the world in large quantities by various commercial ventures. The production equipment, though newly invented, is not very "high

245

tech.'' The equipment can be housed in a standard industrial or manufacturing facility that offers no distinctive sign of the kind of production activity occurring within.

An example: Recent discoveries in mammalian cell culture make possible the growth of mammalian cells on the surface of minute beads, rather than on the inner surface of glass roller bottles. The beads provide the ideal environment for the growth of viruses. One small bottle partially filled with beads can now yield quantities of product that previously would have required much larger production facilities. This single technical advance has effectively erased the distinction between a biological agent production plant and an ordinary-looking small scientific laboratory.

The new type of biological production equipment works fast. Substances suitable for BW use can be synthesized within hours—a day or two at most. Seed stock of BW agent—that is, test tube quantities—can be fermented into large production quantities in three or four weeks. After a production run, the equipment, operating more or less as self-cleaning ovens do, destroys within an hour or two whatever residue there is, thereby preventing contamination of the next production run and, incidentally, making it impossible for anyone to prove that a given substance has been produced.

Soviet Violations

The Soviet Union evidently appreciates the military opportunities created by the biotechnological revolution of recent years. Though U.S. policy remains what it was in 1969 after President Nixon's unilateral renunciation of BW, . . . the Soviet Union has built a large organization devoted to the development and production of offensive BW. At the very time when Soviet officials were negotiating and signing the BWC, a high-ranking Soviet defector has reported, the Politburo decided to intensify the Soviet BW program.

The Soviets retain stockpiles of BW agent produced in pre-recombinant-DNA days. At known biological warfare facilities in the Soviet Union, they maintain highly secured weapons storage facilities under military control. They have, transferred BW to their clients in Southeast Asia. They have themselves used toxins against their enemies in the Afghanistan war. And they are developing new means of biological warfare based on current bio-engineering technologies. In other words, the Soviet Union has not only violated the BWC, but every major prohibition in it.

The scale and seriousness of the Soviet BW program are formidable. There are at least seven biological warfare centers in the USSR under military control, all with unusually rigorous security. One such facility constitutes a veritable city with a large number of residents who work and live there full time, isolated from the rest of society. These residents must possess extraordinary security clearances, a requirement that excludes individuals or ethnic groups considered disloyal. The level of effort committed to research on various natural poisons—such as snake venoms—is far in excess of what could be justified to deal with such substances for purely medical or public health purposes.

Implications

All of this, of course, has implications for both the military and the arms control aspects of the BW problem. The prevailing judgment of years ago that BW is not a militarily significant weapon is now quite unsustainable. BW can be designed to be effective across the spectrum of combat, including special operations and engagements at the tactical level. No field equipment has yet been developed that can detect BW agents, let alone identify them. There are no antidotes now available against many possible agents. And it is not certain that our troops' protective gear would be effective against all such agents.

As for the arms control implications, these divide into two categories. The first can be labeled "crime and non-punishment," the second "technology overtakes the treaty."

The systematic violations of the BWC by the Soviet Union and its clients undermine the treaty and the anti-BW norm it symbolizes. At least equally grave, however, is the international community's unwillingness to take a collective interest in the evidence of those violations. A treaty may survive breaches by some parties. But can it long survive general indifference as to whether it is violated?

Biological Weapons Are Inevitable

The ability to make biological weapons already exists, and cannot be wiped out. There is no alternative but to make every effort to build appropriate defences. Of course, the chain of developments will go on—there will be more sophisticated weapons requiring more sophisticated defences, and the same research will feed both. This has been the case throughout the history of technology, but there is no way of getting out of the cycle.

Brian Stableford, *Future Man*, 1984.

What is unwholesome, I wish to emphasize, is not the failure of many BWC parties to endorse the U.S. government's conclusions about Soviet violations, but their refusal even to inquire into them or urge formal investigation. Some states explain their inaction by asserting that the U.S. government's case is not conclusive. Reasoning like Lewis Carroll's Queen of Hearts, they contend in effect that treaty parties have no responsibility to investigate charges of violations until the allegations are proved. . . .

The major arms control implication of the new biotechnology is that the BWC must be recognized as critically deficient and un-fixable. A state contemptuous of international law and un-constrained by anti-BW public or parliamentary opinion could now maintain an offensive BW capability without violating any of the specific prohibitions of the BWC. (Maintaining such a capability would necessarily violate the BWC's general prohibi-tion; the treaty's purpose, after all, is to ban BW. But if a state refrains from stockpiling large quantities of agent, it would as a practical matter be impossible to prove any such violation.)

Given the ability to produce militarily significant quantities of BW from seed stock within a month or so, it is not necessary to stockpile agent. Such a state need only maintain in a freezer a few hundred test tubes full of seed stock and a production facility which, in the normal course of things, makes agricultural or medical products. In the unlikely event the freezer were discovered, a closed society would have little difficulty character-izing it as part of a research effort for BW defense. In fact, because seed stock can be synthesized in a matter of days, one could get by even without the freezer. . . .

Conclusion

While it in no way excuses or belittles the importance of the Soviet Union's BWC violations, the fact is that their compliance with the treaty's specific prohibitions would not obviate concern about their BW capabilities. Because new technology makes possible a massive and rapid break-out, the treaty constitutes an insignificant impediment at best. Its principal failing, therefore, is no longer the absence of verification provisions or lack of ef-fective complaint mechanisms, the commonly acknowledged shortcomings, but its inability to accomplish its purpose—to en-sure that even states respecting its specific terms pose no BW threat. . . .

It is not a pleasant task to deliver so dismal a report. The material's distressing nature probably accounts in large part for why it is so little treated in the public debate on national security issues. It is axiomatic that the only successful politics in a democracy is the politics of hope. But can one responsibly inflate hope for an escape from the military problems posed by the Soviet BW program? There can be no *deus ex machina* arms control in this arena. In answer to those who crave a constructive sugges-tion under even the least promising circumstances, one can recom-mend only: Defense.

Evaluating Sources of Information

A critical thinker must always question sources of information. Historians, for example, distinguish between *primary sources* (eyewitness accounts) and *secondary sources* (writings or statements based on primary or eyewitness accounts or on other secondary sources). The account from a doctor who has witnessed the horrible effects of biological weapons on military personnel is an example of a primary source. A scientist who used the doctor's account for writing a report that documented the intended destruction and side effects resulting from the use of biological weapons is an example of a secondary source.

To read and think critically, one must be able to recognize primary sources. This is not enough, however, because eyewitness accounts do not always provide accurate descriptions. A government official who wants to end the ban on biological warfare and his colleague who wants to extend the ban may give different accounts of a meeting with Soviet officials to review the ban. The historian must decide which account seems most accurate, keeping in mind the potential biases of the eyewitnesses.

Test your skill in evaluating sources of information by completing the following exercise. Imagine you are writing a report evaluating whether the United States should expand its biological and toxin weapons research for defense purposes. You decide to include an equal number of primary and secondary sources. Listed are a number of sources which may be useful for your research. *Place a P next to those descriptions you believe are primary sources.* Second, *rank the primary sources* assigning the number 1 to what appears to be the most accurate and fair primary source, the number 2 to the next most accurate, and so on until the ranking is finished. *Next, place an S next to those descriptions you believe are secondary sources and rank them also, using the same criteria.*

If you are doing this activity as a member of a class or group, discuss and compare your evaluations with other members of the group. Others may come to different conclusions than you. Listening to their reasons may give you valuable insights in evaluating sources of information.

_____ 1. A book by a genetic researcher entitled _____
*Advances in Biological Warfare Technology
Since 1970.*

_____ 2. A copy of the 1972 Biological and Toxin _____
Weapons Convention. The Convention
prohibited testing and development of
these weapons.

_____ 3. An editorial in the *New York Times* en- _____
titled "Why No One Can Win the Bio-
logical Arms Race," written by a U.S.
senator.

_____ 4. An article in *Time* magazine that traces _____
the history of legislation regulating the
use of biological weapons.

_____ 5. A transcript of congressional hearings to _____
determine the effect of international
biological weapons proliferation.

_____ 6. A televised presidential press con- _____
ference in which the president claims
that the USSR has violated the ban on
biological agent production.

_____ 7. A radio interview of two government _____
officials describing the pros and cons of
the current state of U.S. defenses against
a biological attack.

_____ 8. An official statement from a Soviet de- _____
fector in which he tells what kinds of
biological weapons the USSR has stock-
piled.

_____ 9. A chapter from a book about genetic _____
engineering entitled "How Genetic
Engineering Can Be Used for Military
Purposes."

_____ 10. An article in a foreign policy journal _____
describing the effects on international
economies of increased biological
weapons use.

Periodical Bibliography

The following articles have been selected to supplement the diverse views presented in this chapter.

Barton Bernstein	"The Birth of the U.S. Biological-Warfare Program," *Scientific American*, June 1987.
Elisa D. Harris	"Sverdlovsk and Yellow Rain," *International Security*, Spring 1987.
Melissa Hendricks	"Germ Wars," *Science News*, December 17, 1988.
Jonathan King	"Biology Goes to War," *Science for the People*, January/February 1988.
Lee Lescaze	"Quest for Way to Block Biological Weapons Is Itself Called a Threat," *The Wall Street Journal*, September 19, 1988.
The New York Times	"Lethal Weapons, or Lifesavers?" August 29, 1989.
Colin Norman	"Biological Defense Defended," *Science*, May 20, 1988.
Charles Piller	"Lethal Lies About Fatal Diseases," *The Nation*, October 3, 1988.
Barbara Hatch Rosenberg	"International Biological Weapons Update," *Bulletin of the Atomic Scientists*, January/February 1987.
Seth Shulman	"Poisons from the Pentagon," *The Progressive*, November 1987.
J. Winter Tucker	"Gene Wars," *Foreign Policy*, Winter 1984/1985.
The Wall Street Journal	"A 'Biological Chernobyl,'" September 15, 1989.
Thomas J. Welch	"The Growing Global Menace of Chemical & Biological Warfare," *Defense 89*, July/August 1989.
Susan Wright	"The Buildup That Was," *Bulletin of the Atomic Scientists*, January/February 1989.
Keith R. Yamamoto	"Retargeting Research on Biological Weapons," *Technology Review*, August/September 1989.

Glossary of Terms

amino acids   organic acids that are the building blocks of *protein*

bacteria   class of single-celled *organisms*; often used in *genetic engineering*

biological containment   the use in *genetic engineering experiments* of *bacteria* designed to be incapable of living outside the laboratory

biotechnology   the use of living *organisms* to manufacture products

carcinogen   a substance that may cause cancer

cell   the basic unit of life; the cell is the smallest living thing that feeds, grows, and reproduces independently

cell fusion   the combining of two or more different types of *cells* to become a single *cell* which has the characteristics of both

chimera   an *organism* with a mixed genetic heritage, formed by the merging of *cells* from two or more *embryos* into a unified whole

chromosome   a chain of genetic material in the *cell nucleus*, consisting of *DNA*, *RNA*, and *protein*

clone   a genetic copy of a *gene, cell, bacterium, organism*, etc.

DNA   deoxyribonucleic acid; the genetic material found in all living things; the molecular basis of *heredity* for living *organisms*

E. coli   Escherichia coli, a *bacterium* found in the human colon; commonly used in *genetic engineering*

embryo   animal or plant in the early stages of development; in humans, up to the eighth week of pregnancy

enzymes   *proteins* that speed up chemical reactions in *cells* but are not themselves changed by them

eugenics   the science of controlling and improving the hereditary qualities of a race or breed

gene   the fundamental unit of *heredity*; one segment of *DNA* arranged in a specific sequence which is passed from parent to child

gene splicing   see *recombinant DNA*

gene therapy   the medical replacement or repair of defective *genes* in living *cells*

genetic code   the sequence of *nitrogen bases* in *DNA* which form instructions for producing *proteins*

genetic engineering   techniques that change the characteristics of an *organism* by altering its *genes*; see also *recombinant DNA, cell fusion*

genetic screening   the testing of individuals and populations for genetic abnormalities

genome   the complete set of *genes* in an *organism*

germ cell   reproductive *cell*

heredity   the transmission of characteristics from parent to offspring

monogenic   controlled by or associated with a single *gene*

mutation   the natural or artificial changing of a *gene*; can be induced by temperature extremes, radiation, and certain chemicals

nitrogen base   chemical compounds that make up the "rungs" of the *DNA* ladder; combinations of these compounds form the *genetic code*

nucleotide   the basic structural unit of *DNA* and *RNA*

nucleus   the central mass of a plant or animal *cell* containing genetic material

oncogene   a *gene* that causes cancer

organism   a living being

plasmid   a ring of *DNA* that exists in many *bacteria* separate from the *chromosome,* often used in *genetic engineering* to insert new *genes* into other *organisms*

polygenic   controlled by or associated with more than one *gene*

polynucleotide   chain of *nucleotide* molecules

protein   a complex chemical composed of *amino acids*; proteins make up *cell* structure and control most cell functions

recombinant DNA   the technique of removing sections of *DNA* from one *organism* and "recombining" them with the *DNA* of a different *organism*

restriction enzymes   enzymes that can "cut" a *gene* out from the surrounding *DNA*, used in *recombinant DNA*

RNA   ribonucleic acid; molecules made from and closely resembling *DNA*; they carry genetic messages from *DNA* to the rest of a *cell*

somatic cell   a body *cell* not involved in reproduction

vector   a *plasmid* or *virus* used to carry new *genes* into host *cells*

virus   *organism* made up of a *protein* coat and an inner core of genetic material; can only reproduce inside *cells* of other *organisms*

Organizations to Contact

The editors have compiled the following list of organizations which are concerned with the issues debated in this book. All of them have information or publications available for interested readers. The descriptions are derived from materials provided by the organizations themselves. This list was compiled upon the date of publication. Names and phone numbers of organizations are subject to change.

Agricultural Research Service (ARS)
U.S. Department of Agriculture
Washington, DC 20250
(202) 447-2791

ARS is the research arm of the U.S. Department of Agriculture. It has actively supported research in genetic engineering and believes genetic engineering can help farmers by improving plants and animals. It publishes *Agricultural Research* ten times per year.

American Association for the Advancement of Science (AAAS)
1333 H St. NW
Washington, DC 20005
(202) 326-6400

AAAS supports scientific work in many fields including genetic engineering. It believes that the responsible use of biotechnology has the potential to advance the nation's health, contribute to the food supply, and improve environmental quality. The AAAS Committee on Scientific Freedom and Responsibility Programs has published *Biotechnology: Professional Issues and Social Concerns*.

American Council on Science and Health (ACSH)
47 Maple St.
Summit, NJ 07901
(201) 277-0024

The ACSH is a national organization that contends the lives of people will be improved as a result of genetic engineering. It believes current regulation of genetic engineering is adequate. The Council has a four-part report series on biotechnology/genetic engineering.

Biotechnology Information Center
National Agricultural Library, Room 301
U.S. Department of Agriculture
Beltsville, MD 20705
(301) 344-3218

The Center has a referral service and provides access to a variety of publications covering many aspects of biotechnology such as basic genetic manipulation theory and techniques, plant and animal genetics, monoclonal antibodies, food processing, and biomass applications. It distributes *Agricultural Biotechnology and the Public: A Report on Four Regional Information Conferences, Introduction of Recombinant DNA-Engineered Organisms into the Environment: Key Issues, American Biotechnology Laboratory: USDA Safety Review of Biotechnology Research in Agriculture*, and *BriefSheet*.

Council for Agricultural Science and Technology (CAST)
137 Lynn Ave.
Ames, IA 50010-7120
(515) 292-2125

CAST distributes materials to the public, news media, and government on the science and technology of food and agricultural matters such as biotechnology. It has published a report on plant germplasm and a paper on genetic engineering. It also publishes *Task Force Reports, Special Publications, Comments from CAST, Science of Food and Agriculture,* and *NewsCAST.*

Council for Responsible Genetics (CRG)
186A South St.
Boston, MA 02111
(617) 423-0650

CRG is a national organization of scientists, trade unionists, public health professionals, and other concerned citizens, dedicated to insuring that biotechnology is developed safely and in the public's interest. The organization publicizes social issues and emerging problems, submits comments to executive and legislative bodies on pending regulations, and provides speakers and resources. The Council sponsors a pledge against the military use of biological research. CRG publishes *geneWATCH,* a newsletter which analyzes the politics, ethics, and social impact of genetic engineering.

Eugenics Special Interest Group (ESIG)
2876 Natchez Lane
Memphis, TN 38111

ESIG advocates using genetic engineering to improve the human body. It serves as a communications network to those who are dedicated to improving human genetic quality. It is concerned with issues that affect human evolution, including teenage pregnancy, differential reproduction, immigration, and improved prenatal care. It publishes a periodic *Eugenics Bulletin.*

Foundation on Emerging Technologies (FET)
1130 17th St. NW, Suite 630
Washington, DC 20036
(202) 466-2823

FET was founded by its president, Jeremy Rifkin, a well-known opponent of genetic engineering. The Foundation has supported lawsuits to halt genetic engineering experiments. It distributes information through lectures and offers educational materials on issues such as genetic engineering, biological warfare, industrial and agricultural use of biotechnology, and the effects of biotechnology on human health and reproduction. FET maintains a library and provides a packet of newspaper articles on genetic engineering. It was formerly called the Foundation on Economic Trends.

The Hastings Center
360 Broadway
Hastings-on-Hudson, NY 10706
(914) 478-0500

Since its founding in 1969, The Hastings Center has studied ethical issues raised by advances in medicine, the biological sciences, including genetic engineering, and the social and behavioral sciences. The Center's three goals are to advance research on ethical issues, to encourage universities and professional schools to teach ethics, and to educate the public. It publishes the monthly *Hastings Center Report.*

Humane Farming Association (HFA)
1550 California St.
San Francisco, CA 94109
(415) 485-1495

The Humane Farming Association believes genetic engineering of farm animals harms and abuses animals. The Association's publications include the quarterly magazine *Watchdog* and the books *Animal Liberation* and *Modern Meat*.

Industrial Biotechnology Association (IBA)
1625 K St. NW, Suite 1100
Washington, DC 20006
(202) 857-0244

IBA represents biotechnology companies and promotes cooperation and communication between industry leaders. The Association informs its members of changing governmental policies on commercial biotechnology. The organization publishes *IBA Reports, What Is Biotechnology?, Answers to Commonly Asked Questions About Biotechnology Regulation*, and numerous other materials on biotechnology.

Institute of Laboratory Animal Research (ILAR)
National Research Council
2101 Constitution Ave. NW
Washington, DC 20418
(202) 334-2590

The Institute maintains an information center and answers inquiries concerning animal models for biomedical research. ILAR plans to establish a committee to address many of the complex issues of biotechnology, specifically as it relates to producing transgenic animals, which involves splicing the genes of one species into the genes of another. A committee of the NRC produced a report titled *Introduction of Recombinant DNA-Engineered Organisms into the Environment: Key Issues.* The Commission on Life Sciences, National Research Council compiled *Mapping and Sequencing the Human Genome.* ILAR publishes a quarterly newsletter, *ILAR NEWS*, and proceedings of conferences.

Monsanto Company
800 N. Lindbergh Blvd.
St. Louis, MO 63167
(314) 694-1000

Monsanto is a major U.S. corporation that is actively researching and developing agricultural biotechnology products. It advocates biotechnology as a way to improve farmers' harvests and animals' health. The company publishes numerous materials such as *Of the Earth: Agriculture and the New Biology*, the quarterly *Monsanto Magazine, Chemical & Engineering News*, and *The Promise of Biotechnology*.

National Center for Education in Maternal and Child Health
38th St. and R St. NW
Washington, DC 20057
(202) 625-8400

The Center disseminates instructional materials to professionals and the public on maternal and child health and medical genetics. It provides a directory of sources with pro and con viewpoints on genetic engineering. It aids in developing and evaluating educational programs. The Center's publications include *Human Genetics—A Guide to Educational Resources, Comprehensive Clinical Genetic Service Centers: A National Directory*, and *Guide to National Genetic Voluntary Organizations*. It also produces a periodic newsletter as well as guides and bibliographies.

National Center for Policy Alternatives
2000 Florida Ave. NW, 4th Floor
Washington, DC 20009
(202) 387-6030

The Center's members include state and local government officials and community activists interested in restructuring public policies on the state and local level. The Center believes that genetic engineering is hazardous, particularly when it requires the introduction of new organisms into the environment. It has compiled a briefing paper on the need for stricter regulations on commercial biotechnology. Its publications include the quarterly newsletter *Ways and Means*, periodic *Legislative Briefs*, periodic *Policy Memos*, and periodic *Resources*. It also publishes monographs, reports, books, manuals, and bibliographies.

National Council of the Churches of Christ in the USA (NCCC)
475 Riverside Dr.
New York, NY 10115
(212) 870-2290

NCCC is an organization of Protestant, Anglican, and Eastern Orthodox denominations composed of over 100,000 churches. The Council contends that the development of genetic engineering is too rapid and unpredictable. It holds that the manipulation of genes for the purpose of creating a better human being violates the sacred worth of human life and the values of fairness, justice, and love. NCCC has published a policy statement, "Genetic Science for Human Benefit."

Office of Technology Assessment (OTA)
Congress of the United States
Washington, DC 20510-8025
(202) 224-8996

OTA is an analytical support agency of the United States Congress. It explores issues in fields such as genetic engineering and provides Congress with a summary of the work being done in this area. Summaries of OTA reports on biotechnology are available as are the *OTA Publications List* and the following special reports: *Patenting Life—Special Reports*, *Field-Testing Engineered Organisms: Genetic and Ecological Issues—Special Report*, *Ownership of Human Tissues and Cells—Special Report*, and *U.S. Investment in Biotechnology—Special Report*.

Psychologists for the Ethical Treatment of Animals (PsyEta)
PO Box 87
New Gloucester, ME 04260
(207) 926-4817

PsyEta members include psychologists, graduate students, institutions, animal rights organizations, and interested individuals. This organization seeks to develop procedures to reduce the number of animals used in research, education, and farming. It has supported legislation to instate a moratorium on the patenting of animals.

Science Resource Center Inc. (SRC)
897 Main St.
Cambridge, MA 02139
(617) 547-5580

SRC believes that commercial biotechnology has many potential hazards that warrant strong public involvement in controlling the destiny of that technology. SRC devoted an entire issue of its magazine, *Science for the People*, to the topic of biotechnology and distributed it to educators and legislators. In addition to its bimonthly magazine, the Center publishes *Decoding Biotechnology, Biology as a Social Weapon*, and *Science and Liberation*.

Bibliography of Books

Walter Truett Anderson — *To Govern Evolution*. San Diego: Harcourt Brace Jovanovich Publishers, 1987.

Elizabeth Antébi and David Fishlock — *Biotechnology: Strategies for Life*. Cambridge, MA: The MIT Press, 1986.

William Bains — *Genetic Engineering for Almost Everybody*. London: Penguin Books, 1987.

Nigel Calder — *The Green Machines*. New York: G.P. Putnam's Sons, 1986.

Leonard Cole — *Clouds of Secrecy*. Lanham, MD: Rowman & Littlefield Publishers Inc., 1988.

Bernard D. Davis — *Storm over Biology: Essays on Science, Sentiment, and Public Policy*. Buffalo, NY: Prometheus Books, 1986.

Paul DeForest, Mark S. Frankel, Jeanne S. Poindexter, and Vivian Weil, eds. — *Biotechnology: Professional Issues and Social Concerns*. Washington, DC: American Association for the Advancement of Science, 1988.

Jack Doyle — *Altered Harvest*. New York: Viking Penguin Inc., 1985.

John Elkington — *The Gene Factory*. New York: Carroll Graf Publishers Inc., 1985.

Robert Esbjornson, ed. — *The Manipulation of Life*. San Francisco: Harper & Row, 1984.

Joseph Fletcher — *The Ethics of Genetic Control: Ending Reproductive Roulette*. Buffalo, NY: Prometheus Books, 1988.

John R. Fowle III, ed. — *Applications of Biotechnology: Environmental and Policy Issues*. Boulder, CO: Westview Press, 1987.

Robert T. Fraley, Nicholas M. Frey, and Jeff Schell, eds. — *Genetic Engineering of Agriculturally Important Crops: Progress and Issues*. Cold Spring Harbor, NY: Cold Spring Harbor Laboratory, 1988.

Erhard Geissler, ed. — *Biological and Toxin Weapons Today*. Oxford, UK: Oxford University Press, 1986.

David Goodman, Bernardo Sorj, and John Wilkinson — *From Farming to Biotechnology*. New York: Basil Blackwell Inc., 1987.

Cynthia S. Gross — *The New Biotechnology: Putting Microbes to Work*. Minneapolis: Lerner Publications Company, 1988.

Stephen S. Hall — *Invisible Frontiers: The Race to Synthesize a Human Gene*. New York: Atlantic Monthly Press, 1987.

Henk Hobbelink — *New Hope or False Promise? Biotechnology and Third World Agriculture*. Brussels, Belgium: International Coalition for Development Action, 1987.

Neil A. Holtzman — *Proceed with Caution*. Baltimore: The Johns Hopkins University Press, 1989.

| D. Gareth Jones | *Brave New People*. Grand Rapids, MI: William B. Eerdmans, 1984. |

Calestous Juma — *The Genehunters: Biotechnology and the Scramble for Seeds*. Princeton, NJ: Princeton University Press, 1989.

Carol Kahn — *Beyond the Helix*. New York: Times Books, 1985.

Martin Kenney — *Biotechnology: The University-Industrial Complex*. New Haven, CT: Yale University Press, 1986.

Daniel J. Kevles — *In the Name of Eugenics: Genetics and the Uses of Human Heredity*. New York: Alfred A. Knopf, 1985.

Marc Lappé — *Broken Code: The Exploitation of DNA*. San Francisco: Sierra Club Books, 1985.

Ruth McNally and Peter Wheale — *Genetic Engineering: Catastrophe or Utopia?* New York: St. Martin's Press, 1988.

Karl H. Muench — *Genetic Medicine*. New York: Elsevier Science Publishing Company, Inc., 1988.

National Research Council — *Biotechnology and the Food Supply*. Washington, DC: National Academy Press, 1988.

National Research Council — *Mapping and Sequencing the Human Genome*. Washington, DC: National Academy Press, 1988.

J. Robert Nelson — *Human Life: A Biblical Perspective for Bioethics*. Philadelphia: Fortress Press, 1984.

Eve K. Nichols — *Human Gene Therapy*. Cambridge, MA: Harvard University Press, 1988.

G.J.V. Nossal — *Reshaping Life: Key Issues in Genetic Engineering*. New York: Cambridge University Press, 1985.

Steve Olson — *Shaping the Future: Biological Research and Human Values*. Washington, DC: National Academy Press, 1989.

Charles Piller and Keith R. Yamamoto — *Gene Wars: Military Control over the New Genetic Technologies*. New York: Beech Tree Books, 1988.

President's Commission for the Study of Ethical Problems in Medicine and Biomedical and Behavioral Research — *Splicing Life: The Social and Ethical Issues of Genetic Engineering with Human Beings*. Washington, DC: U.S. Government Printing Office, 1982.

S.B. Primrose — *Modern Biotechnology*. Boston: Blackwell Scientific Publications, 1987.

Richard Noel Re — *Bioburst: The Impact of Modern Biology on the Affairs of Man*. Baton Rouge, LA: Louisiana State University Press, 1986.

Jeremy Rifkin — *Algeny*. New York: The Viking Press, 1983.

Alan M. Russell — *The Biotechnology Revolution: An International Perspective*. New York: St. Martin's Press, 1988.

Nicholas A. Sims — *The Diplomacy of Biological Disarmament*. New York: St. Martin's Press, 1988.

Patricia Spallone

Beyond Conception. Granby, MA: Bergin & Garvey Publishers Inc., 1989.

Brian Stableford

Future Man. New York: Crown Publishers Inc., 1984.

David Suzuki and
Peter Knudtson

Genethics: The Clash Between the New Genetics and Human Values. Cambridge, MA: Harvard University Press, 1989.

Edward J. Sylvester and
Lynn C. Klotz

Genetic Engineering and the Next Industrial Revolution, rev. ed. New York: Charles Scribner's Sons, 1987.

Robert Teitelman

Gene Dreams. New York: Basic Books, 1989.

Indra K. Vasil, ed.

Biotechnology: Perspectives, Policies, and Issues. Gainesville, FL: University of Florida Press, 1987.

David Weatherall and
Julian H. Shelley, eds.

Social Consequences of Genetic Engineering. New York: Elsevier Science Publishing Company Inc., 1989.

Raymond A. Zilinskas and
Burke K. Zimmerman, eds.

The Gene-Splicing Wars. New York: Macmillan Publishing Company, 1986.

Burke K. Zimmerman

Biofuture: Confronting the Genetic Era. New York: Plenum Press, 1984.

Index

263